MUSIC AND BALLET

THE AUTHOR, 1933
[*Elliott & Fry photograph*]

MUSIC AND BALLET

Recollections
of

M. D. CALVOCORESSI

NOVERRE PRESS

First published in 1933

This facsimile reprint published in 2013 by
The Noverre Press
Southwold House
Isington Road
Binsted
Hampshire
GU34 4PH

© 2013 The Noverre Press

ISBN 978-1-906830-60-1

To
LITTLE ETHEL GREY
THESE MAINLY PRE-NINETEEN SIXTEEN
REMINISCENCES

CONTENTS

CHAPTER I *page* 17
Musical Paris in the 'nineties—Currents and cross-currents—Official circles hostile to new music—Franck and Debussy ostracized—Progressive activities in the teeth of opposition.

CHAPTER II *page* 23
My childhood—Paris schools in the 'eighties and 'nineties—Unhygienic conditions and splendid teaching—Three masters I gratefully remember.

CHAPTER III *page* 33
Wagner's music gives me my first thrill—Piano lessons—Bach—Pierre Louÿs and Debussy—José-Maria de Hérédia—Other musical experiences—My studies interrupted—My début as a critic.

CHAPTER IV *page* 46
My first meeting with Ravel—We study Russian music together—His path to the Prix de Rome barred by official opposition—His views on music—His admiration for Liszt the composer.

CHAPTER V *page* 55
Ravel and our circle—Florent Schmitt—A meeting with d'Annunzio—A ballet that was never written—Albert Roussel—My share in his Evocations—Déodat de Sévérac—Léon-Paul Fargue and his ways—Manuel de Falla and his first opera—Ravel's first two pupils: Maurice Delage and Roland Manuel.

Contents

CHAPTER VI   *page* 66
Ravel at work—The Miroirs *and the* Histoires Naturelles
*—His indifference to criticism—A lecture on Ravel and an
over-zealous champion—First anonymous performance of
the* Valses Nobles et Sentimentales, *and a moral.*

CHAPTER VII   *page* 74
*How Ravel came to write the Sonatina and the Greek Folk-
Songs—Inception of* Daphnis et Chloé*—Schemes for operas
that came to nought—Pity for a condemned criminal—
Vaughan Williams comes to Paris for lessons from Ravel.*

CHAPTER VIII   *page* 82
Arthur Bles and his Weekly Critical Review*—Pierre
Aubry, scholar and gourmet—His appalling death—My
first lecture—Lecturing at Marseilles.*

CHAPTER IX   *page* 90
*Grieg's last visit to Paris—His interest in Debussy's music
—How he took an offensive article by Debussy—A glimpse
of Sibelius—Felipe Pedrell, an overlooked pioneer and master—Albeniz—His personality and plans—The story of an
unfinished set of songs.*

CHAPTER X   *page* 98
*André Caplet—He gives me lessons—His early prejudices
and speedy evolution—Achievement and promise of his religious music—Ianco Binenbaum—First performance of his
chamber works in Paris—His retiring disposition—A ballet
on Poe's* Masque of the Red Death *and a cupboard full of
unpublished manuscripts.*

CHAPTER XI   *page* 107
Henri Duparc—His strange neurasthenia—His unfinished
Roussalka*—His views on Liszt.*

Contents

CHAPTER XII page 111
Vincent d'Indy—My admiration for his Fervaal—A portrait of Charles Bordes—D'Indy's second symphony—A disciple who was more royalist than the King—D'Indy's Treatise of Composition—His views on Debussy's Pelléas et Mélisande—A letter on Mussorgsky's Boris Godunof.

CHAPTER XIII page 118
Claude Debussy—His sensitive and suspicious nature—An article of his commissioned and then rejected—A lampoon on Pelléas circulated on the day of the Press rehearsal—A talk on contemporary music—Evils of premature discussion.

CHAPTER XIV page 124
Erik Satie, composer, jester, and practical joker—He challenges the manager of the Paris Opéra to a duel—Pranks and stories—Significance and influence of his early works—Ballets with and without characters on the stage—Satie after the war.

CHAPTER XV page 132
Gabriel Fauré—His great and beneficial influence on French music—Revolutionary innovations which official vigilance overlooked—The fate of his music outside France—Diaghilef tries to obtain a ballet from his pen—Bourgault-Ducoudray, a forgotten promoter of the modern renaissance of French music—Influence of his history class at the Conservatoire.

CHAPTER XVI page 140
Camille Erlanger—His Juif Polonais—A glimpse of Victor Maurel and one of Caruso—Chaliapin in the 'nineties and after—The interpretation or the music?—Raoul Gunsbourg.

Contents

CHAPTER XVII page 148
Russian music—Balakiref's Islamey *and* Tamara*—Mussorgsky revealed by the d'Alheim couple—Russia's attitude to his music in the 'nineties—My early work on Russian music—An option on Boris Godunof disdained—My book of 1908 on Mussorgsky.*

CHAPTER XVIII page 157
Balakiref as seen from France—My correspondence with him—His isolation and the ingratitude of his fellow countrymen—His plans for a Rhapsody on Greek folk-tunes—His tone-poem In Bohemia*—His views on modern French music—Celebrating Chopin's centenary.*

CHAPTER XIX page 165
Diaghilef in 1907 and after—His ideas—His advisers and helpers—Their wonderful team-work—His catholicity and mutability of outlook—My opinion of his production of a Tamara *ballet.*

CHAPTER XX page 172
The Russian concerts of 1907—Russian composers in Paris—Rimsky-Korsakof on Boris Godunof, *on French music, and on his own opera* Sadko*—Felix Blumenfeld—Glazunof—A French critic's blunder—A glimpse of Scriabin—I become Diaghilef's second-in-command He decides to produce* Boris Godunof*—Impossibility of producing it in its genuine form.*

CHAPTER XXI page 181
Boris Godunof *at the Paris Opéra—Ruthless excisions—A stuffed parrot as compensation for a suppressed episode—I prevent the cutting out of the Revolution scene—Rehearsing under difficulties—A Press rehearsal of an unusual kind—Impromptu scene-shifters—An angry editor—Triumph rewards our efforts.*

Contents

CHAPTER XXII *page* 195
Relaxations during the Russian season—At the Louvre with Bakst—The Bal des Quat'z-Arts—*A memory of Mata-Hari—Scenes and costumes at the* Bal des Quat'z-Arts.

CHAPTER XXIII *page* 205
The début in Paris of Diaghilef's Ballet—Fokin at work—Scarcity of suitable music and how it was overcome—The Igor *dances and* Cleopatra—*First Act of Glinka's* Russlan and Liudmila – *Rimsky-Korsakof's* Maid of Pskof *produced under a new name—Nijinsky, Pavlova, Karsavina—Memorie of Caran d'Ache—Our plans for a London Season and a visit to London—My first break with Diaghilef.*

CHAPTER XXIV *page* 218
Differences adjusted—The 1910 Ballet Season at the Opéra—Stravinsky's Fire-Bird—Shéhérazade—*Revival of Adolphe Adam's* Giselle – *My final break with Diaghilef and a memory of an earlier quarrel—The first performance of Stravinsky's* Rite of Spring—*The Diaghilef version of* Khovanshchina—*Diaghilef on possessions.*

CHAPTER XXV *page* 227
I start on a journey to Petrograd—A visit to Schönberg in Berlin—His views on the use and misuse of modern devices—His paintings—Schönberg amid his pupils—His Handbook of Harmony—*The Russian customs.*

CHAPTER XXVI *page* 232
Petrograd—A visit to Glazunof—César Cui—Ziloti—Gretchaninof, Liapunof, and a surfeit of pancakes—A manuscript of Mussorgsky revised by Balakiref—The home of the Rimsky-Korsakofs—Wonderful hospitality—Karatyghin and Mussorgsky's Salammbô—*Findeisen—Import-*

Contents

ance of his work as critic, historian, and editor—Young Russian composers—I am arraigned for my opinions on Tchaikowsky—Vain attempt to examine the Boris Godunof *manuscripts—Street dialogues.*

CHAPTER XXVII *page* 246
A parenthesis on my musical likes and dislikes—My impressions of Richard Strauss's music—The value of first impressions—Spontaneous, taught *and* caught *opinions—The critic and his readers.*

CHAPTER XXVIII *page* 257
Arnold Bennett in Paris—His interest in music—His home at Fontainebleau—A poem by Meredith discussed—What I discovered in Bennett's diary—My preface to a privately printed booklet of his—Plans for opera libretti—Bennett at work and play—Questions of attire—Bennett on Boris Godunof.

CHAPTER XXIX *page* 265
Criticism—My meditations on the vocabulary of my craft—The effect of a misused word—My lectures on "programme" music and criticism—A course on contemporary music—First Paris performance of a Bartók quartet—A perplexed board—A would-be critic checked in his career—A handicapped music-lover—My books on Musical Taste and on Criticism.

CHAPTER XXX *page* 279
How I came to be attracted by England—Early attempts at writing for the English public—First visits to England—Thomas Hamond—At the Royal Academy of Music—Professor Corder on French taste—Vaughan Williams and Ravel—A music Congress in London—Bathing in the Serpentine in 1911.

Contents

CHAPTER XXXI *page* 291
My situation in 1914—Léon Vallas and the Revue Française de Musique*—The war—I join the British Intelligence—Results of studying Edgar Allan Poe—Code-picking—Examining candidates—My marriage.*

CHAPTER XXXII *page* 299
Reverting to music after the war—Musical France and England: retrospects and comparisons—The Press and public, there and here—On hissing at concerts—The genuine Boris Godunof *published—What broadcasting may do.*

INDEX *page* 314

AUTHOR'S NOTE

Portions of chapters I and XIII appeared in *The Nineteenth Century and After*; of chapters IX, XIV, and XV in *The Monthly Musical Record*; of chapter VII in *The Listener*. Permission to reprint is gratefully acknowledged.

M. D. C.

ILLUSTRATIONS

THE AUTHOR	*frontispiece*
MAURICE RAVEL	*to face page* 80
ALBENIZ AND HIS DAUGHTER LAURA	97
HENRI DUPARC	101
POSTCARD WITH BLACK-AND-WHITE DRAWING FROM DUPARC. THE MUSIC CONSISTS OF THE BEGINNING OF A PHRASE IN HIS SONG "LA VIE ANTÉRIEURE", MERGING INTO THE "JEWELS" AIR FROM "FAUST" (*see page* 108)	108
IANCO BINENBAUM	112
FIRST PAGE OF AUTOGRAPH MANUSCRIPT OF A "SARABANDE" BY SATIE	129
BALAKIREF, WITH A FEW BARS FROM HIS "TAMARA"	160
RIMSKY-KORSAKOF, WITH A QUOTATION FROM HIS OPERA "TSAR SALTAN"	177
CHALIAPIN AS IVAN THE TERRIBLE (1909). FROM AN ORIGINAL PRINT BY DE LOSQUES	206
NIJINSKY IN "SHÉHÉRAZADE"	209
LOPOKHOVA IN THE "IGOR" DANCES (1910)	213
GRIGORIEF AND BOULGAKOF IN "THE FIRE-BIRD"	220
DANCERS IN "THE RITE OF SPRING" (1913)	224
ETHEL (1933)	292
THE AUTHOR FISHING THE LAC DE TIGNES	301
THE AUTHOR AND HIS WIFE, AT THE COL DU PALET, ABOVE THE LAC DE TIGNES	301

CHAPTER I

Musical Paris in the 'nineties—Currents and cross-currents—Official circles hostile to new music—Franck and Debussy ostracized—Progressive activities in the teeth of opposition.

I

Paris in the 'nineties and after was a wonderfully active and stimulating centre—stimulating by virtue not only of all the splendid music that French composers were writing, of the speedy growth of a live interest in music old and modern, and of all the new ideas and aspirations that were afloat, but also of the very cross-currents that convulsed it and of its atmosphere of violent partisanship and combativeness.

There can be no doubt that when the history of musical evolution and progress from the 'eighties to the first decade or so of the present century comes to be seen in its true perspective, the leading part played by France will be acknowledged. New, live forces, it is true, were breaking out all over Europe; but nowhere was activity as great and as far-reaching as in France—a country which, in the course of a very few years, had risen from a deplorably low level to a high one, and was still rising fast.

Even so, it may well be asked why all the fuss and flurry, the organized campaigns and guerilla warfare, which, viewed from afar, seem merely so many storms in a tea-cup (Romain Rolland described the situation picturesquely and satirically in the volume *La Foire sur la Place* of *Jean Christophe;* but he showed the true significance of the whole movement in the chapters *Le Renouveau* of his *Musiciens d'Aujourd'hui*). In England, too, a musical renaissance started taking place almost at the same period. But it began and continued without violent reactions or sudden explosions: from the days of Parry and Stanford and Mackenzie in his youth to those of Bax, Bliss, and Walton, progress was marked by no tumultuous upheaval, not even by abnormal excitement. Enthusiasm and apathy, approval and disapproval rubbed along together without much friction.

But then, England was simply a country which had sunk into bad habits passively. She had no musical officialdom always prompt to rise in arms against progressive composers, as in France the Académie des Beaux-Arts and the Conservatoire against Franck, Debussy, and, a little later, Ravel. Nor were the new works of her composers, as they appeared, denounced and derided by journalists at home and abroad. We may smile to-day, or raise our eyebrows, and put it all down to French overexcitability: but looking deeper, we shall soon realize that the issues were not so trifling as might seem to casual observers. Indeed France was, in many respects, the worst possible field for a musical renaissance—not merely a field that had long remained almost unproductive and untilled, but one that, besides being overgrown with tenacious weeds, was held in force by active foes of progress: so that pioneers felt that they had not only many things worth fighting for, but good reasons to fight lustily.

II

It was of paramount importance, for instance, to oppose the influence of musical officialdom. The Conservatoire, the official upholder of what was supposed to be the true French musical tradition and official distributor of musical education, was little more than a stronghold of time-worn conventions and blind prejudices. The one object of its curriculum (apart from the instrumental classes, which were excellent) was to turn out composers of conven-

Official circles hostile to new music

tional operas and operettas. Ambroise Thomas, who was its director from 1871 to 1896, once gave, to a suggestion that the art of composing instrumental music might be included in the programme of studies, the highly characteristic reply that "No musician of standing would condescend to become a mere teacher of symphony." This was, let it be noted, at a time when César Franck was in charge of an organ class, and had long been teaching composition to private pupils, some of whom, such as Vincent d'Indy, had already made their mark in instrumental music. But then Franck, while exercising a beneficial influence second only to Wagner's, was practically ostracized by the powers that were.

I remember entering one day the library of the Conservatoire (a library open not to students only, but to the public) in order to read some of his scores. To my amazement I found out that the library possessed no score of his symphony, his piano quintet, or his string quartet. And the attendant to whom I had handed my slips looked at me very much askance, making me feel that thenceforward I was to be a suspicious character for having dared to expect to find music of that kind in those august precincts (this was, I believe, in 1898).

All composers whose practice ran counter to the rules of the musical game as played, compulsorily, at the Conservatoire were considered undesirable when not actually banned. In the counterpoint classes, pupils were warned not to be influenced by Bach's "irregularities". Many things of Beethoven, too, were thought to set a bad example; and Wagner's music, naturally, even more so. A story told, years later, by Widor, the famous organist, shows how little some of the official leaders knew of the great classics. After hearing one of Bach's chorales played at an examination, Ambroise Thomas was greatly moved. "What wonderful music!" he exclaimed. "How can it be we know nothing about it? Where does it come from?"

Franck and Debussy ostracized

III

Debussy, of course, was absolutely taboo, despite the fact that the Académie had sanctioned his right to existence by awarding him the Prix de Rome. As I shall relate in another chapter, the Académie was careful not to commit a similar mistake with Ravel; and let it be recorded that even before Debussy had come back from Rome, his official sponsors were deploring, in reports published at the taxpayers' expense for all to read, that he should be "bent on achieving the weird, the unintelligible, the impossible to perform."

Nor was this hostility short-lived. In 1902, at the Press rehearsal of his *Pelléas et Mélisande*, I heard a well-known professor at the Conservatoire say in an angry voice to a group of his pupils assembled around him during an interval: "Le premier qui apporte cette cochonnerie de partition dans ma classe, le premier qui s'en autorise pour faire des fautes d'harmonie, je le f—— à la porte de ma classe, et je le fais f—— à la porte du Conservatoire." He was, no doubt, merely letting off steam: later, I think, he developed a genuine liking for *Pelléas*. But his attitude that day represented exactly the official stand taken by the Conservatoire. A little later one pupil, by name Emile Vuillermoz (who has since made a great reputation as a critic) was actually expelled, at another teacher's request, for having been found in possession of the forbidden score while attending a class.

IV

While modern music, despite the pundits, was making headway, a strong reaction against the neglect of old masterpieces was taking place under the leadership of a few enthusiasts, among whom the foremost was the admirable Charles Bordes. He founded, in 1892, the Association des Chanteurs de Saint-Gervais, and, two years

Progressive activities in the teeth of opposition
later, the Schola Cantorum. Thanks to him, and to others too, it became possible for music-lovers to acquire a reasonable degree of familiarity with Bach, Palestrina, Josquin des Prés, Orlando Lasso, and many others. A little later the pianist Blanche Selva, a pupil of d'Indy, started doing very much what Harold Samuel is doing nowadays in England—giving recitals of Bach's music, and playing it simply, straightforwardly, with a thorough intelligence of its style and quality. Wanda Landowska appeared. She played Bach and other old masters on the harpsichord. Vincent d'Indy revealed to us Monteverdi's *Orfeo*. All these experiences, and many others with them, were the more thrilling for us because we felt full well that every one of them was the direct outcome of a successful move in the campaign against the prevailing routine—again an object well worth fighting for, and a good reason to fight with a will. Eventually a few of the combatants—especially among those engaged in fighting for modern music—developed a taste for warfare for its own sake, and indulged in fighting around modern music rather than for it; this after all, is intelligible even though it does seem ridiculous. The most preposterous was that the "pro-moderns", instead of forming a united front, split up into clans which fought one another—as when attempts were made to down Ravel in Debussy's name, and later to oppose Ravel to Debussy; or when the Schola-Cantorum clique (consisting, as cliques usually do, of underlings and hangers-on) stealthily strove to undermine the growing influence of both Debussy and Ravel. Nobody who did not live in Paris in those days could realize how true and free from exaggeration Rolland's description in *La Foire sur la Place* is. But all the same, music and interest in music were growing speedily and healthily.

It was in that atmosphere that I learnt to love music and began my career. Before going further, I shall relate the circumstances that led to my being first a spectator of,

Progressive activities in the teeth of opposition and later, to a small extent, an actor in that musical life of Paris whose characteristics I have attempted to sketch as a background to these reminiscences.

CHAPTER II

My childhood—Paris schools in the 'eighties and 'nineties—Unhygienic conditions and splendid teaching—Three masters I gratefully remember.

I

I was born at Marseilles on 2 October, 1877. My father was a Greek, a merchant, and had settled in that town, where he married my mother, also of Greek blood, but born at Marseilles, whither her family had come after fleeing from Chio at the time of the massacres (1821). An old servant, who as a girl of fifteen had accompanied my great-grandmother in that flight, was still with the family. I can see her still, a sweet frail little dame in semi-national costume (with beribboned bonnet and elaborate black apron), spending hours in the nursery, telling her beads and crooning, for my delight, old songs in a curious patois, not always Greek. One of them began, I remember:

> Donda, palonda,
> Setti passi l'onda;
> Sia Maria,
> La mbarka no ze mia . . .

Some of them, maybe, would constitute, did I remember them in full, valuable additions to the repertory of Mediterranean folk-tunes. But it did not occur to me at that time that here was an early opportunity for a future student, in a mild way, of this subject.

I should like to have characteristic anecdotes to tell of my childhood. A friend of my wife has assured us that

My childhood

her daughter, when a tiny baby, used to show great delight when her father was playing Bach, but start whimpering whenever he switched on to other music, even not startlingly contrasting in style. I wish I could tell some similar story about myself. It is the very kind of thing that would look well as a start to the memoirs of a music critic. But the only one I remember which might serve as a substitute is that when the time came for me to be taught the piano (I must have been about seven), after a few lessons I declared that I did not want to play the little pieces in the *Méthode* provided by my governess, because they were too silly. This, I think, was ominous enough. The lessons, by the way, were soon given up, because I was not in the least interested, and made no headway.

All the music I had heard so far was that played by my mother, an excellent pianist, but one whose repertory, apart from a few things by Chopin, consisted entirely of drawing-room pieces. I liked to hear her play—especially Prudent's *Danse des Fées* and a fantasy on motifs from Weber's *Oberon*. To this day the page's song from that opera has preserved a special significance for me. A little later I had my first experiences of orchestral music at Aix-les-Bains, where my mother went to take the waters (my father by that time had been dead four years). The Colonne symphony orchestra gave regular concerts at the Casino; and every day, at two o'clock, a small contingent of its members played lighter music. At ten minutes to two, I was sure to be seen rushing towards the Casino with my governess in tow. I listened with rapture to all they played. Once or twice I was taken to the symphony concerts: but I did not like these so well. I was also allowed, one night, to stay up for the first two acts of *Carmen* at the theatre. But these left no musical impression. It was some eight years later that the revelation of music was to come to me.

If I showed no disposition for music, I did well in the

Paris schools in the 'eighties and 'nineties

matter of languages, thanks to my mother's eager care. As soon as I was able to talk, I was taught Greek, Italian, and English as well as French. During all my childhood, I read far more English books—from nursery rhymes and *Alice in Wonderland* upwards—than French. I thoroughly appreciated my merits as a polyglot, apparently: for my mother has told my wife that one day, at the age of four, I was taken by the maid to a draper's shop and, upon the draper's beaming and saying: "Quel gentil petit garçon!" the nice little boy drew himself up and said proudly: "Et je sais quatre langues!" At eight I was put on to German: but by then, my first nurse, who was from Naples, having long left me, I had forgotten Italian, so that I was unable to boast that I knew five languages.

II

In the Autumn of 1886 we left Marseilles for Paris, where my mother was to undergo an operation. It was the beginning of a twenty-odd years' fight against various ailments which, alas, gradually led to total blindness.

The following year I entered school—not as a boarder, but as a *demi-pensionnaire*, going to the school every morning and leaving in the evening. In those days the usual schools to attend, for boys (aristocratic or plebeian, rich or poor) going in for a thorough classical education, were the *lycées*, State institutions under the direct control of the Ministry of Education. These were run on very backward lines in all respects except one: that of teaching, which was splendid. No attempt was made to develop character or to foster a sense of responsibility—not even a pretence. There was, in fact, nobody who could have done any such thing. Apart from the *professeurs*, who came to the school only to hold their classes, the only masters to be in daily contact with the boys were the *maîtres d'études* (as a rule, either men who were reading for an examination or awaiting a better appointment, or

Paris schools in the 'eighties and 'nineties

older men who had failed to obtain a degree). Their sole duty was to sit at the desk during prep. hours and patrol the recreation ground and refectory in order to maintain discipline. One of them, I think, slept in each dormitory. But there was no call for them to speak to the pupils except to issue instructions or to admonish. The head and his second in command, the *censeur des études*, we never saw except from a distance, when they came into the classes to read out competition results, or when we were in for either a wigging or a piece of advice. In short, all that the masters did was to make us work and keep us in order. There was no one to whom a boy could take his troubles—except such troubles as might arise over a piece of work, when a *maître d'études* would perhaps stretch a point and give first aid if capable of so doing; and any one of us who might have sought help on a personal matter would surely have been considered a freak and a nuisance.

Even self-respect formed no part of the education scheme. At the *lycée* I eventually went to, no accommodation for washing was provided except in the dormitories, and nobody was allowed there between getting up and bed-time. This meant that we all had to sit at lunch and "tea" (bread and water, with the possibility of buying chocolate from the porter) with unwashed hands. The boarders—who, by the way, were never allowed outside the school building except on Sundays, to visit their families—could not wash before dinner either. Nor could we change or wash before or after gym (compulsory) or fencing lessons (optional). We did everything in our town clothes and starched shirts and collars; so that often, at the end of the day, even those of us who had started quite clean were sorry sights to see.

However, this was to be for me a later experience. The first school I attended was a big private one, the Ecole Monge, run by a progressively minded man, Aimé Godart by name, who had, among other things, sounder notions of decency and hygiene than the then Ministry of Education. Every day before lunch we were actually marched off to lavatories where cold water and towels (but no soap) enabled us to wash our hands. And the beautifully illustrated prospectus of the school proclaimed: "Les internes prennent deux bains de pieds par semaine, et un grand bain tous les quinze jours." But, even at the Ecole Monge, it was impossible for a pupil to wash at other times, or to get a drink of water except at meals.

Godart was the first to institute outdoor games for the boys, the *lycées* following suit a year or two later. He also showed initiative in other directions—arranging for concerts to be given at the school, for instance. But this meant extras on the bill, and the concerts, owing to lack of support, had been given up before my time.

I stayed there four years. My best recollections of the period are the excellent lessons in natural history which we received. The professor, Léon Gérardin, was capital at his job. During these four years, we were taken through elementary botany, geology, zoology, and anatomy. He encouraged us to collect and taught us to identify plants and stones and fossils (there are splendid fossil beds all around Paris, and I spent my holidays in Auvergne, where interesting minerals abound; and the school had a botanical garden of its own). Geology and mineralogy remained favourite hobbies of mine. This splendid tuition, and the fact that I had a cousin who was a doctor, and never wearied of answering my questions and providing me with well-chosen primers on the natural sciences, physics, and chemistry, made me decide that I should become a doctor. And this was my ideal until music came and swept it away.

III

At thirteen, I left the Ecole Monge for the *lycée* Janson

Three masters I gratefully remember

de Sailly. No more lessons in natural history for me, but I was fortunate in being put under a first-rate master, Gabriel Vauthier, for French, Latin, and Greek. He was a lovable man and a fine scholar. He had eccentricities—very strange ones—which amused us as much as they bewildered us. He remained an impish schoolboy at heart, and we felt this and loved him all the more for it. He hated to hear a pen squeak. He would creep stealthily towards offenders, jerk the penholder out of their hands (thereby remorselessly adding to their inkiness) and break it. But the bereft owners were expected to go on taking notes, so that it was well to be provided with plenty of spares.

When he had to take two classes consecutively, he used to remain in the room during recreation interval. Once I came in from the playground to get a handkerchief from my overcoat pocket. He was standing in the centre of the room, looking surprisingly innocent. I went to my peg. The coat was not there. I looked round, and saw on the floor, in front of him, a shapeless, very dusty bundle. Feeling in need of a little relaxation, he had tied several of our overcoats together by the sleeves, and had been kicking this substitute for a football all round the room. "But, Monsieur Vauthier," I exclaimed, "you've got *my* overcoat there!" "Well," he retorted calmly, "what about it?" What indeed! I untied the bundle, got my handkerchief, and ruefully hung my coat on its peg. I wonder whether it was allowed to remain there after I had left the room.

But he loved teaching, and he *could* teach! He spared neither himself nor us. Finding me promising, he asked me whether I should care to do extra work in order to train for the Concours Général, the yearly inter-schools competition. I readily agreed, and was invited to come to his house on Sunday mornings for private lessons. I did not realize that this meant for him sacrificing part of the very little spare time he had; and of course no mention

Three masters I gratefully remember

was made of a fee, nor would he have accepted one. But then, he was a glutton for work.

When I had become a music critic, I was brought back into contact with him. His wife, a music teacher and composer, often asked me to their house. He was working harder than ever. After the war, while on a visit to Paris, I took my wife to see them, for I wanted her to meet the old master of whom I had spoken to her so often. He had long been pensioned off, but was still hard at work: no longer on literature and the classics, but on historical research, a lifetime passion which he was able to indulge in freely at last. He toiled, his wife told us, sixteen hours a day, and hated interruption. But he consented to make an exception for us, and we were admitted into his sanctum. To lure him out of it was, we heard, an almost impossible task.

But to revert to my schooldays: I am glad to be able to record that I was fortunate enough not to disappoint him, for I took the first prize in Latin version and a minor reward in another subject. I was the first pupil of his to score such a success at the Concours Général; and later, he told me that I had brought him luck. The following year, a boy in his class took two first prizes, and another boy one. These first prizes consisted of fine sets of bound volumes and a laurel wreath (made of gilt paper) which was solemnly placed on our brows the day of the distribution—an imposing ceremony in the Grand Hall of the Sorbonne, with military band and all. To this the *lycée* added a silver medal. And a distant relation of ours, Mrs. Julie Ralli—she and her family were the best friends my mother ever had, and were to do us many kindnesses—insisted on coming to witness the show and afterwards presented me with a hundred francs—four whole pounds, an unparalleled tip to me.

But even more important than the prize was the training which had placed it within my reach. Vauthier had

Three masters I gratefully remember taught me not only the true craft of translation, but the right way to tackle languages, by wasting no time, at the outset, over their surface, but forthwith getting to grips with essentials—investigating spirit and modes of structure and articulation. It was, of course, years later that I realized this; and whatever small ability I may have shown in both directions I owe almost entirely to him.

More generally speaking, the tuition we received was capital, and the standard of knowledge and efficiency we were encouraged to achieve very high. Too high, I have been told since, because it meant too great a strain on young minds. I do not agree. Those of us who were not up to the mark were not compelled to do more than the minimum required for examination purposes; the others were taken as far as they could reach.

I could have benefited by that tuition far more than I did. After having won my prize, I was considered a great asset to the school (what we used to call a *bête à concours*, an animal trained for exhibition purposes), and availed myself of the ensuing privileges to work as little as possible at the things that bored me—history and mathematics, for instance. Later, I was to regret having neglected the latter, and had to study them afresh before I could find my way through the intricacies of acoustics. And having become slack in certain respects, I grew slack in others. I remained a *bête à concours*, but never won another prize at the Concours Général.

IV

Another master to whom I must pay a grateful tribute is André Lalande, whose pupil I was for philosophy during my last year at school. His course was wonderfully stimulating and, though elementary, so admirably clear and thorough—especially in matters of psychology, æsthetics, logic, and methodology—that to this day I find myself constantly referring to the notes I then took. When

Three masters I gratefully remember
I became a lecturer at the Ecole des Hautes Etudes Sociales, he was a member of the Board, and gave me invaluable advice and criticism on my lectures and also my writings.

Long after my settling in England my wife and I were having a holiday in Dauphiné. During a climb with friends, I heard them talking of having seen Lalande the previous day. "Do you mean André Lalande, the philosopher?" I asked. "Is he here?" They told me that he was spending the summer in the next village. I was so excited that when I came back I barely took time to change before rushing to the next village to hunt him up. After that I saw him nearly every day, and we often played bridge with him and his wife in the evening. My *Principles and Methods of Musical Criticism* had just appeared. I had sent him a copy, and here was the opportunity to discuss things with him. I had already started preparing complements for an eventual second edition. Writing the book, and reading or hearing what other people had to say about it, had made me painfully aware of the difficulties of the subject, and of the need to explore certain avenues more carefully than I had done. I took all my perplexities to him, and he gave me a list of books to read, especially on the psychology of imagination and problems of judgment —which was the very thing I needed. One of my troubles, I said, was the difficulty of ascertaining exactly the differences in the meanings which various authors gave to the same terms. "Well," he replied, "perhaps I can help you. I have compiled a vocabulary of philosophical terms and will send you a copy." I imagined that he was referring to a pamphlet or small handbook, and was amazed when I received in London the two stout volumes of his *Vocabulaire Technique et Critique de la Philosophie*, that splendid guide through the maze of philosophical theories and terminology.

By the time I became his pupil, I had begun to study music; and I benefited all the more by his teaching thanks

Three masters I gratefully remember to the patience with which he used to reply to all my questions about the philosophy of music, and mainly about Wagner. One branch of his course was æsthetics, it will be remembered; but I fear that, even when he was dealing with metaphysics, I now and then dragged in Wagner.

CHAPTER III

*Wagner's music gives me my first thrill—Piano lessons—
Bach—Pierre Louÿs and Debussy—José-Maria de Hérédia—Other musical experiences—My studies interrupted—
My début as a critic.*

I

Until the year 1893 or thereabouts, I had never given a thought to music, nor derived any impression from the little I must have heard at times—although I remember nothing about it. Then it happened all of a sudden. One Thursday morning (Thursday was half-holiday) a schoolfellow of mine said to me: "Are you going to the Trocadéro festival this afternoon, to hear Melba?" I stared at him; but he—already a confirmed concert-goer—was so enthusiastic that he persuaded me to go. At the booking-office I found that the cheap seats were sold out. Only stalls, at ten francs, remained. Never mind: as I had come to hear Melba, and happened, by a miracle, to have ten francs, hear Melba I would. I heard her. I did not listen much to her singing. The "festival" was a gala concert of the Concerts Lamoureux, and the programme consisted chiefly of Wagner excerpts: the *Lohengrin* prelude, I think, the prelude and Good Friday music from *Parsifal*, and *The Ride of the Walkyries*. Other things too. I don't remember exactly . . . I was absolutely carried off my feet. Returning home I could think of nothing else. Within a few days I had bought books on Wagner and decided to study music. Soon afterwards I bought the vocal scores of *Rheingold* and *the Walküre* and a complete set of Wagner's writings

Piano lessons

(how glad I was that I knew German!). In the Autumn my mother presented me with a season ticket for the Concerts Lamoureux, and I arranged for piano lessons with the school's music teacher, Eugène Claveau.

I was lucky, for in him I found not only a good instructor—he was a violinist in the orchestra of the Opéra; later I went through all Beethoven's violin sonatas with him, and a terrible ordeal it was for the poor fellow, who had to set me right while playing—but a man wise in his ways. When at the third lesson or so I arrived with the vocal score of *Rheingold* (in Klindworth's transcription, not in the easier one—the best was just good enough for me) and said: "I want to learn to play this," he never turned a hair, but left me to find out for myself that my ambition was premature. Realizing how eager I was to make headway, he urged me on. But when he suggested to me, the following year, that I should learn to transpose Bach's *Inventions* and *Preludes* at sight (Bach had been my next love, owing to my discovery, in a bundle of my mother's music, of an old copy of the *Forty-Eight*) I felt that he was hardly playing the game. But he insisted; and this and other tasks of a similar kind went a long way towards helping me to coordinate and use the theoretical knowledge I was eagerly acquiring from books.

This picture of an absolute tyro led by his intuition straight to Wagner and Bach, and thus entering a world of pure joy, with the result that he developed a vocation for music would be impressive indeed were I not compelled to confess that I was not attracted in the least by Mozart or Haydn or Chopin (all that was to come later), and that Beethoven's symphonies left me with very mixed impressions. Not so, however, his quartets. I shall speak elsewhere of my other early loves and how they were born.

Pierre Louÿs and Debussy

II

In those days, we were living in a flat at 147 Boulevard Malesherbes, on the second floor. Pierre Louÿs, the writer, occupied one on the fourth floor. He was very keen on music, and played the piano a good deal. I could hear him quite plainly. One of his favourite things was the first Act of *Siegfried*. Visitors came to see him, and they too played. At times I heard music which sounded very peculiar to me, and which I was quite unable to identify. Many years later, I solved the riddle: I learnt that Debussy was one of his intimate friends, and, being at the time engaged in composing *Pelléas et Mélisande*, used to play excerpts from it, and other works of his as well, for Pierre Louÿs' benefit. I must have crossed Debussy many times on the stairs.

If I had only known, how eagerly I should have listened! I wonder whether *Pelléas* would have appealed to me at the time—even without ceilings in between. Debussy's very name was unknown to me. I was saturated with Wagnerian ideals. Even my first experiences of Russian music were yet to come. But at least, I might have acquired a small measure of familiarity with Debussy's style; and, when *Pelléas* was performed, eight years or so later, I should have been prepared for its wonderfully novel strains instead of having had a mere twenty-four hours to run through the vocal score before attending the Press rehearsal.

I never spoke to Pierre Louÿs or, to my knowledge, saw him. This is all the more strange for the reason that, later on, he married a daughter of José-Maria de Hérédia, the poet, whom for a long time I used to meet almost weekly, together with his daughters and his other two sons-in-law, Henri de Régnier and Maurice Maindron, at the house of a friend, where we played billiards. Whenever I missed an easy stroke, de Hérédia would throw

José-Maria de Hérédia

back his shoulders, beam on the assembly, and hold me up to shame in a loud voice. I can still hear him shouting: "Ce descendant de Périclès joue au billard comme un Iroquois!" A fine-looking man he was, alert of features, brown of skin, with wonderfully silky pepper-and-salt hair and beard. He had great charm. He had written very little, but earned a big reputation on the strength of beautifully chiselled poems which were widely diffused long before being collected in the volume *Les Trophées*. But one had the impression that there was great power, as well as knowledge, in his forceful personality. He was the custodian of the Bibliothèque de l'Arsenal, which fact led me at one time to go to work there. He was very kind and helpful.

Henri de Régnier—aristocratic, lean of face, bald, with a drooping moustache and an eyeglass—was as silent and intent on the game as de Hérédia was jovial and flamboyant about it. His wife had already earned a reputation as a writer under her *nom de plume*, Gérard d'Houville. I lost sight of them for many years, but in the days of the Russian ballet called on her to ask whether she would care to attend the shows. She accepted and, as we hoped, devoted to them an article or two which were among the very best of the many that appeared at the time.

III

I met Debussy for the first time in 1902. During the first years of my musical studies my piano teacher was the only musician whom I knew. But I was acquiring a great variety of experiences. The dealer from whom I got my music, Eugène Fromont, was the agent for Schott's, the publishers of Wagner's works, and this was how I came to patronize his shop. Realizing my eagerness—evinced by many questions and much excitement while I inspected the treasures on his shelves—he very kindly allowed me unlimited credit, for which I should never have dared to

Other musical experiences

ask, and gave me the choice of the complimentary tickets which he received for displaying concert-bills. I went to many recitals and to the concerts of the Société Nationale, devoted to new music, mainly French. And, of course, Lamoureux played other music besides Wagner's. This I often regretted, but at times it meant new thrills. There were many new thrills in the air. It was the moment when d'Indy's and Debussy's music was gaining ground, and Ravel's appearing. The battle around Wagner was subsiding, but hardly any works of his except *Lohengrin*, *Tannhäuser*, the *Walküre*, and—a little later—the *Mastersingers* were to be heard at the Opéra. When about to produce the *Walküre* for the first time in France, in 1892 or 1893, the manager of the Opéra, struck by the notion that perhaps the public might wish to know something of *Rheingold*, had arranged for one lecture on this work, illustrated by excerpts, to take place at his theatre. The excerpts were given with piano accompaniments, and one of the players was Debussy. For most of our knowledge of Wagner's music, we were indebted to the initiative of the conductors Colonne and Lamoureux. What an excitement it was when at their symphony concerts, excerpts —sometimes, O bliss, a whole act and more—of *Tristan* or *Parsifal* could be heard!

Claveau used to give me tickets for the Opéra on Wagner nights. The players were allowed (incredible as it may seem) occasionally to bring friends into the orchestra pit so far as floor-space permitted; and in that pit I sat many a time, learning all I could from watching the players and conductor at work. In those days, the conductor's desk was right against the proscenium—a survival of the times when the singers alone mattered—and he conducted with his back turned to most of the players, and only his profile visible to the remainder.

Other musical experiences

IV

Other memorable experiences were provided by performers, at the Salle Pleyel, of Liszt's *Faust* and *Dante* symphonies in piano arrangements (Edouard Risler and Cortot were the players). These were as seldom to be heard in their orchestral form in the Paris of the 'nineties as they are in twentieth-century London. And to this day I am glad that I had that opportunity of an early acquaintance with them. I owe it mainly to a dear friend of mine, Fred Partington, who later married a daughter of the Marquis de Casa-Miranda, and, according to Spanish custom, succeeded to the title. He was a keen music-lover, and, being acquainted with Téodor de Wyzewa, had received much valuable advice and information from that most well-informed, enlightened, and versatile critic—now remembered chiefly as joint author, with G. de Saint-Foix, of an admirable book on Mozart.

Fred used to come to many concerts with me, the tickets provided by the kind Fromont being usually for two. He exercised, then as well as later, a great influence on my evolution, acting as both moderator and fellow scout; he was far more sober and wise than I, although no less enthusiastic. He urged me not to miss those two concerts, assuring me that the symphonies, whose very existence was unknown to me, were splendid, and that it was a great pity that Liszt should be known mainly by his poorest compositions and judged accordingly. After having heard the *Faust* and the *Dante*, I became as keen on Liszt as he was.

When I started writing, one of my first concerns was to call attention to his neglected or underrated masterpieces. The first book of mine to appear (1905) was a small one on Liszt.

In 1899, Lamoureux gave the first Paris performances of *Tristan and Isolde* in a small theatre rented for the

My studies interrupted

occasion. A little later, Cortot, suddenly blossoming into a very fine conductor, gave, in another theatre, *The Dusk of the Gods*. Cortot told me at the time that on hearing of the scheme the manager of the Opéra, who probably felt that a march was being stolen upon him, and who was —quite rightly—proud of the singer in his company who took the part of Wotan in the *Walküre*, exclaimed: "Je voudrais bien savoir qui est-ce qui va lui chanter Wotan dans son Crépuscule des Dieux!"

Then there was the revelation of Russian music: of Balakiref's *Tamara* and Rimsky-Korsakof's *Antar* and *Shéhérazade* and of various works of Borodin at the symphony concerts (no question, as yet, of Russian opera) and of Mussorgsky's songs suddenly sprung on the Parisians in 1896 by the d'Alheim couple (of whom more hereafter). In 1898, d'Indy's *Fervaal* was given at the Opéra-Comique, meeting with more censure than praise, but creating a profound impression upon a few of us. D'Indy too was one of the first composers on whom I wrote.

V

Medicine, of course, was thoroughly forgotten. Having discovered that music was my main interest in life, I went on listening, reading, and studying, but without forming any definite plans of action. I had a vague idea of becoming a composer, but no strong inclination in that direction—later, I found out that I was too keenly interested in the music written by others ever to be able to develop an individuality of my own. Conducting would have become my ambition had I not realized that I had started my musical studies far too late to be able to entertain any hope of acquiring all the needful knowledge. I also felt that I should hate having to conduct any music which I did not love; and I had no reason to suppose that I had any natural gift for conducting. In short, all my thoughts centred in learning as much as I could about

My studies interrupted

music and hearing more music. It is curious that, whereas I loved to talk about music, the idea of writing about it should not have entered my head.

I was not encouraged to take up music as a profession: very much the reverse. My mother loathed the idea; and considering how late and how suddenly my inclination had cropped up, she was not unjustified in suspecting that it might be merely a temporary infatuation. She discussed the matter with relatives and friends, who told her it would be madness. As I had no money to speak of, and she very little, I was urged to study law, after which a situation would be found for me; this, it was pointed out, would not prevent my keeping up music as a side-line. I matriculated at the École de Droit, but six months later was studying harmony at the Conservatoire. Then I was offered a job in a bank. I tried it and did not like it. My cousin the doctor (who was very fond of music but wished me, he said, to do well in life while cultivating Art) found me another, this time with an *agent de change*—the equivalent of the English stockbroker, but with the additional prestige of being one of a closed corporation of forty members, ranking high, and all appointed by the State. My new employer had been impressed, apparently, by what my cousin had told him of my musical abilities. He was a kind man, and gave me paternal advice. "Maybe you will not like the work much", he told me, "but stick to it. It gives you a status, and you'll get promotion. Et puis, vous êtes joli garçon, vous êtes artiste, et sûrement vous pourrez faire un beau mariage."

Alas for those high hopes! What money I earned (quite a reasonable amount) did not go far. We young clerks were not discouraged from "operating" on the Stock Exchange. Quite on the contrary, we were allowed special rebates on commissions. We also imagined that we had inside information. The temptation to try whether I could pick up money enough to be able soon to return

My début as a critic

to music was great. I took a flutter, and then another, came a cropper or two, and finally, the experience having proved costly, reverted to music with my mother's full approval. We decided to restrict our expenditure to the utmost and hope for the best. I got one or two odd jobs from publishers. Then one day a friend of mine, Binet-Valmer, the novelist, told me (probably after having had to endure a particularly long disquisition of mine on some musical topic) that I ought to become a musical critic. I was startled; I asked him if he really thought it would be possible. He urged me to go ahead, and gave me an introduction to Octave Maus, the proprietor and editor of the *Art Moderne*, a Belgian weekly of international repute. Maus, generously but rashly, accepted me as Paris musical correspondent, my instructions being to deal, as a rule, with new works only, because the paper was a small one and little space was available for musical topics. A few months later, Binet-Valmer founded in Paris *La Renaissance Latine*, a monthly (it lasted three years) and appointed me its musical critic. He too expected me to deal mainly with new or little-known works; and I may as well add, although I shall deal with the point in another chapter, that in Paris there existed very little demand for criticism of interpretations, and the supply was not only small, but often most peculiar. So there I was, at the age of twenty-four, launched all of a sudden in the very midst of the fray.

VI

My work brought me into closer contact not only with music, but with a good many composers and other musicians; and thereby I added, little by little, to my slender stock of knowledge. My previous experiences, while teaching me various things and stimulating in me a keen desire to help in the investigation of the many new problems that confronted everybody at the time, had not

My début as a critic

all been equally beneficial. Indeed, some ot them hampered me as much as they helped. For instance, my fiery enthusiasm for Wagner had blinded me for a time to the beauty of a good deal of other music which happened to stand, or appeared to stand, far away from his—Mozart's and Chopin's, for instance. I was only half-way towards recovery—thanks, mainly, I think, to Ravel, whose sharp rebukes had shamed me into reconsidering those views of mine and many others as well. I had been delighted with Debussy's *Prélude à la'près-midi d'un faune*, although not very deeply impressed. The first time I heard his string quartet (in 1897 or so, played by the Quatuor Ysaye, and therefore, I should think, splendidly) I was utterly bewildered. Fred Partington, who had come with me, asked me what I thought of it. I replied: "I wonder whether it is I who am mad, or the players, or the composer." And his reply was: "That is exactly what I feel." Later the memory of that experience was to be useful to me, not only as a reminder not to judge music in haste, but as a warning to have patience with people to whom things that are perfectly clear and sensible to me may seem obscure and senseless. Six years or so elapsed before I had another opportunity to hear Debussy's quartet; and then I wondered what could have baffled me at the first hearing.

Ravel's music attracted me from the outset and never rubbed me the wrong way, as Debussy's quartet had done. I have already alluded to other early loves of mine. And I may add, on the credit side, that I had developed a great keenness for Beethoven's piano sonatas and string quartets.

VII

As can be seen, I was, all told, as inexperienced as I was enthusiastic. And in order to cope more or less adequately with the musical events of that period, a good

My début as a critic

deal of experience would have been needful—especially as I was not treading the easier path. I did not begin by writing on safe subjects such as the well-known classics performed at symphony concerts, with regard to which even the veriest tyro need never go wrong so long as he restricts himself to elementary considerations, since he can find all the guidance he requires in easily accessible books.

I had to obey my instructions; and, as it happens, these corresponded exactly to my preferences. Even later, when I had found outlets for long special articles on subjects of my own choosing, it never occurred to me to write one on my beloved Wagner; plenty of other writers were doing justice to his genius and throwing light on the trend and various aspects of his art. And the same thing happened to me, for similar reasons, with regard to Bach, despite the growing attraction which his music exercised over me. I had studied with delight, among other things of his, *The Art of Fugue* and the *Musical Offering*, to which nobody except a few specialists was paying attention at the time, and I remember copying, from the Bach Society edition, the solutions of all the canons in the latter work. But instead of trying my hand at turning out something of my own on the subject, I made translations of the German writings which I had hunted up to help me in my study—translations which I did not succeed in getting published.

In short, whenever I considered that the very things which I felt were already said and well said, and that there was no opposition or indifference to overcome, I had no desire to play a part which would have been, to my mind, that of a fly on a wheel. But to write on Liszt and d'Indy and Ravel and the Russians, among others, was a different matter. I knew that there was a lot to be said, and felt that I had things of my own to say.

Had I been able to deal only with subjects in which I

My début as a critic

felt at home, all might have gone well. But while learning to swim, I was not allowed to choose my own pool. I had been thrown into the deep, swiftly moving, open waters of contemporary music and was compelled to keep afloat as best I could. Naturally, some of my efforts were very poor.

For instance, it was in May, 1902—exactly four months after my first Paris letter to the *Art Moderne* had appeared in print—that Debussy's *Pelléas et Mélisande* was first produced. There indeed was a chance for a tyro critic to display acumen and balance, and to fight for the new music against the prevailing hostility and routine! But, alas, I missed it! To this day I can but wonder how I missed it so thoroughly. Like all decent-minded people I had been roused to indignation by the unspeakable attitude of part of the audience at the Press rehearsals, by the murmurs and sniggers mingling with the music, the hissing at the end of nearly every act, the loud angry or derisive comments during every interval. And I was interested in a way, though not in the least moved. I felt that here was something boldly original and worthy of earnest attention. But it was my mind which told me this; my imagination had not been appealed to. As regards dramatic music, I was still far too exclusively under the influence of other, and very dissimilar, tendencies, to be able to realize the true significance of Debussy's lovely score. And in the end, all I managed to turn out was a notice, neither fish nor flesh nor good red herring when it was not gross misrepresentation, the very recollection of which makes me, even now, feel hot under the collar, so plainly did it betray my annoyance at being up against something which I could neither place nor understand. A few months later, after having heard *Pelléas* several times, I tried to make amends, as best I could, in another article: but, by that time, *Pelléas* had overcome all opposition; and I remained with the feeling that I had badly

My début as a critic

failed in the first important test to which my critical abilities had been put. My one solace was the hope that my first article might have remained unnoticed or soon be forgotten: I was, after all, only an insignificant speck in that turbulent, changeable, but eager and active musical Paris of thirty years ago.

CHAPTER IV

My first meeting with Ravel—We study Russian music together—His path to the Prix de Rome barred by official opposition—His views on music—His admiration for Liszt the composer.

I

Ravel and I first met in 1898 or thereabouts at an "At Home" to which I had been taken by a painter friend; and we frequently met there during a year or so. Our acquaintanceship—as later we confessed to one another—was marked from the first by reciprocal suspicion, because, although the hosts were altogether simple, worthy, and likable people, their "At Homes" used to be attended by quite a number of queer characters. Soon afterwards this suspicion became dislike: on his part because of the stupid remarks I used to pass on Debussy's music, on mine because of his sharp strictures on the music of Wagner, César Franck, and d'Indy.

Then, for a time, we lost sight of one another; but eventually we met again in the courtyard of the Conservatoire. He was still in Fauré's composition class, and I had obtained permission to attend Xavier Leroux' class of harmony for a time in order to rub up my technical knowledge; we started discussing music recently heard. The talk having veered round to Russian music, I suddenly asked him: "Do you remember *Tamara* at the Concerts Lamoureux?" His eyes shone. "Wasn't it lovely?" he replied. A few seconds later, to my surprise and delight, he burst out: "Look here: I've got the piano-duet score. Let's meet and play it together." I accepted

Ravel and I study Russian music together eagerly. Poor Ravel! He little knew what he was letting himself in for. I was (and have remained) a vile bungler at the piano, and especially in duet playing. Anyhow, we met, and we played *Tamara* again and again, and after that a quantity of other Russian music. And in our love for this music we found a first common bond. By tacit agreement we ceased discussing Wagner, Franck, and d'Indy (having, I presume, given up one another as hopeless); and we soon became great friends.

II

In 1901 he was awarded the second Grand Prize for composition, missing the first, or Prix de Rome, by a narrow margin of votes. But, at that time, he was practically without a friend in the musical world. His *Sites Auriculaires* for two pianos, performed in 1898 at a concert of the Société Nationale, had been received very coldly. Years later he revealed the fact that the performers, playing from a none too legible manuscript, had committed a number of serious mistakes—and the far-fetched, rather affected title may have prejudiced some of the listeners. In 1899 his overture *Shéhérazade* was described by one of the very few critics who condescended to notice it as "du Rimsky-Korsakof retripatouillé par un Debussyste qui serait jaloux d'égaler Erik Satie"—a pronouncement which most people, at that time, must have held to entail no less than three "distinct damnations, each one sure if the other two failed."

He was generally considered a dangerous revolutionist and iconoclast, and absolutely disliked in the official musical circles whose general attitude towards innovations in music I have outlined in the foregoing chapter. His outspoken, but usually shrewd and well-weighed utterances on music old and new, many of them expressing views that may have been novel at the time, but are by now almost universally held, were bandied about in

Path to Prix de Rome barred by official opposition
strangely distorted forms. I remember that one day Georges Marty (who was then a conductor at the Opéra and later became the conductor of the Concerts du Conservatoire) said to me: "Oh yes! Ravel—he's the fellow who says that Beethoven couldn't score for nuts!" And Marty was a genuine, open-minded artist and man, who did not incline in the least to side with the enemies of progress, and who, had he been personally acquainted with Ravel, would soon have realized how far the gossip he happened to have heard in Conservatoire circles was from the truth. What Ravel would actually say and repeat, as I have often heard him do, was that Beethoven's scoring, especially as regarded the brass, was not always free from imperfections. But, as I have said, Ravel, at the Conservatoire, was a marked man, against whom all weapons were good. And in consequence he was never awarded the Prix de Rome, which usually follows as a matter of course upon the obtaining of the second Grand Prize, and ensures the holders seven years of financial independence on a modest scale besides certain privileges as regards performance of their future works.

Twice again he was admitted to compete for it. And this, as he pointed out to me, involved each time a heavy financial sacrifice: for the candidates had to spend a whole month immured within the precincts of the Château de Compiègne, while composing their Cantata, and were given only house-room and a grant in aid of one hundred francs (then four pounds) towards their upkeep—which, as it happened, cost them five or six times that amount. And in 1905—the year after which, having reached the age limit, he could no longer compete—he was not even passed at the preliminary examination, whose sole object is to eliminate insufficiently competent candidates.

That the holder of a second Grand Prize should suddenly have become incapable of satisfactorily performing the two simple tasks (the writing of a fugue and a chorus)

Path to Prix de Rome barred by official opposition
of which this preliminary examination consisted was in itself incredible. But when one remembers that Ravel had to his credit, among other things, the *Jeux d'Eau*, the Song-set, *Shéhérazade* (which bears no relation to the Overture of the same name, performed in 1899 but never published) and the String Quartet (first performed in 1904 and published the same year), it becomes quite clear that the verdict in question was simply the expression of the hostility of the authorities.

Indeed, aggravating circumstances made it quite clear that the jury really wished to eliminate Ravel for good and all. Apart from the fact that Ravel was the only candidate nearing the age-limit (a consideration which often led the jury to stretch a point), it happened that the composer who had been awarded the Prix de Rome in 1904 had resigned his privileges in order to get married (such were the regulations in force: bachelordom was compulsory not only for candidates, but also for holders of the Prize until the end of their compulsory sojourn at Rome). In consequence, the jury had the right, that year 1905, to fill the vacancy by awarding two Prix de Rome, and so could have passed Ravel without impairing the normal chances of the other candidates. And on the other hand, a precedent for leniency (had it been needful) at the preliminary examination had been created by the fact that the jury, three or four years before, had passed a candidate who had proved unable to finish his fugue in the appointed time, because that candidate was nearing the age-limit.

One of the members of the musical section of the Académie des Beaux-Arts, apparently, had said on a previous occasion: "Il ne faut pas que M. Ravel s'imagine qu'on peut se moquer de nous." If the rumour is true, the attitude of the Académie is accounted for in a way. The texts of the competition cantatas were written to order by some poetaster or other in view of the usual conventional setting. Ravel may have written his settings

Path to Prix de Rome barred by official opposition
with his tongue in his cheek; indeed, one cannot imagine his having written them otherwise. Once, after being released from confinement at Compiègne, he informed us with glee that one of the lines in the text with which he had had to cope ran:

"Alcyone! Alcyone! Aimée! Aimée! . . . Hélas!"

but he certainly was far too experienced a composer not to have written them in the required style, and in perfectly workmanlike, musicianly manner. It must have been some uncomfortable consciousness that he, of all people, could not believe in the kind of stuff he had to write for competition purposes that led the jurors—some of whom turned out stuff of the same kind in all good faith, and often with very profitable results—to see parody when none was meant, to resent it, and to take summary revenge on the helpless composer.

The whole thing was so obvious that even the critics who had been, and were to continue to be, most hostile to Ravel's music raised a hue and cry. Nothing could make up, of course, for his loss of his last chance; but at least moral reparation of a kind was granted him. So strong a current of opinion arose that shortly afterwards the Director of the Conservatoire and a professor of composition at the same establishment, who, being also a member of the musical section of the Académie des Beaux-Arts, was impugned for having led the opposition against Ravel, handed in their resignations; and a thorough reform was carried out, Gabriel Fauré being appointed the Director. Soon afterwards Ravel was sitting on the examination and competition juries, and would, no doubt, have been appointed a professor had he so desired. After the war, I hear, he was invited to stand for election at the Académie des Beaux-Arts, but declined the honour.

III

To revert to the earlier days: he was then exactly as

Ravel's views on music

he is in the present year 1933, except that his hair was raven black and that he wore a beard. He carried out a good many experiments with that beard before deciding to do away with it for good and all. When first I knew him, he displayed a combination of moustache and short whiskers *à la Franz-Josef*. Then he tried a two-pointed beard, and later on a single-pointed. When one came into contact with him, the first impression was almost sure to be that of dryness and aloofness—very different from the semi-shy, semi-ironical reserve that was Debussy's first line of defence. He was endowed with a great capacity for indifference and also contempt, but—as one found out quite soon—as great a capacity for admiration; and I was to realize, a little later, that behind the cutting manner, the irony, and the aloofness, there lurked an even greater capacity for affection.

He had matured early, both in temperament and in musical outlook. Indeed, he is one of the few composers of whom it may be said that their earliest works are thoroughly representative both in spirit and in idiom. He had a marked taste for the recondite, which people who did not know him well considered a sign of affectation. He was aware of this, but it did not worry him in the least. One day, however, he said to me, rather impatiently: "Mais est-ce qu'il ne vient jamais à l'idée de ces gens-là que je peux être 'artificiel' par nature?" And there can be no doubt that with this remark he defined one of his idiosyncrasies quite accurately—one that is, however, more apparent in his early works than in the later.

IV

Many people alleged that the care he took to exclude from his music all that might resemble a direct expression of emotion was one of the signs of this artificiality. Once, in reply to a question of mine, he said that if he himself had to point out, in his music, passages in which the

Ravel's views on music

direct expression of emotion, far from being excluded, had been deliberately attempted, he would begin by selecting the opening of *Asie* in *Shéhérazade*, (*la goélette*), then *l'Indifférent* in the same set of songs, and, in the *Histoires Naturelles*, *le Martin-Pêcheur*, and the end of *Le Grillon*. He did not mention other obvious instances such as the slow movement of his String Quartet and the *Oiseaux Tristes* in *Miroirs*.

In his assessment of the music of other composers there was very little room for doubts, for half-hearted views, or even for any change of views. He may have learned, now and then, to like things which he had begun by not liking, but this must have occurred very seldom; and certainly he never came to dislike anything he had liked. His reasons for liking or disliking were definite, and for him final. To hear him pick to pieces a musical work, and then, by a swift process of reconstruction, deliver judgment, was an experience as instructive as it was fascinating.

His chief concern was with points of originality in idiom and texture. When calling attention to some beautiful thing, he would often wind up with: "Et puis, vous savez, on n'avait jamais fait çà!" Questions of form seemed to preoccupy him far less. The one and only test of good form, he used to say, is continuity of interest. I do not remember his ever praising a work on account of its form. But, on the other hand, he was very sensitive to what he considered to be defective form. Once he gave rise to great indignation by declaring, in the course of an article, that Franck's form often was "appallingly poor."

V

I have just referred to the rare interest of his verbal comments on music. Curiously, when writing critical articles (which in later years he was often asked to do, but hardly ever did unless pressed) he either did not trouble,

Ravel's views on music

or remained unable, to recapture the lucid, subtle, and illuminating terms in which he accounted for his views when talking. Indeed, he sometimes tended to drive his points home with a bludgeon rather than with the rapier which anybody would have considered to be his natural weapon, and which he could, when he chose, wield skilfully and with devastating effects. In one article, he dismissed Beethoven's *Missa Solemnis* with the sole epithet: "cette œuvre médiocre", leaving his readers to puzzle out his reasons for this unqualified verdict. Another time, he concluded a notice of d'Indy's *Fervaal* with the following remark: "Even more significant than the composer intended it to be is the symbol of Fervaal, who, while proclaiming the victory of life and love, climbs the heights with the dead body of a woman in his arms."

His dislike for much of d'Indy's music did not prevent his considering the *Symphonie sur un thème montagnard* a very fine work. There was little he admired in Wagner's music, but that little he admired very greatly. At a time when Gounod's music used to be sneered at in "advanced" circles, he passionately called attention to the lovely things to be found in it. During the early years of our friendship, my impression was that he set no great store by the music of Saint-Saëns: the only two examples of it which he used to mention with praise were the symphonic poems *Phaéton* and *La Jeunesse d'Hercule*. But in 1910 or 1911 I began to notice, rather to my surprise (for the music of Saint-Saëns leaves me quite indifferent), that he was evincing great interest in it. And, indeed, signs of the influence which it eventually exercised upon him (a definite, although not very great one) are to be found in his Piano Trio of 1915, and in his Sonata for violin and 'cello of 1922.

VI

On Russian music, he and I were in almost complete

Ravel's admiration for Liszt the composer

agreement. We gave pride of place to Mussorgsky, Borodin, and Balakiref. We loved Rimsky-Korsakof's music, especially his tone-poems and some of the early operas. We were not interested in Tchaikowsky, and we belonged to the number of the few who held Glazunof's early works in high esteem—especially his tone-poems *The Forest, Stenka Razin,* the *Oriental Rhapsody*, and the second and third symphonies. Of course, we were not blind to their derivative character: yet we felt that Glazunof displayed strong personality and fine imagination.

Another bond between us was our love of Liszt's music. We both felt very strongly on the matter, and were often driven to exasperation by the utterances of the people who were clear-sighted enough as regards the obvious defects of Liszt's music, but utterly incapable of seeing its equally obvious merits. The writing of a concert-notice gave Ravel the opportunity to refer to the matter in the following terms:

"It is to Liszt's defects that Wagner owes his turgescence, Strauss his churlish enthusiasms, Franck his ponderous ideality, the Russians the tinsel which occasionally mars their picturesqueness. But it is also to him that all these dissimilar composers owe the best of their qualities."

He found little to admire in the music of Berlioz. He was extremely keen on that of Chabrier and Fauré; and he was, with Debussy, one of the very first to realize the interest of Satie's—it was he who gave me the idea of studying it at a time when hardly anybody knew it, and very little of it was published.

CHAPTER V

Ravel and our circle—Florent Schmitt—A meeting with d'Annunzio—A ballet that was never written—Albert Roussel—My share in his Evocations—*Déodat de Sévérac—Léon-Paul Fargue and his ways—Manuel de Falla and his first opera—Ravel's first two pupils: Maurice Delage and Roland Manuel.*

I

Soon after our friendship had begun to ripen, Ravel introduced me to his family. He was living, then, with his father, mother, and brother, in a small flat, Boulevard Péreire (those were lean times for all of us), and I became a frequent visitor to their home. He also introduced me to some of his friends, and soon afterwards a small informal circle of music-lovers was formed. We used to meet of an evening to read and discuss music. The reading was done at the piano chiefly by Ravel and Ricardo Viñes, but occasionally by other, less expert, players, the worst of whom was certainly myself.

The other regular members of the circle were, at first: Paul Sordes, a born art-lover and painter, who, although he worked slowly and fitfully (for by nature he inclined to contemplation rather than action) has turned out some very delightful pictures; Florent Schmitt, Maurice Delage, and Inghelbrecht, the composers; Léon-Paul Fargue, the writer; and Emile Séguy, the designer. Later on, one or two of these dropped out and others appeared either as regular attendants or frequent visitors: Albert Roussel, Déodat de Sévérac, and Manuel de Falla were among the latter.

Florent Schmitt

II

Florent Schmitt, who had been awarded the Prix de Rome in 1900, at the age of thirty, was the eldest of the "regulars". He was not much of a talker, but very keen in his enthusiasms and forcible in the expression of his dislikes. It was he who, at the Press rehearsal of Debussy's *Pelléas et Mélisande*, yelled from the gallery to a party of smartly dressed women who sat fussing and sniggering in the stalls: "Allez donc au Casino de Paris!" He had a villa somewhere in the Pyrenees, quite near the Spanish border. After the execution, in Spain, of the revolutionist Francesco Ferrer (which many people considered, rightly or wrongly, a political murder pure and simple) he renamed his house, by way of public protest, "Villa Francesco Ferrer". A few years later, in his enthusiasm for Stravinsky's music (an enthusiasm so great that once, after the first performance of a work of Stravinsky's at a concert, I heard him mutter: "C'est à décourager tous les autres d'écrire de la musique!") he changed the name to "Villa Oiseau de Feu".

He was impulsive, rather than self-critical, in all things, not excluding composition. This trait helps to account for the fact that his output is as unequal in quality as diversified in character. Now and then he would allow his ideas to run away with him, as when he wrote his piano quintet—a really splendid work, but one whose performance takes an hour without a break (I think he has, since then, slightly compressed it).

As a composer he stood, and still stands, very far apart from all those around him. His music is as remote from that of Debussy and Ravel as from that of Franck and d'Indy; nor can it be connected in any way with that of Saint-Saëns, or of the French "verists" such as Charpentier and Bruneau. In fact, he was more directly influenced

A meeting with d'Annunzio

by the German romantics than any other French composer of any standing. It is true that he was also influenced, to no small degree, by Balakiref, Glazunof, and Chabrier. But none of these influences prevented him from asserting an individuality characterized at times by ruggedness, at others by subtlety, and often very striking. At that time and long after, some of us, in the strength of his *Psalm 46*, his Quintet, his *Musiques de Plein Air* for orchestra, and his *Tragédie de Salomé*, were convinced that he was, of the French composers of his generation, the one whose music would find the quickest and widest diffusion abroad. I, for one, thought so highly of him that later, when Ida Rubinstein, who had commissioned d'Annunzio to write for her *Le Martyre de Saint-Sébastien* (in which she was to take the title-part, calling for both acting and dancing) asked me whom she could commission to write the music should Debussy, with whom she was negotiating, refuse, I unhesitatingly suggested him.

He accepted in principle, and, at Ida Rubinstein's request, I took him to her house to meet d'Annunzio for a preliminary discussion. This is the only occasion on which I met d'Annunzio. He began by informing us that, as the whole of Europe was eagerly awaiting the disclosure of the subject of his forthcoming play, and it was essential that there should be no premature revelation of the secret, he had to ask us both to pass our word of honour that we should divulge nothing of what we were about to hear. Schmitt passed his word of honour as requested. I, seeing no reason why my part in the whole affair should extend beyond the act of introducing Schmitt, offered to retire then and there, if d'Annunzio preferred. But with a wave of the hand he brushed the suggestion aside; and so did it come to pass that I heard, that afternoon, the story which the whole of Europe was breathlessly awaiting.

Albert Roussel

A few days later, the news came that Debussy had agreed to write the music of *Saint-Sébastien*.

In 1909 I wanted Schmitt to compose a ballet for Diaghilef, and he agreed to do so on a libretto entitled *Urvasi* that I wrote for him. It was even announced in the Press that he was at work on it. Then he gave up the idea. I had long forgotten all about it until, during the war, I received from an American writer, who was preparing a book on Schmitt, a letter asking for particulars about the ballet *Urvasi*. I wrote back that the ballet had not been and would never be composed. To my intense amusement, he replied: "Never mind. Could you not tell me just the story of the plot for me to put into my book?"

III

Albert Roussel, too, was and remains a composer whose music baffles classification, although the influence of d'Indy's teaching can be felt in his early instrumental works, and although he shows no trace of having undergone, like Schmitt, any non-French influences. We all liked him very much. He was, in conversation, no less laconic than Schmitt, but as restrained and tactful (even diplomatic) on the subject of music which he did not like, or of views which he did not share, as Schmitt was blunt and hyperbolic. As often as not, it was just by a quiet smile that he would reveal his unfavourable opinions or, as the case might be, show that he stuck to his guns. He had been a naval officer before devoting himself to composition, and in the course of his voyages had become acquainted with the music of the East and Far East. Indian music attracted him strongly. In 1908 or thereabouts, he visited India again, and on his return I had the good fortune to become a collaborator of his in the following circumstances.

It had occurred to me, some time before, to arrange certain passages of a translation of Kalidasa's works into

My share in Roussel's "Evocations"

short prose poems suitable for musical settings. Five of these, more or less remodelled for the purpose, had been used by Eugène Grassi, the Siamese composer, in his lovely *Chansons Populaires Siamoises*. The remainder I showed to Roussel, who took them away and, to my great delight, told me a few days later that they had given him the idea of using human voices in the finale of a symphonic triptych which he was composing. He selected three, of which he used two exactly as they stood. But he wished the third to keep to a certain rhythm throughout—the rhythm of a psalmody which he had heard a fakir singing—so that he rewrote it practically from end to end. Thus it is that I had a small share in the genesis of his admirable *Evocations*.

In the main, Roussel has changed almost as little as Ravel with the passing of years. But the works of his later maturity betoken the gradual development of a more austere philosophy of outlook, a tendency to grapple with new problems of texture and structure, which leads certain people to label his music "difficult"—a view which I find quite unaccountable, for nothing could be more straightforward than his ends and the means he applies to achieving them. But he has not yet been the subject of much critical discussion, and his music is comparatively little known outside France: so that, although he is the eldest of that little circle which I am describing (he was Florent Schmitt's senior by a year) he remains, in a way, a composer to be "discovered".

IV

Déodat de Sévérac was, like Roussel, a pupil of d'Indy, and, like him again, as much a favourite with us all—both as a man and as a composer—as in the Schola-Cantorum circles. He brought with him, wherever he went, a delightful atmosphere of robust simplicity and breeziness. He loved the South, of which he was a native, and pro-

Déodat de Sévérac

bably never felt quite at home in Paris, where he would stay as little as possible. He is the only one of the circle who is no longer with us; and I was deeply pained when I heard of his death, in 1921, at the age of forty-eight.

His first characteristic works, the piano suites *Le chant de la terre* and *En Languedoc*, created a deep and altogether special impression. One felt that they sprang straight from the soil, teeming with sap, irradiated with sunshine, and that the quality of suggestion and expression in them was altogether Sévérac's own—entirely distinct from anything in the music of any other composer. So, great admiration, and even greater confidence in his future, were aroused. The high praise which his music won at that time and later has appeared excessive, I find, to a number of critics in other countries. This may be accounted for, at least partly, by the fact that his published output is comparatively small. It is incredible how many things he composed which he never troubled to set on paper (I remember a lovely *Elégie sur la mort de Gauguin* of which he used to play us bits, not very skilfully, at the piano), or lost the manuscripts of, or composed only partly, or planned and dreamt of without going any further. Then, there are works of his, such as his lyric tragedies *Héliogabale* and *La fille de la terre*, which were composed specially for production at the Open-air Theatre at Béziers, and cannot be assessed fairly unless from actual performance under the intended conditions.

Perhaps those of us who knew not only his finished works, but his sketches and plans, were inclined, now and then, to anticipate the future in their praise of him, and were influenced by their memories of him when there was no longer any future to anticipate. Yet, all told, I do not think we were far wrong in our judgment. Sévérac is so eloquent a poet, so thoroughly himself in his simple, straightforward eloquence, so subtle and genuine in his originality, that even if only a small part of his not very

Maurice Delage

big output survives, that little will certainly continue to rank high.

V

Maurice Delage was introduced to our circle a year or two after its birth. His was a truly remarkable case. He had reached the age of twenty-three without even giving a thought to music, and he suddenly developed a passion for it after hearing Debussy's *Pelléas et Mélisande*. I do not know which instinct, or which happy combination of circumstances, led him to Ravel for tuition: but to Ravel he went straight, and he certainly could have made no better choice. Ravel—who, so far as I know, had never done any teaching before—was interested in him from the first, and handled him with infinite skill, tact, and patience. Tact and patience were very needful—for, like many beginners (and especially beginners who make a late start under the influence of irrepressible enthusiasm), Delage was eager to plunge forthwith *in medias res*, and impatient of the weary discipline of technical training. Ravel managed to keep him interested and to encourage him while never yielding to his impatience. Delage used to tell me all about his ordeals with counterpoint, blessing and cursing Ravel in the same breath. He made splendid headway; and, after a voyage to India, conceived a plan of a musical play—a kind of ballet—inspired by Kipling's *Bridge-Builders*. He made a splendid start with it, and more than once we heard him play excerpts which were most forcible and original. Then, as I heard, difficulties arose with regard to the required permission. I remember no details; but I believe that a misunderstanding arose as to the extent to which Delage proposed actually to draw upon the tale. Anyhow, the difficulties proved insuperable to him, and he had to give up his plan. This was a great pity, for the impulse which had prompted him was a powerful one; and no doubt, had things gone otherwise,

Léon-Paul Fargue and his ways

he would not only have written a fine work (one with which Diaghilef, in the days of Fokin, would have done wonders), but been stimulated to further efforts at the very outset of his career. As it is, he must have been bitterly disappointed, though he hid it well. Eventually, most of what he had written was used in a "choreographic tone-poem on Indian themes" which was performed in Paris after the war.

VI

Léon-Paul Fargue was the only professional writer in our little circle, exactly as I was the only professional critic. He was then known to very few people, owing to his extreme reluctance to appear in print. He used to read to us, from very scrappy manuscripts (bits of paper such as the Montmartre "Chansonniers" draw from their pocket-book before starting to sing) his exquisitely wrought prose poems. He was very simple and lovable despite many peculiarities, of which the most striking was an almost incurable incapacity to make up his mind about the things of everyday life—an incapacity which seemed greatly to amuse him and with which (as indeed with his other peculiarities) he toyed as gleefully as a child instead of trying to conquer it. Once, for instance, he told us, without ever batting an eyelid, that he had missed by three hours an important appointment, entirely by his mother's fault. "She knows me well enough," he explained, "yet what did she do but put out two pairs of boots for me to choose from!"

For a long time he made a practice of carrying about, day and night, a small camera (never filled), as people carry a walking stick: "pour me donner une contenance", he said. He not only was an expert at compressed jokes (which often took the shape of nonsense verse, never printed, but very much alive in my memory), but had a knack for defining impressions, or the qualities and defects of

Viñes

people, by means of terse, startlingly apposite verbal images. One of the most whimsical jokes of his that I can remember is hard to beat for its simplicity. Ravel, after the first performance of his String Quartet, had received from a friend (Mme. Louise Cruppi, the wife of the politician, and a most keen and active music-lover), by way of memento, a pocket-book on which was stamped the date of the performance. He showed it to us; and we were commenting upon the charming form given to the tribute when Fargue took hold of the pocket-book, gave it a tug or two, and remarked approvingly: "Et puis, c'est du bon cuir: c'est solide!"

VII

Viñes, alert and cheerful, ever on the track of new music and new ideas, as keen on literature and painting as on his own art, was, whenever he turned up, the life and soul of our meetings. We loved his childlike ingenuity as much as we admired his playing and appreciated the colossal amount and rare quality of his disinterested work as a pioneer. He played in public the piano music of Debussy and Ravel years before any other pianist dreamt of touching it. Indeed, for a long time, all the first performances of these two composers' piano works were given by him, as well as countless first performances of music by other composers, French, Russian, and Spanish.

This unselfish devotion won him much kudos, but he also had to pay the penalty of it. People grew accustomed to think of him only as an interpreter of new music, and lost sight of the tremendous amount of splendid work he put into his playing of the classics. He never could resist a request to play a new work; and the tradition was established, as a matter of course, that he was always available when wanted. To the present day, he is chiefly engaged in introducing works of young composers; and he has done far more for others than for himself.

Manuel de Falla and his first opera

VIII

It was he who brought Manuel de Falla to one of our meetings. De Falla had just come from Spain with the manuscript score of his opera *La Vida Breve*, which had just been awarded the first prize in a Spanish opera competition. There being no chance, despite this success, of getting it published or performed in his native country (where publishers and lyric theatres were few and unenterprising), he had decided to try Paris. He played the work to us, and we were struck by the fine musicianship he had displayed in spite of the rather conventionally "veristic" subject and treatment of it by the librettist. Soon afterwards, we heard that he had found a publisher. In 1913 the first performance took place at Nice; and thenceforth, De Falla made continuous headway.

Delage having taken a bungalow in a part of Auteuil which was still semi-countrified, our meetings soon began to take place there. Then, Ravel introduced us all to new friends of his, both keen music-lovers, Cyprien and Ida Godebski; and gradually the meetings were diverted to their house. What they lost thereby in intimacy they gained in variety of scope and character. We used to meet there a number of writers and painters; among the latter was Georges d'Espagnat, who in 1910 conceived the notion of painting a group of us: Viñes at the piano, and around him Ravel, de Sévérac, Roussel, Schmitt, Godebski, his little son, and myself. The picture was painted in 1911.

It was round about that time that Roland Manuel, a pupil of Ravel, joined us. Soon afterwards he wrote an excellent little book on Ravel, which he inscribed jointly to Vuillermoz and to me—explaining that it was great fun thus to associate the names of the two critics who had been the first to write in praise of Ravel, but had done so from widely different angles. As a composer, he did not

Roland Manuel

assert himself until after the war. Nowadays, when I meet in Paris the friends I have just mentioned, it is usually at his house, to which Milhaud, Honegger, Poulenc, and other younger composers are frequent visitors.

CHAPTER VI

Ravel at work—The Miroirs *and the* Histoires Naturelles *—His indifference to criticism—A lecture on Ravel and an over-zealous champion—First anonymous performance of the* Valses Nobles et Sentimentales, *and a moral.*

I

To his intimate friends Ravel never grudged the pleasure of watching his new works grow. And, although he never invited comment, it was clear that he liked us to like his music. As a rule, we were responsive enough. Only once, in those early days, did a work of his bewilder us for a time. It was *Oiseaux Tristes*, which he played to us again and again without our being able to understand what he was after. He was rather disconcerted to find us indifferent to a piece in which he had put so much of himself. Sordes summed up the humour of the situation by drawing a verbal picture of Ravel hawking about, on his extended finger, two forlorn little birds with whom nobody would have anything to do. But, after a while, we all learnt to love *Oiseaux Tristes*; and I, for one, cannot help wondering how I could have failed to enjoy it from the first.

When the set *Miroirs*, of which *Oiseaux Tristes* is part, was finished, Ravel inscribed one of its numbers to each of us: to Viñes, *Oiseaux Tristes*, because, he said, "it was fun to inscribe to a pianist a piece that was not in the least 'pianistic' "; to Fargue, *Noctuelles;* to Delage, *La Vallée des Cloches;* to Sordes, *Une Barque sur l'Océan;* and to me, the *Alborada del Gracioso*. As can be seen, Ravel inscribed the *Alborada* to me because I was one of his close friends, and not at all, as has been averred on one or two

The "Histoires Naturelles"

occasions, because I happened to be the first critic to stand for him and challenge his censors. Besides, at the time, I had not done much in the matter—merely called attention to his music in the course of concert-notices and of one or two not very long articles, and expressed my admiration for it. I had been very much interested in it from the first, and so my early comments on it were free from the doubtfulness which had coloured my first articles on Debussy. But it is only in 1907 when, on the occasion of the first performance of his *Histoires Naturelles*, Ravel had again been denounced as a slavish imitator of Debussy, that I really took up the cudgels, writing for the *Grande Revue* an article entitled *Maurice Ravel et l'imitation Debussyste* (I had deliberately selected this ambiguous title so as to lure his opponents into reading it in the hope of finding in it a confirmation of their assertions) in which I did my best, by comparing idiosyncrasies of style, idiom, texture, and structure, to show that the allegation was utterly unfounded. It may seem ludicrous to-day that it should have been needful to devote a whole long article to demonstrating this one point. But needful it was, if only to counteract the favourite manœuvre of Ravel's detractors.

II

While I am on this topic, I may as well tell a little story which perhaps will interest collectors of documents on the ethics of criticism.

When Ravel's *L'Heure Espagnole* was produced at the Opéra-Comique (in 1911) one detractor again accused him, in a long, merciless article, of imitating Debussy. Eleven years later, this work having been revived at the Opéra, he devoted to it an equally long article which was the finest bit of camouflage—and camouflage of a very unusual kind—that I have ever seen. It did not disparage Ravel, but praised him. It ran, however, on exactly the same lines as the previous one, practically every sentence of which was repeated almost word for word: but, by virtue of a few changed epithets and of a few skilful adjustments, it was made almost as laudatory as the other had been devastating, without containing one word of retractation.

If that article was intended as a peace offering, it signally failed of its purpose. Shortly afterwards Ravel, taking up the cudgels in favour of a fresh victim of the same critic's animadversions, denounced him as making a practice of trying to crush young composers under the weight of older ones: "To-day", he said, "he is using poor me against So-and-so exactly as he has tried to crush me under the weight of Debussy, and Debussy under the weight of Wagner."

III

I sometimes was given the opportunity of discussing Ravel's music with critics who were hostile to it. One of these—a very good friend of mine—used to deride me mercilessly for thinking otherwise than he did; but one day he gave me the surprise of my life. As I was entering his room, he gripped me by the shoulder, shook me by the hand warmly, and said: "Calvo, you were right: Ravel's music is stunning (épatante)." And he began to tell me why. A fortnight or so later, he was explaining to me that I was utterly incapable of understanding Ravel's music, and that he alone could realize its significance to the full. He was a queer fellow, as unbridled in his prejudices as in his enthusiasms. As soon as he took to championing Ravel, he began to find fault with everything that other people wrote about him, either because they did not praise him enough, or because they praised him for the wrong things or in the wrong way. But he was so ingenuous about it all that one never could be angry with him.

A lecture on Ravel and an over-zealous champion

One day Ravel called upon me and said: "Engel and Bathori are giving a concert of my music, at which I am to play the piano. They are longing for you to deliver an introductory lecture, but are shy about asking you because they can offer no fee: so I undertook to approach you on their behalf." I accepted with delight. Apart from my enjoying the prospect of lecturing on Ravel's music, nothing could have pleased me better than the notion of cooperating with Emile Engel and Mme. Jane Bathori, two singers whose talent and disinterested devotion to modern music I greatly admired.

The next day, the posters announcing the concert and my lecture were up, and I received from the enthusiastic champion of Ravel a telegram urging me to call upon him that night. As he was kept busy all day by his work, it was an understood thing among his friends that he paid no calls but was to be seen at his own home when desired —late at night for choice. I went, and, without even a greeting, he started: "Calvo, are you quite mad?" and explained to me that by lecturing on Ravel at a concert at which Ravel was to appear on the platform, I was going to render him the laughing-stock of the whole musical world. Vainly I strove to argue that, after all, he might credit me with a little tact: "You will make his name stink in everybody's nostrils"—that I had given my promise: "You must get out of it!"—that Ravel himself had asked me: "Ravel doesn't know what he's about." His entreaties followed me while I walked down the stairs, and on the day of the concert I received from him a telegram beseeching me "in the name of our common admiration for Ravel" not to commit an irretrievable blunder.

When I arrived at the concert-hall, I found him awaiting me in the artists' room. He said to me, eagerly, almost humbly: "Calvo, you're still in time; can't you develop a sudden hoarseness or headache, make your ex-

A lecture on Ravel and an over-zealous champion
cuses, and go home?" I do not remember what my reply was. He did not realize in the least the extreme unfairness of his action. Had I happened to have been in the least nervous or inexperienced in the technique of lecturing, he might well have unnerved me beyond repair.

But worse was to come. When I appeared on the platform, there he was, conspicuous in one of the front rows of the stalls, his chin resting on the knob of his stick, frowning, glaring, fidgeting, a picture of gloom and indignation. Consciously or not, he kept making the funniest faces at me throughout my lecture. It was all I could do to refrain from bursting into laughter.

After the concert he reappeared in the artists' room to congratulate Ravel and the singers. When he came to me, I said: "Well, B——, it was not so bad after all, was it?" He gulped, gave me a last scowl, and replied in a voice hoarse with conflicting emotions: "Anyhow, you shouldn't have done it." Then he shook my hand quite cordially and took himself off.

Ravel, whom I kept informed of the various stages of the affair, did not, of course, interfere in it, but remained an amused spectator from end to end.

IV

His attitude towards criticism, favourable or unfavourable, was and has remained one of absolute, often contemptuous, indifference. Generally speaking, composers may be divided into two categories: those who declare themselves unaffected by criticism, and those who aver that they pay the greatest attention to it. But the majority of the former, even if they do not change their ways under the influence of anything that appears in print (and why indeed should they?) are now and then pleased, or hurt, or angered—which, after all, is only human; and an immense majority of the latter are either deluding themselves or—which is far more likely—offering a sop to Cerberus.

The "Valses Nobles et Sentimentales"

Ravel, who has often proclaimed his indifference to criticism, is as good as his word: he may experience a natural pleasure in finding his friends (whether they be critics or not) responsive to his music, but the only opinions to which he ascribes a more general importance are those of the composers whose music he thinks well of. And, if I remember right, in his early days the only other critical judgments (quite apart from the question whether they referred to his own work or not) regarded by him as not altogether negligible were those which, belonging to what is usually described nowadays as the "sensitized-plate" type (that is, not aiming at expressing anything but their writer's reactions), struck him as worthy of praise from the literary point of view.

He was, from the very outset, quite sure of himself, of his purpose, and of his technique. The one thing he cared to say about his music was that he knew exactly what he wanted to do, and why. One day he said to me: "I may confidently aver that I never release a work until I am quite certain that I have done my utmost and could not in any way improve one single detail in it." This accounts for the surety of touch to which even his earliest works testify, and also for the fact that, with few exceptions (possibly, in his pre-war output, the *Noctuelles* in *Miroirs*, and one or two songs), all his music is thoroughly representative of him.

V

One of Ravel's works, the *Valses Nobles et Sentimentales*, was first launched into the world under unusual circumstances, providing him with an experience which would have brought ample confirmation, had it been needed, of his views upon the value of critical judgments. The Société Musicale Indépendante, in order to show how far knowledge of the authorship could influence an audience in the matter of placing and assessing musical works,

The "Valses Nobles et Sentimentales"

gave a chamber concert of music all new except (I cannot imagine why this one exception) for three Scarlatti Sonatinas, without revealing the names of the composers responsible for the numbers on the programme—the titles only were given.

I do not know whether it was because no other new works by more or less well-known composers were available at the moment, or because Ravel alone proved willing to contribute to the experiment: but the fact is that all the other works heard on that memorable occasion were by little-known composers, many of whom were tyros.

This rendered the experiment less instructive than it would otherwise have been. But, as regards Ravel, it was instructive enough. Many people who would have applauded the *Valses* with the utmost vigour had they known that Ravel had written them remained indifferent; and unfavourable comments arose freely, during the interval, from lips usually ready to sing Ravel's praises. On the forms provided together with the programmes for everyone to write down, as he guessed it, the authorship of the works played, some people ascribed the *Valses* to Kodály (whose piano pieces Op. 3, played shortly before at another concert of the same Society, had met with a most unfavourable reception), and others to Erik Satie. I cannot remember whether a majority found for Ravel, but I doubt it. What I remember quite well is that I did not.

Very few notices of the concert appeared in the Press —partly because the music critics of most of the daily papers were not expected to attend, as a matter of course, anything but the big symphony concerts (I shall revert to this matter in another chapter), and were given very little space even to notice these. By the time my own article appeared, the authorship of the *Valses* had ceased to be a secret, and my comment, in the main, took very much the form I have given it here.

The "Valses Nobles et Sentimentales"

In theory, the authorship remaining unknown, a musical work ought not to be more difficult to assess, either objectively (if such a thing be at all possible) or subjectively, than a book or a painting—and nobody could reasonably assert that a book or a painting cannot be assessed unless its author is known. But in practice, we know so little about the mainspring of music and relation of musical art to our own experiences that there are many special difficulties in the way of musical criticism.

As regards the question of authorship pure and simple, it can be said that if there are composers whose works are so characteristic that their authorship can be inferred from internal evidence Ravel, as I was pointing out a while ago, is surely one of them. And the *Valses Nobles et Sentimentales* are most characteristic of him, but in a way that (apart from the impossibility of judging a work adequately after a single hearing) set a trap in the way of judges. One of Ravel's main idiosyncrasies is his eagerness always to cover fresh ground in the matter of both scope and technique; and his progress, from the early works to the *Valses*, had been steady and logical enough. But, as it happens, those *Valses* represent an altogether new stage in his evolution: for instance (I feel very guilty for allowing technicalities to crop up in this book) the texture is more tenuous, and the harmony far more elliptical, than in any of his previous works. And it is mainly by a process of induction, on psychological grounds, that it might have been possible to proclaim, in 1911, that nobody but Ravel could have done exactly thus and not otherwise, retrenching here, adding there, and proceeding —so to speak—from given premisses to almost unavoidable conclusions.

CHAPTER VII

How Ravel came to write the Sonatina and the Greek Folk-Songs—Inception of Daphnis et Chloé—*Schemes for operas that came to nought—Pity for a condemned criminal—Vaughan Williams comes to Paris for lessons from Ravel.*

I

Whatever the usefulness of my critical work on the subject of Ravel's music may have been, I think that I may claim to have been useful—if not to Ravel himself, at least to lovers of his music—in that circumstances led me to provide the incentive which induced him to write several of his works.

The first of these works was the piano Sonatina, or at least the first movement of it. In 1903 an enterprising man, Arthur Bles by name, founded in Paris the *Weekly Critical Review*—an Anglo-French weekly devoted to literature, music, and the fine arts. The list of contributors included Arthur Symons, John Runciman, Ernest Newman, Rémy de Gourmont, and, among the lesser lights, myself. Bles, who was very keen on music, gave it a lion's share in the paper. One of the stunts he imagined to promote circulation was an international competition for the first movement of a piano Sonatina, the length not to exceed seventy-five bars. The prize was to be a hundred francs. I suggested to Ravel that he should enter the competition, and so he did, turning out in a very short time what is now the opening movement of his published Sonatina. But, alas, this movement consisted of seventy-seven bars, instead of the prescribed maximum of seventy-five; and, no other competitor having come forth, Bles,

How Ravel came to write the Greek Folk-Songs
whose *Review* was nearing financial collapse (he paid his contributors generously and did not find among the public the support which he deserved) decided to cancel the competition. Ravel accepted the inevitable with good grace, took his manuscript back, and completed the Sonatina a couple of years later.

II

Then, one day in 1904, my colleague and friend Pierre Aubry came to me post-haste for help. He wanted some Greek folk-songs, and a singer to sing them by way of illustrations to a lecture of his arranged at short notice, for a special purpose—propaganda in favour of the oppressed Greeks and Armenians. For some reason which I forget, he did not wish to use examples from Bourgault-Ducoudray's published collection; and, apart from that, there was little to draw upon except Hubert Pernot's admirable *Chansons populaires de l'Ile de Chio*. These were not translated, but I knew a singer, Louise Thomasset, whom I could teach to sing them phonetically. The trouble was that she could not, or would not, sing them without accompaniment. So, eager to oblige Pierre Aubry (I was very fond of him, and indebted to him for much encouragement and advice), I turned to Ravel and asked him to provide accompaniments, explaining the need for haste. We selected five songs—four from Pernot's book, and one (the delightfully humorous sketch whose French title is *Quel Galant!*) from a collection published at Constantinople. I gave him the meaning of the words, and within thirty-six hours he turned up with the accompaniments almost exactly as they are known to the world to-day (*Cinq Chansons Populaires Grecques*). Needless to say I was amazed at seeing what he, who had never yet turned his mind to harmonizing folk-songs, had been able to achieve. Tunes and accompaniments simply seemed to have grown together.

Inception of "Daphnis et Chloé"

Meanwhile, the singer had learnt the words from a phonetic transcription, so that she was ready to set to work, with Ravel at the piano and myself as coach. On the appointed day, Pierre Aubry was able to deliver his lecture with illustrations all complete.

A little later Durand, the publisher, offered Ravel an agreement for the first refusal of all his compositions to come, and expressed a wish to publish a work from his pen as soon as possible. The only thing which Ravel had ready at the moment was that set of songs. I was asked to provide French translations, and thus Ravel and I, hand in hand, entered into business relations with the firm A. Durand et fils.

III

It would be absurd to mention on a similar plane the ballet *Daphnis et Chloé*. Diaghilef, who began scouring France as well as Russia for suitable composers as soon as he started his ballet seasons, would have been sure to come into contact with Ravel at an early date. Indeed, his Russian advisers—Walter Nouvel and Alfred Nourok—knew Ravel's music quite well and had given it pride of place at the Contemporary Music Evenings organized by them at Petrograd. But, as a point of fact, it was I who, as early as 1907 introduced Ravel and Diaghilef to one another, and one of my reasons was (for at the time, Diaghilef had given no sign of having any use for music by non-Russian composers) that I wanted Ravel's help in persuading him to concentrate his efforts, the following year, on Mussorgsky's *Boris Godunof*. Naturally, as soon as I heard of Diaghilef's plans for the future, Ravel was among the very first whom I suggested. At the same time, I recommended that Fauré and Florent Schmitt should be approached; but for some reason or other nothing came of these other suggestions.

Inception of "Daphnis et Chloé"

IV

The two facts that the Greek songs were Ravel's first venture in the harmonization of folk-tunes, and that one of his most important works is a ballet on a Greek subject, have given rise—though not very generally, it is true—to the idea that Greek subjects may have had some special attraction for him. There is absolutely no foundation for this idea. *Daphnis et Chloé*, like the Greek folk-songs, owes its existence to purely accidental circumstances, and Ravel did not think of the subject himself.

Besides, as soon as one begins to see him as he really is, it becomes almost impossible to think of him as capable of being attracted, for creative purposes, by anything not French. I am not referring, of course, to the influence exercised upon him by the rhythms and colours of Spanish music, which, like many other French composers, he was often tempted to use; nor to the mainly technical influence of Liszt, Balakiref, Rimsky-Korsakof, and Borodin. I am thinking of essentials—outlook and modes of thought and expression, character, and atmosphere: his "Spanish" music, for instance, is as French as can be—and as French as Rimsky-Korsakof's or Glinka's "Spanish" music is really Russian.

Ravel must be thought of as French first and last. At the time of which I am writing, he knew no single word of any language but French, though nowadays he can speak a few words of English, which he utters with a wonderful combination of the French and American accents. He had studied neither Greek nor Latin; all his acquaintance with the classics and with foreign authors he owed to French translations, and I am sure that often the French flavour conferred by these translations played a part in his enjoyment of them.

For instance, he had been, at an early date, greatly attracted by Gerhardt Hauptmann's play, *The Sunken Bell*,

Schemes for operas that came to nought

and had started setting A. Ferdinand Hérold's French translation of it to music. Nothing of what he composed for it was ever written down, although he kept working at it, during many years, at irregular intervals, and used to play us excerpts which we liked very much. I have often wondered whether, knowing German, he would have been equally attracted by the original text; and indeed I remember his commenting lovingly upon the rhythm, colour, and musical quality of passages which were, of course, quite different from anything he would have found in the German.

As regards *Daphnis et Chloé*, he surely loved Amyot's delightful old French quite as much as the story itself. I also remember discussing with him the *Arabian Nights* and discovering to my amazement—simply because I felt otherwise—that, leaving aside the relative value, from the purely narrative point of view, of the French translations available, he far preferred Galland's eighteenth-century version, in which atmosphere, colours, and happenings are quaintly altered in accordance with French taste and habits, to modern translations such as that of Mardrus (then in course of publication) which attempted to preserve at least the illusion of a purely Eastern character.

More generally, he also loved the character that Greek, and likewise Chinese art, had acquired at the hands of their French imitators. When after the war he had taken, at Montfort l'Amaury, a house of his own, which he was able to furnish after his own heart, I had an amusing instance of this bent. He took my wife and me round the house, and while showing us one room exclaimed with glee: "Voyez: ici, rien que du faux Grec!" And then, as he opened another door: "Et ici, rien que du faux Chinois!"

Exceptionally he once entertained the idea of learning Spanish, in order to be able to read *Don Quixote* in the original and to extract from it the libretto of an opera

Schemes for operas that came to nought
which he dreamt of writing. No translation, he said, and no librettist, could give him exactly what he wanted. But he never carried out this plan, and I have often thought how deplorable it was that he should have given it up. A *Don Quixote* from his pen would have been a work on a grand scale, certainly most racy and stimulating, and very probably true to the spirit of outward irony and latent compassionate tenderness which characterizes Cervantes' masterpiece—a spirit which no music inspired by it has to my knowledge ever succeeded in suggesting, even faintly.

V

But to revert to *Daphnis*. Ravel never thought of dealing with this particular subject in any form until 1909, when it was offered to him by Diaghilef, who, with the help of his advisers, had been eagerly casting round for subjects as well as for composers. Various libretti, all of them very conventional, had been outlined, and were submitted to Ravel to choose from. I well remember him, Diaghilef, Fokin, Bakst, Benois, and myself in Diaghilef's little sitting-room (red plush and mahogany, alas!) at the Hôtel de Hollande as it then was, finally deciding for *Daphnis* and offering suggestions as to particulars of plot and incidents, Fokin eventually casting the libretto into shape to Ravel's satisfaction.

I also remember that the very first bars of music which Ravel wrote were inspired by the memory of a wonderful leap sideways which Nijinsky (who was to be Daphnis) used to perform in a *pas seul* in *Le Pavillon d'Armide*, a ballet produced by Diaghilef that very season; and that they were intended to provide the opportunity for similar leaps—the pattern characterized by a run and a long pause, which runs through Daphnis's dance, pages 26 and after of the piano score.

Pity for a condemned criminal

VI

I will add to this chapter one memory of Ravel, which has nothing to do with music, but which I think worth recording because it refers to one of the rare occasions on which I saw him lose his self-possession, and the only one on which I have known him display, publicly and actively, concern in, and sensitiveness to, purely human events outside the circle of the people he was individually interested in. I was not acquainted with him at the time of the famous Dreyfus affair; and it stands to reason that I am not referring to his activities and feelings when the war came.

It was after the passing of the death sentence on a French criminal named Liabeuf. Liabeuf, who was being constantly watched by the police because he was known as an anarchist, had been arrested for living on the earnings of prostitutes, and sentenced to imprisonment despite his protests of innocence. Released from prison, he had manufactured leather wristlets and shoulder-pads all covered with steel spikes, and, equipped with this formidable obstacle against arrest, had shot the two detectives responsible for his previous arrest and conviction. Several policemen were wounded before he was overpowered.

Hardly had the death sentence been passed that a petition was set afloat by a few people who, believing him to have been wrongly sentenced in the first place, considered that his revenge did not deserve capital punishment. Ravel was among the most eager to secure a reprieve. He would have liked me to sign the petition. He was, he told me, against the death penalty always. Quite apart from that, he averred that Liabeuf had been the victim of a trumped-up charge simply because he was an anarchist, and the blind fury which had led him to avenge his honour by shooting his accusers was understandable.

After Liabeuf's execution, Ravel was so upset that for

MAURICE RAVEL
[*Elliott & Fry photograph*]

Vaughan Williams at Paris for lessons from Ravel
a few days he shut himself up in his home, refusing to see anybody.

VII

There is another little-known aspect of Ravel on which I could say a good deal had I not partly wasted a rare opportunity which came my way. This was when Ralph Vaughan Williams, upon my suggesting it, decided to take lessons from Ravel—the full story shall be told later. As a special favour I was allowed to attend the lessons, and although pressure of work prevented my attending them all, I heard, during the few at which I was present, much that shed light on the personalities of both composers. I wish it had occurred to me to take notes. Ravel is very lazy in the matter of writing, as all people know who have tried to get articles out of him. Of late years, Roland Manuel has jotted down many sayings of his; the results (which appeared in various French periodicals) show how very illuminating a book by him on the technique of music would be. Recently I suggested to him that he should write one on orchestration, and he promised to do so. Shortly afterwards, he even told me that he had started jotting down ideas for it. I wonder whether he will ever find time to carry it out.

He has done very little teaching. Vaughan Williams was, I think, the first after Delage to receive advice from h m on composition. Since then, he has had a few private pupils—among whom, after the war, Nikolai Obukhof, that strangest of young Russian composers; and it is a great pity that his advice to the privileged few who have worked with him should not be recorded.

CHAPTER VIII

Arthur Bles and his Weekly Critical Review—*Pierre Aubry, scholar and gourmet—His appalling death—My first lecture—Lecturing at Marseilles.*

I

I mentioned, in the foregoing chapter, Arthur Bles and Pierre Aubry. Both of them proved very helpful during the early years of my career. It was Bles who, after Binet-Valmer, gave me my best chance to make headway, and one of my earliest chances to earn money by my writings. The fees he paid in connection with the *Weekly Critical Review* were far in excess of anything paid by French periodicals; and he gave me many concert notices to do besides publishing as many articles as I could write for him, including the first articles I wrote in English. Unfortunately, he did not find for his *Review* the support he had hoped for—maybe because, on account of half of its contents being in English and the other half in French, it fell between two stools instead of appealing to the reading public of both countries—and it disappeared, after a game struggle, at the end of two years or so.

This, by the way, was a blow to me as well as to Bles. Between the *Renaissance Latine*, the *Weekly Critical Review*, and occasional contributions to other papers, I had been making, for a time, quite a good income for a beginner. My earnings for 1903 and 1904 exceeded by far the salary which I had received as an *agent de change's* clerk, and already I felt that the world of musical criticism was my oyster. But after 1904—the *Renaissance Latine* having also gone under—things became very difficult. French

Pierre Aubry, scholar and gourmet

musical journals paid stingily when they paid at all; and as practically no other work was forthcoming, it looked for a time as if I should never be able to earn more than pocket money. Then things began to right themselves: thanks chiefly to my work on Russian music, my first articles on which had appeared in the *Weekly Critical Review*, commissions for articles, translations, and—later on—lectures, started coming in. Bles, with his readily open columns and his liberal cheques, had done me a really good turn at the time when I needed it most, and I remember the fact gratefully.

Soon after the collapse of his *Review*, he founded another, devoted to motors and motoring. I kept in touch with him, though no longer as a contributor, and we remained great friends until the war. Later, he became the art critic of an illustrated French fortnightly of which I was the musical critic. We both held these posts until August, 1914. Then for a time we lost sight of each other; but one day, in 1915, we suddenly met in London, in a corridor of the War Office. I was working there, and he was a captain in the British Army. We had a brief chat. He was leaving for France the next day, and since then I have had no news of him. I should like our paths to meet again.

II

I first met Pierre Aubry at the Schola Cantorum. He was a splendid scholar—a specialist in both mediæval music and folk music—and a delightful man, always ready to encourage other workers. Being very wealthy, he was able to indulge freely in his passion for research work and to undertake, at his own expense, things such as the publishing, in collotype facsimiles, of important musical manuscripts, for instance. After I had helped him in the matter of the Greek folk-songs to illustrate a lecture of his, he suggested to Romain Rolland, then the Director

Pierre Aubry, scholar and gourmet
of the music section at the Ecole des Hautes Etudes Sociales, that I should be invited to join the staff of this section. From that moment on, a close friendship developed between Pierre Aubry and me, and we found ourselves ever consulting one another. His library and files were invaluable to me, and from time to time I was able to give him some information on Russian or Greek folk-tunes. His hobbies, apart from music, were fencing (of which I had done a good deal before relinquishing it for boxing), shooting, and gastronomy. Having discovered that this last was, in a small way, one of my hobbies too, he used to invite me to dine at his house whenever there was something special going, another favourite companion on these solemn, though informal, occasions, being a young barrister named Paul Albert Martin. Martin was keen on fishing, and so was I (how his descriptions of tackle by Hardy brothers and Farlow and others, and of his fishing expeditions in many waters, excited my envy!), so that I could, in a measure, swop fishing yarns with him as well as fencing yarns with Pierre Aubry. But when the talk veered round—as it often did —to food, I could no longer compete, and had to preserve an awed silence except perhaps for an occasional question. To hear these two discussing blends and contrasts and order of courses and vintages, recollecting past menus, and making plans for future gastronomical adventures, was a liberal education.

Anticipations aroused by their forecasts were seldom disappointed. One day, however, I was summoned to sample a rare and wonderful dish from South America— a dish with a name as cryptic and as long as anything in musical criticism—of which, by a stroke of luck, Pierre Aubry had been able to procure a large tin. I arrived, duly licking my chops. Our host (Martin had been asked too, of course) rushed out to meet me and said in a plaintive voice: "Calvo, it's just stewed beef and beans! But

Pierre Aubry—his appalling death

never mind," he added, "there's plenty of other things." And indeed there were.

Happening to like me and my work, he did his utmost to find opportunities for me. Once, hearing of some vague hope I had of becoming the editor of a musical periodical, he said: "As soon as your plans mature, let me know, and I'll find thirty thousand francs (£1200) for the paper."

In 1910, just before the summer holidays, he told me of a big plan of his own—a collection of books of folk-tunes from all countries—for the carrying out of which he asked me to join forces with him. The carrying out of the plan, he added, would take many years. I accepted joyfully, and he suggested that we should start work in October. Alas! In the train that was carrying me back to Paris, on September first, I opened a newspaper and saw the headlines: *Terrible Accident d'Escrime. Mort de M. Pierre Aubry*. He had been taking part in an épée tournament at Dieppe. During an interval he started demonstrating to a friend a certain lunge of his own. As he was throwing himself forwards (he was a tall, very heavy man) his friend's weapon got caught (probably through a small tear) between the two thicknesses of canvas of which the sleeves of fencing jackets are made, and, thus directed straight at his armpit, had pierced, button and all, through lining and skin and inflicted a wound (all this was explained to me later by an eyewitness). Not feeling badly hurt, he went back to his hotel, then suddenly collapsed, and died shortly afterwards. He was only thirty-six years of age. I arrived in Paris just in time to attend his funeral.

III

Romain Rolland having fallen in with Pierre Aubry's suggestion, I made my début at the Ecole des Hautes Etudes Sociales in 1905, with two lectures on Russian

My first lecture

music. I have a vivid memory of that first experience on the platform—or, rather, in the professorial chair. I was, naturally, a little nervous, never having spoken in public before. Moreover, at the eleventh hour the date of my first lecture was changed: Antoine, the famous actor-manager, who had been booked to speak on some contemporary play, being unable to appear, I was asked to step into the breach.

Well, on that day of days, a large audience, consisting mainly of people connected with the theatre, turned up to hear Antoine, all unaware of the substitution. Members of the general public were allowed to attend the lectures on payment of a small fee; and from the secretary's room, in which I sat awaiting the moment to appear, I could hear them talking in the entrance hall. "Oh! Not Antoine? What's on? Russian Music . . . by Cal-vo-co-res-si. . . . What a bore! Let's be off.—Well, lots of things are to be played and sung. Since we are here, we might as well stay."

The moment came. The secretary ushered me in. The hall was crowded, and the audience very noisy. I started speaking. Right in front of me, a set of three or four ladies continued their conversation quite unabashed, with much rattle of handbags and beads. It was rather disconcerting. Another two minutes, and the infection would surely spread. But all blessings on my dear friend Jehan Adès, the actor, who had undertaken, at my request, to teach me the art of lecturing! He had made a most thorough job of it, too. With almost uncanny prescience, he had told me how to deal with any emergency which might arise. Remembering his instructions, I ceased to address my audience at large, and, concentrating upon the offenders, started telling them in a confidential tone all about Russian folk-songs and their influence on Glinka. This worked according to plan, and splendidly. Within a few seconds, the whole audience were craning their

Lecturing at Marseilles

necks to find out to whom I was devoting so exclusive an interest. The ladies, realizing that they had become the centre of attention, looked all of a sudden very uncomfortable and held their peace.

The sporting spirit in which many people who had been attracted by Antoine remained to hear my lecture did not go unrewarded, thanks to the splendid support I was given by Viñes, Marguerite Babaian, and, I think, Ravel, though I cannot remember exactly whether he contributed to the illustrating of that first lecture; but I know that, either then or later, he played with Viñes the piano-duet arrangement of Glazunof's *Stenka-Razine*.

IV

As regards my adventures as a lecturer, I have very few memories worth recording. What I think is my best "lecturer story" I told in the foregoing chapter. But the following one is, to me, no less amusing.

In 1911, the Committee of the Marseilles Symphony Concerts invited me to take part, as lecturer, in their celebration of Liszt's centenary. They would be particularly glad, the secretary wrote, if I, a native of the city and the author of a book on Liszt, could see my way to accepting. I accepted, naturally, and, arriving at Marseilles the day before the lecture, called upon the secretary at the Committee's office. He told me that he was delighted to see me, and that they had all been delighted at my acceptance. "You see, Mr. Calvocoressi, you are our last hope—positively our last hope. We have had lecturers at various of our concerts during the past few years, and all of them were failures. Our public doesn't seem to care for lectures. The last man who came from Paris was all but booed off the platform." I expressed my appreciation of the trust they were kind enough to put in me, and, mightily cheered at the prospect of the morrow, took myself off. In the street I met an old friend of mine,

Lecturing at Marseilles

Zouros by name, the part-author, under a pseudonym, of several successful light plays.

"Hullo, Calvo," he said; "fancy you coming to lecture here! What devil possessed you? We don't want lectures at our concerts—they bore us." After which he dragged me into a café and told me the story of that other lecturer —a well-known novelist, journalist, and poet. Apparently he had begun the day by taking too much at lunch, and at the appointed time (4 p.m. or so) had stumbled on the steps leading up to the platform, glared at the audience who were laughing aloud, and after that given a rather sorry display of verbal pyrotechnics which didn't quite come off. I assured Zouros that I would be temperate at lunch and watch my step. The encouragement he had given me, I added, was the very thing I stood in need of.

Despite all fears to the contrary, the lecture came off quite well, and the public applauded heartily. When all was over, the secretary clapped me on the back and insisted on my promising to come again to Marseilles soon. And I had excellent Press notices. One, after praising my lecture, went on to say (to my glee and to that of Ravel, Fargue, and all others to whom I showed it): "M. Calvocoressi a le profil d'un jeune moine érudit et fouilleur de merveilles." In short, I had conquered the prejudice which the fair city of Marseilles entertained against lecturers. But I was never asked to lecture there again.

One more recollection of the picturesque order may find a place. In 1908, a few days before the first performance of *Boris Godunof*, a charming Paris hostess, the wife of a Russian diplomatist, gave, at Diaghilef's special request, a great propaganda reception at which Chaliapin and other members of the Russian company sang, and I delivered a talk on Mussorgsky. There was a huge crowd. To me befell the task of opening fire. But, despite my loud and firm "Mesdames, Messieurs," the hubbub of conversation went on unabated. No using Adès's receipe

Lecturing at Marseilles

that time: I should have had to take about four roomfuls of people into my confidence. So I went on quietly, knowing quite well that nobody, except maybe a dozen or so of guests sitting quite close to me, would hear a single word I said. When I had finished (which was made perceptible by my bow to the audience) there was loud applause. And presently the hostess, coming to me from the next room but one or two, exclaimed warmly: "Oh, Monsieur, que de choses intéressantes et nouvelles vous nous avez dites sur notre Mussorgsky!"

CHAPTER IX

Grieg's last visit to Paris—His interest in Debussy's music —How he took an offensive article by Debussy—A glimpse of Sibelius—Felipe Pedrell, an overlooked pioneer and master—Albeniz—His personality and plans—The story of an unfinished set of songs.

I

On the occasion of Grieg's last visit to Paris (in 1903) when he conducted a programme of his works at the Concerts Colonne, I, who longed to meet him, was fortunate enough to get from the editor of an illustrated monthly a commission for an interview. Otherwise, I should probably not have gained access to him. He was, at that time, very much annoyed because certain newspaper reporters had raked up, à propos of this visit, a letter which he had written some years before, at a time when the "Affaire Dreyfus" was raging, to Colonne, refusing an invitation to come to Paris on the grounds that he was indignant at the way in which Dreyfus had been persecuted. There had also been, at the concert, an attempt or two at hostile demonstrations; so that he fought shy of unknown visitors, and remained safely ensconced in the flat of a friend of his, the publisher, Albert Langen.

He welcomed me very charmingly, and, besides replying to my questions, gave me a musical autograph and a signed portrait. When I had finished interviewing him, he started interviewing me on modern French music. We had been talking for quite a long time when he began to ask me questions about Debussy, whose *Pelléas et*

How Grieg took an offensive article by Debussy

Mélisande he did not know and would be unable to hear during his short stay in Paris. I offered to lend him the vocal score, and also the full score of the *Nocturnes*. The conversation continued; and then, suddenly, disaster came. Debussy had just published, in the *Gil Blas*, an article on Grieg which was unkind and heavily jocular. It began with a reference to Grieg's attitude at the time of the *Affaire* and proceeded to poke fun at his personal appearance and at the mannerisms in his music (it is republished in the volume *Monsieur Croche, Anti-Dilettante*). Grieg, speaking of the reception he had found in Paris, said something which I obtusely took to be an allusion to this article; so that I mumbled something to the effect that Debussy was known to be rather whimsical and that nobody paid attention to his quips. Alas! Grieg had not seen the article, and it was my unfortunate remark that first called his attention to it.

II

A few days later, he returned the scores I had lent to him, together with a letter of which here is the translation in full, except for one paragraph in which embarrassingly kind references are made to my own work:
"Dear Sir,
"I do wish you had not called my attention to Mr. Claude Debussy's article on the Concert Colonne. I have now read it; and I am positively amazed at the tone which he, an artist, dares to adopt when speaking of a fellow artist. Of course, I likewise deplore his utter lack of comprehension of my art; but this is not the main point. The main point is his venomous and contemptuous tone. A genuine artist ought to strive to maintain a high level in all things of the mind, and to respect the point of view of other artists.

"As regards the political question: I never said, as he alleges, that 'I wanted never again to set foot in a country

A glimpse of Sibelius

which, etc. . . .' I said that *at the time* I felt I could not come to Paris. It is altogether unworthy of so gifted an artist as Mr. Debussy consciously to utter an untruth in order to disparage a colleague.

"I emphatically say, 'so gifted an artist'. I am fortunate enough not only to remain uninfluenced by his utterances on me, but to be able to feel in sympathy with his music. I read his three *Nocturnes* with great interest. They show a fine sense of colour, and high imaginative qualities. I thank you very much for having given me the opportunity to become acquainted with this work. I hope to conduct a performance of it in the North.

"As regards *Pelléas et Mélisande*, I hardly feel that I can form an opinion on the strength of the vocal score only. I hope to hear it performed in Berlin. But of course there again I acknowledge the earnestness and genuineness of his outlook. And it is this earnestness, which he denies, wrongly, to my musical outlook, that attracts me towards him, because it is my own ideal. I am sure that you . . . will fully understand me."

As Léon Vallas points out in his book, *The Theories of Claude Debussy*, Debussy, eleven years later, made some kind of amends by lauding in print the "engaging melancholy" and suggestive power of Grieg's music. At an earlier date—but yet after Grieg's death—he had also taken part in a performance of Grieg's Violin Sonata. What will strike many people as surprising is that, since he lived to correct the first proofs of his *Monsieur Croche, Anti-Dilettante*, it did not occur to him to suppress or modify certain portions of his unfortunate article of 1903.

III

Associated with this memory of Grieg is that of a meeting or two with Sibelius (I cannot remember the date) at the house where the Swedish composer Sjögren was staying in Paris. I had heard, and very much liked,

Felipe Pedrell

his tone-poems *The Swan of Tuonela* and *Pohjola's Daughter*, and I wished to know more about his output. On the other hand, I had received from a German publisher a number of his songs, which, I must confess, did not impress me much; and the instrumental music was practically impossible to procure in France. Had I seen more of Sibelius, this particular obstacle might have been overcome with his help; and even otherwise, it might have been had I displayed greater activity in the matter. But I had my hands full with other urgent work, so that I put the scheme aside for the time being, promising myself to take it up again at some more favourable moment. That moment never came, and to the present day I regret that I did not seize the early opportunity which had come my way to study the music of one of the most significant composers of our time. I regret it all the more for the reason that no critic in France, either then or later, called attention to it. Maybe if someone had at least set the ball in motion, others would have followed suit. I believe, contrary to the opinion entertained by many people, and, I understand, by Sibelius himself, that his music, and especially the symphonies, would have made great headway in France if given a proper chance to become known. And anyhow, to overlook it was a bad break for me, who, ever since my first thrilling experiences of modern Russian and French music, had been longing to investigate the contemporary output of all other European countries.

IV

Not only this desire, but also what I had heard and read concerning the activities of Felipe Pedrell led me to enquire, right at the beginning of my career, into the condition of things in Spain.

Pedrell's work had already begun to attract notice outside his country, which, at the time when he appeared, had no share whatever in the musical life of Europe, and

Felipe Pedrell

hardly any musical life of her own worth mentioning. Her position was even worse than that of England just before the days of Stanford and Parry; and one heard that Pedrell, alone and amid general indifference, was striving to bring her back to a consciousness of her old and fine musical tradition, and to raise Spanish music once again to a high, and genuinely national, level.

All this sounded very exciting and prompted me to get into touch with him, which I did by letter. He sent me, among other things, his opera, *Los Pireneos*, and, later, another, *La Celestina*. For several years we corresponded at irregular intervals. I could not help being attracted by his personality as revealed in his letters: he worked so hard, against incredible odds, towards his lofty ideals, and he was so simple, so unassuming about it all. There was a tremendous lot to be learned from his scholarly editions of old Spanish masters such as Cabezon and Victoria and Guerrero and Morales, and much to be admired in the compositions of his maturity—of the early ones I know nothing. Critics of several countries had commented favourably upon his works, but few of these were ever produced in Spain or elsewhere. I doubt whether another instance could be found of a composer so highly praised by writers of undoubted discrimination and standing, and so utterly overlooked by the remainder of those upon whom rests the responsibility of bringing musical works to the notice of the public. It is pathetic—and to him it must have been very painful—to read, in the stout volume of collected essays entitled *Escritos Heortasticos* which appeared in 1921 on the occasion of his eightieth birthday, the tributes paid to him by critics of almost every country and every possible attitude of mind, when one thinks that none of his works has been given a chance to become known.

This, of course, leads one to wonder whether his music is of a kind that can be read with interest and enjoyment,

Albeniz

and praised for quite good reasons, but lacks the incisiveness and compelling power by virtue of which it might appeal to audiences. But without a doubt it has intrinsic beauty of no common order. Excellent judges—among whom Manuel de Falla, and, in Italy, Tebaldini, who in 1897 produced at Venice, with grand success, the Prologue of *Los Pireneos*—have praised it for its evocative quality and the high sense of musical characterization and dramatic expression which it evinces. And I feel sure that well-chosen excerpts from *Los Pireneos* and *El Conde Arnau*—to name only these two operas, in which there are splendid orchestral and choral ensembles—would prove telling enough on the concert platform. Solo songs from *Los Pireneos* were given as illustrations to lectures of mine in Paris and elsewhere; and, judging by the favour with which, on every occasion, they were received, there seems to be no reason why experiments on a more ambitious scale should not meet with success. And if I mention in this book Pedrell, of whom I have no personal recollection—for I never met him, and my relations with him consisted solely in the passing of a few letters on purely musical matters—it is mainly in the hope of inducing enterprising concert-givers to try.

V

Of Albeniz I have few recollections, but the few I have remain singularly vivid. He was a most attractive person, with many baffling and elusive features in his make both as man and artist. From what his French biographer, Henri Collet, records, anyone having known him during the whole of his picturesque, restless career would have a rich store of memories to draw upon. But when I met him, he had settled down in Paris and was working as hard as his failing health allowed. I saw a good deal of him during the last year or two of his stay there, and also of his charming wife and daughters. He was

Albeniz

lovable, affectionate and impulsive in a quiet, yet demonstrative way. His aristocratic grace of manner and speech struck me as almost feminine in quality. One day he said to me: "There are only four men in the musical world whom I really love"—and he named them, but I can only remember three: Fauré, Dukas, and Bordes. "I wonder whether you will be the fifth?" And the way in which he said it made it quite clear that he was voicing a thought, not paying a subtly worded compliment.

He was full of ideas on music and of schemes, many of which were not to materialize. One of the tragedies of his musical career was that he longed to write for the stage and could not find really suitable libretti. He set to music legendary dramas, altogether northern in atmosphere, which, whatever their merits may have been from a general point of view, were the very last kind of thing he of all people would have tackled successfully—including even a *Merlin*. That, it is true, was at a time when, under the influence of the post-Wagnerian movement, nearly everybody in France was composing legendary operas, and, as often as not, operas in which Merlin the enchanter played a part. What he stood in need of was a supply of typically Spanish subjects with plenty of action, like that of his *Pepita Jimenez*.

VI

He told me many things about Spanish music in general, and about his own. I took a good many notes, which I still have, but they are too disjointed to be of much use. He was much concerned with separately defining the various influences that had contributed to the forming of his style, and making clear the differences between his ideas and aims and those of Pedrell. He spoke of his heredity—Andalusian on his mother's side, Basque, and further back Arabian, on his father's.

"There are in me", he used to add, "two composers,

ALBENIZ AND HIS DAUGHTER LAURA

Albeniz

the nationalist and the non-nationalist." He alluded to his operas, *Henry Clifford* and *The Magic Opal* performed in England; to two "very bad" string quartets, written at an early period; to a set of *English songs* of 1888, in which "quite modern things" were to be found. He was, of course, deeply interested in his work on national lines, of which an outstanding example was the recently completed set of piano pieces *Iberia*. He felt that he was just finding himself and that *Iberia* represented his aims fully. Its only defect was, he remarked, that he had written it "more like a piano duet than as music for one player only". He intended to guard against this over-fullness in the future, and also to carry further his researches as to the exploitation of Arabian ornamentations and the avoidance of runs in piano music.

But he had plans also for "non-national" work. And for one of these—which was partly carried out—a move of mine happened to provide the original impulse.

Mrs. George Swinton, an English singer whom I knew, and whose talent and lovely contralto voice I greatly admired, had been appearing in Paris at a concert which Albeniz, who longed to hear her, was too ill to attend. I asked her whether she would come to his house and sing for him, and to this request she willingly agreed. He was so impressed by her singing that he started then and there composing a set of twelve songs, to poems by Francis Coutts, specially for her. These he wished to inscribe to her; and he had asked her through me whether she would accept the dedication. Four of them were completed in manuscript when he died. But for some reason or other his executors had them published with a dedication to Fauré.

CHAPTER X

André Caplet—He gives me lessons—His early prejudices and speedy evolution—Achievement and promise of his religious music—Ianco Binenbaum—First performance of his chamber works in Paris—His retiring disposition—A ballet on Poe's Masque of the Red Death *and a cupboard full of unpublished manuscripts.*

I

When, in 1925, the news came of André Caplet's death, I was deeply grieved, not only because he was the first of my comrades to go (and I loved him dearly) but because his career, already rich in fulfilment, and even richer in promises of still finer things, had been so suddenly cut short.

I knew him first at Xavier Leroux's harmony class at the Conservatoire. Although his senior by three years, I was among the less advanced pupils when he had become our master's assistant. As such, he was usually responsible for the overhauling of my tasks. He also gave me private lessons, for which I paid at the rate of four francs (three shillings and twopence) an hour. These took place in a small cheerless room in the Rue de Dunkerque, which he shared with his brother. It was a bitterly cold winter and, not being able to afford a fire, he used to wear woollen mittens even when at the piano.

I was, in Leroux's class, a rather suspicious character because of my lack of respect for the reigning ultra-Conservative tradition and also my interest in Wagner's music (only one other member of the Class, Alfredo Casella, and he, like myself, a junior, dared to show his

André Caplet—he gives me lessons

interest in Wagner). Caplet, being a dutiful pupil, and keenly feeling his responsibility as an assistant teacher, inclined to share the general view that the germs of musical modernism were playing havoc with my mind. I remember how one day Leroux, exasperated by something I had done or said, asked another of his assistants: "What *is* to be done with this Calvocoressi? He's not unmusical, far from it: but he's absolutely hopeless." And the assistant replied: "Well, perhaps he might be sent to work with Vincent d'Indy, who, I understand, teaches music d'une drôle de façon." Caplet suggested no such drastic measure. He taught me with kindness, but not without a certain amount of constraint.

II

He progressed speedily, but was rather slow in finding himself as a composer. He was awarded the Prix de Rome in 1901 and went to Italy. By that time I had lost sight of him and almost forgotten him. His early works—among which I remember a *Suite Persane* for wind instruments, composed at a time when it was not yet usual to write for small combinations of these instruments without admixture of others—betokened a sound, and certainly not unattractive musicianship, and fine technical ability, but showed no sign of originality. I heard that he was making great headway abroad as a conductor, but I did not see him for several years.

One night, during the interval of a concert, I felt a hearty clap on the back, and, turning round, saw him beaming upon me. "Oh, Calvo," he exclaimed, "I *am* glad to see you! I've been reading articles of yours and enjoying them, and wondering when we should meet. Do you know, I've changed a lot. I think you are no end of a fine fellow and I feel about music exactly as you do. I hope that perhaps you'll like the music I'm writing now."

All this with that well-remembered twinkle in his eyes

Caplet's early prejudices and speedy evolution
which in earlier days had so often seemed to be tinged with a shade of ironic reproof for the error of my way—for he was endowed with a quality rare in musicians: a keen sense of humour. But even then I could not help being fond of him. He was a man of great charm—rather insipid in appearance at first owing to his pale, almost pasty complexion and flaxen hair, until you looked into his eyes and heard him speak. Then you realized how alert and sensitive and warm-hearted he was.

He showed me his new works, and certain of these I heard at concerts. In telling me that he had discarded the old Conservatoire superstitions, he had spoken the truth. Later I found out that it must have been chiefly owing to the influence of Debussy's music that this change had taken place in him—but a purely liberating influence, which had helped him to find his own path: there was no trace of "Debussy-ishness" in anything he had written.

I was particularly interested in his settings of Fables by La Fontaine, crisp, supple and telling; by a very original and beautiful septet for female voices and bow-instruments, which he wrote in 1909 but, for some unfathomable reason, decided not to publish; and by his Fantasy for harp and bow-instruments inspired by Edgar Poe's *Masque of the Red Death*. I suggested to him that he should develop the last-named work into a ballet for Diaghilef (who liked the idea when I mentioned it to him) but the notion did not appeal to him.

I was more fortunate—at least at first—with other schemes which I submitted to him. I longed for him to write an opera buffa; his lightness and surety of touch, in combination with that subtle and ready sense of humour to which I have alluded, would, I felt, enable him to do so splendidly. And I also thought that he ought to write a fairy opera, in which he would further exploit the possibilities of those combinations of instruments and human voices used instrumentally (as in Debussy's *Sirènes*) which

HENRI DUPARC
[*Photo. Pirou, Paris*]

Caplet's achievement and promise of religious music
he had so successfully started exploring in his Septet.

Both these plans interested him; and for a while the possibility of a collaboration between us was discussed. But nothing came out of it all. And, in fact, it was in an altogether different direction that his future as a composer lay.

III

After the war—in which he was wounded and badly gassed—he turned his attention to religious music, possibly under the influence of his war experiences, possibly in consequence of his intimate contact with Debussy's *Saint-Sébastien*, which he had helped to score, and had conducted in 1911 at the Théâtre du Châtelet and on other occasions.

His first characteristic works in this new direction—foreshadowed by a few songs written during the war, and the *Prières* for voice and piano—were the *Messe à Troix Voix* and the *Miroir de Jésus*, heartfelt and restrained, reverently thought out and exquisitely wrought, devotional and mystical, and as true to tradition as they were original.

What might not have followed had he been spared? He had barely passed the threshold of maturity, and seemed to be just coming to his own. During a visit to Paris I heard him conduct a concert, and never have I known finer conducting. The programme consisted of works by Mozart, Beethoven, Debussy, and Ravel.

I had long chats with him, and he talked of many plans. He seemed full of vitality, and launched at top speed. Recognition, too, had come to him. And when the sad news came, everybody in France felt, I am sure, that he had died at a time when he was only beginning to show of what he was capable both as conductor and as composer.

Ianco Binenbaum

IV

The notion of a ballet founded on Poe's *Masque of the Red Death* had remained strong in my mind and, soon after Caplet had rejected it, I submitted it to another composer—whose nature, as it happens, was as different from Caplet's as could be—Ianco Binenbaum by name.

There is a legend to the effect that when Messrs. Philip Heseltine and Cecil Gray first organized a concert of works by Bernard van Dieren, a certain London critic, to whom this composer's name was unknown (as it was, indeed, to many people), and who deeply mistrusted the organizers because their views on music differed fundamentally from his own and they took no pains to conceal the fact, suspected that there existed no Bernard van Dieren, and that the name had been invented for the dire purpose of hiding the real authorship of the works played at the concert.

Now, as I prepare to speak of Ianco Binenbaum, I have an uncomfortable feeling that in this country I, in turn, may incur a similar suspicion. Not one note of Binenbaum's music is published; not one note of it has been heard in England; and, so far as I know, the only articles mentioning his name (for instance, in Dent's *Dictionary of Modern Music* and in Cobbett's *Encyclopedic Survey of Chamber Music*—Mr. Cobbett having very kindly consented, upon my suggestion, to waive the rule that only published works should be mentioned in it) are from my pen. So that in sheer anticipatory self-defence I feel compelled to mention that he is known both in Germany and in France, where he lives; and that many of his works have been performed in these two countries and also in the United States of America.

To me the first intimation of his existence came in April, 1912, with the playing at the Société Musicale Indépendante of a piano quintet of his, which I found magnificent.

Binenbaum's retiring disposition

I got hold of a member of the Society's Committee and started questioning him about the composer. "Binenbaum?" he replied. "Oh, there he is." And he pointed to a quiet, gloomy-looking man of about thirty, dressed in black, with a long clean-shaven face and a big bush of crinkly black hair, sitting alone on a bench in a corner of the promenade. I was introduced, and Binenbaum submitted with perfectly good grace to a fire of questions.

Within the first three minutes of our talk, his gloomy appearance had turned out to be quite deceptive. His voice and manner were cheerful and brisk, his features alive, and he seemed delighted at the chance to talk freely about his works and adventures. He told me that he was born at Adrianople (then under Turkish rule), had studied at Munich, and won in 1902 a medal and a travelling scholarship in a competition in conjunction with the Wagner Festival at Bayreuth; that in 1905 he had given at Munich a concert of his own orchestral works (an Overture and two Symphonies) and had come to Paris in 1910. Two string quartets of his had already been played in Paris at the Chamber concerts of the Quatuor Oberdoerffer (I had noticed no announcement of these).

Another meeting was arranged, and he showed me the manuscripts of the Quartets and of other work. I did not like them all, but even those that left me baffled or indifferent struck me as worthy of notice in some way or other. I met him again and again, I studied his music, and shortly afterwards had the pleasure of lecturing upon it at the Ecole des Hautes Etudes Sociales and also at a concert organized by Oberdoerffer, his first French champion.

Then, I tackled him on the subject of the *Masque of the Red Death*. The dramatic eloquence which was the most striking feature of his chamber music made me feel sure that the subject would suit him to perfection. And indeed it appealed to him forthwith. In a very short time he had

"*Masque of the Red Death*"

turned out the score—grim, forcible, impressive, extraordinarily dynamic music, the very music I was expecting on the strength of his Quintet. But by that time, Diaghilef, whom I intended to approach on the matter, despite my rupture with him, had announced a *Masque of the Red Death* by another composer. And so Binenbaum's work remained shelved until the spring of 1914, when Fokin came to Paris. He too had left Diaghilef by then; and he had great plans for forming and running a company of his own. On my suggestion, Binenbaum showed him the *Masque*, and he was so impressed by it that he promised to submit it at once to the Committee of the Moscow Imperial Theatre. Needless to explain why nothing came out of this scheme.

V

On the other hand, it may be asked why, if indeed Binenbaum's music is worthy of attention, it remains so very little known. That an earnest, original, and prolific composer should reach the age of fifty and over without having a single work published, and without having become a subject for discussion among writers on musical topics, is a most unusual phenomenon in these days of swift information—and, it should be added, highly coloured assertions. The reasons may be partly his nationality and the fact that he lives in a country not his own. Technically, he is a Turkish subject, and he narrowly escaped being interned as such during the war. He had made a good start in Germany, and maybe would have had a better chance there than in France, where he stands in isolation, and bereft of opportunities that might naturally come his way if he was a French subject. This of course is bound to be the case, however favourably inclined towards new music by foreign composers a country may be.

Another reason is, perhaps, that his music, tense, fierce,

"Masque of the Red Death"

and overladen, and conveying, even in its occasional serene moods, the impression of a continuous grappling both with the possibilities of the medium and with complex, unformulated problems of thought and expression, is anything but easy. It is more difficult to play than to follow, however; for it is as convincing as it is forcible. It has affinities with German classicism and is definitely romantic in character; it is bold but not deliberately modern according to any formula. Thus, defying classification and exemplifying none of the "tendencies" which writers and the more ambitious members of the public are accustomed to consider, it loses the benefit of being carried on with some current or other, as a good deal of far less interesting stuff often is nowadays.

But the real reason is, I think, his reluctance to hawk his wares about. I soon discovered that it was practically impossible to get him to write letters and offer his manuscripts to publishers and concert-givers. Those composers —they are not many—who never do anything to make themselves known can be as exasperating as those who are for ever pushing themselves forwards.

Recently I made a move to get a work of his proposed for performance at an International Festival of the Contemporary Music Society. I asked him to send the manuscript to Henry Prunières, the President of the French section, who had told me that he remembered Binenbaum's pre-war works quite well and was wondering what had become of him—and this ten years after Binenbaum's return to France after the war! Binenbaum's characteristic reply to me was: "All right. I'll do it. I am glad, not for the thing in itself, but because I see what a faithful friend you are."

At the time of writing, I do not know whether he sent the manuscript, and, if so, what happened. I am compelled to end this section of my recollections with an interrogation mark. As long as Binenbaum's output re-

A cupboard full of unpublished manuscripts

mains untested and undiscussed, nobody can really foretell what kind of a future lies in store for it. Will he, deprived of the possibility of hearing his music played and surveying it, so to speak, from without, further develop the tendency to introspection and solitary dreaming which is already strong in him? Will this be to the good or to the bad?

One thing is certain: his mind is live and buoyant, his inner world is richly peopled with emotions and fancies, and he has sufficient grit to be able to carry on without encouragement of any kind. Anybody more cheerful and more confident could hardly be imagined. I saw him not long ago in the little country house at Orsay, near Paris, where he lives with his wife and two grown-up daughters —and so youthful in aspect and spirit he and his wife are that one could swear that all four belong to the same generation. There were many new manuscripts in his cupboard; and while I was scanning them, he remarked: "Bah, all these will come out sooner or later." I earnestly hope that they will, and soon. When they do, it will certainly be through no fault of his own.

CHAPTER XI

Henri Duparc—His strange neurasthenia—His unfinished Roussalka—*His views on Liszt.*

I

My friendly relations with Henri Duparc are among my most treasured memories. It was, I think, Viñes who introduced me to him in 1902 or thereabouts. As everybody knows, Duparc was a pupil of César Franck —one of the first batch, which also comprised d'Indy, Bordes, and Alexis de Castillon. He gave, in his youth, the greatest hopes. He had composed a dozen songs— among them masterpieces such as *L'Invitation au Voyage, Phidylé*, and *La Vie Antérieure*—one fine, but not outstandingly significant tone-poem, *Lénore*, a 'cello Sonata (unpublished; a few bars of it were used in *La Vie Antérieure*), and was at work on an opera, *La Roussalka*, when suddenly he had a nervous breakdown, followed by some kind of permanent neurasthenia which compelled him to give up composition without, seemingly, having otherwise affected his general health. Indeed, nobody would have suspected him of suffering from any kind of infirmity, physical or mental. He was tall, broadly built, stout, rather florid, with rosy cheeks, a golden moustache, a hearty voice and manner, and ever a twinkle in his eyes. He liked his friends to come and see him of a morning, and his conversation would always prove lively and stimulating. His interests were widespread. He followed musical developments closely and keenly, and was always ready to break a lance for or against new works as they appeared. He had an inexhaustible stock of stories about

Henri Duparc

César Franck and his group—I have forgotten most of them, but wish I had written them down at the time. He always loved a joke. One of his favourite ones was to parody his own music or that of some other composer by starting a passage in grim earnest and then suddenly branching off into something quite different and, for choice, ludicrous (it is not he, however, who is responsible for the idea of tacking the *Blue Danube* waltz on to the opening bars of the *Parsifal* prelude). When he had found a combination of this kind that pleased him particularly, he would send it to his friends, neatly written on post cards which he illustrated with some highly conventional drawing in black and white.

II

He was greatly interested in painting, and owned a number of modern pictures of which he was very fond. Among them were landscapes by Charles-Marie Dulac—pieces of mountain scenery, mystical in character, with wonderful effects of diffused light emanating from a setting or rising sun. Then there were his Japanese trinkets—netsukés and lacquerwork. He would take them one after another out of their show-cases, and talk of them as lovingly as he would talk of his pictures.

Such was he—to all appearances hale, strong, and merry, without ever a care and enjoying to the full the use of all his capacities. It was hardly credible that he should have lost the ability or the will-power to think out music or to set pen on paper. I remember talking the matter over with his wife. "Yes," she said, "when his friends call, they find him at his best, and many of them are deceived by appearances. He chats, he laughs, and they leave under the impression that he is in perfect health. But, ten minutes after they have gone, he comes to me and says: 'Oh! I am a fool: So-and-so came to see me, and

POSTCARD FROM DUPARC
WITH BLACK-AND-WHITE DRAWING
THE MUSIC CONSISTS OF THE BEGINNING OF A PHRASE
IN HIS SONG "LA VIE ANTÉRIEURE", MERGING INTO THE
"JEWELS" AIR FROM "FAUST" (*see page* 108)

Duparc's unfinished "Roussalka"

instead of being nice to him I was sullen and boorish—he will never come again!'"

A few years later he did try to do a little work. He put the finishing touches to a small orchestral Prelude, to three or four songs, to arrangements for two pianos of Bach fugues. As for *La Roussalka*, nobody except the companions of his youth knows how much or how little of it was actually written, or has heard one note of it. Sometimes, encouraged by his kindness and by the care-free way in which he talked of this *péché de jeunesse*, I asked him to show it to me. Then he smiled, shook his head, and the matter was left at that. Once, however, his hand—how eagerly my eyes followed its motion!—went to a drawer, and he had half turned the key when he shook his head and said: "Non, décidément, ce n'est pas à montrer."

When my book on Liszt appeared, I received from him a letter in which he deplored that many "good musicians" should be prejudiced against Liszt the composer.

"This", he wrote, "may be on account of his having been the most extraordinary of pianists. But those people were wrong who did not realize that if he was so wonderful an interpreter, it was because the virtuoso in him was inspired by his musical genius. I do not refer to his occasional acrobatics at the piano; but those who have heard him play in private will ever remember the experience: one forgot all about his virtuosity, which was for him the mere means of revealing the very soul of the composers whose music he played. When he played a Beethoven sonata, it was not Liszt, but Beethoven that one heard, and almost imagined to be sitting at the piano. No other pianist—not even Rubinstein—has produced so great an impression on me. And this is because he alone among pianists was a musician of genius—short-winded now and then, maybe, but nevertheless inspired. Often, in his music, a splendidly set-forth idea may stop short in

Duparc's views on Liszt

its course instead of soaring further; or there may be mechanical repetitions and stereotyped developments. But at every page of it you recognize genius. How direct a precursor of Wagner he was is not sufficiently known. I myself realized it only at a time when I knew practically the whole of Wagner's output; and the revelation amazed me."

Eventually, Duparc left Paris for good and all, settling down in a house on the Swiss bank of the lake of Geneva. The last communication I had from him was a post card in which he said that his eyesight was gradually failing him. Later, I heard, he went to live somewhere in the Pyrenees. He is now eighty-five years of age, and, I was glad to hear, in good health.

CHAPTER XII

Vincent d'Indy—My admiration for his Fervaal—*A portrait of Charles Bordes—D'Indy's second symphony—A disciple who was more royalist than the King—D'Indy's* Treatise of Composition—*His views on Debussy's* Pelléas et Mélisande—*A letter on Mussorgsky's* Boris Godunof.

I

In 1898 I attended, quite by chance, a performance of Vincent d'Indy's lyric drama *Fervaal* at the Opéra-Comique (or, more accurately, at the Théâtre des Nations, then temporarily occupied by the Opéra-Comique pending the rebuilding of its own premises, destroyed by fire in 1886). As I have said, the work had met with a very mixed reception at the hands of both critics and public. It had been freely described as a slavish and dull imitation of Wagner. There were in France at the time, as there had been in the 'seventies and 'eighties, a number of critics who saw imitation of Wagner in all kinds of music—even in Gounod. Bizet and Delibes had been upbraided for "Wagnerism": but it must be acknowledged that, superficially considered, *Fervaal* seemed to deserve the denunciation, for it was a heroic, legendary drama in the music of which leitmotifs were freely used. And, apart from this pretext, there was the fact that d'Indy was already marked as a composer who trod a path far different from any path sanctioned by musical officialdom.

Under the influence of the prevailing hostility, I was quite prepared—although I had enjoyed various symphonic works of d'Indy, such as *Wallenstein, Istar,* and especially the lovely *Symphonie sur un thème montagnard*

Vincent d'Indy—My admiration for his "Fervaal" français—to remain indifferent to *Fervaal*. But, contrary to my anticipations, the music gripped me from the very beginning; and by the time the performance was ended I had developed a keen enthusiasm. I studied the score; and soon I felt convinced that, although d'Indy had indeed undergone Wagner's influence, he asserted a strongly marked and most distinctive personality. Fifteen years later, when *Fervaal* was revived at the Opéra, I attended as many performances as I could; and I was delighted to see that many critics, by that time, had reconsidered their verdict of 1898. And, even although *Fervaal* seems to have little chance of an immediate future, I am sure that it will, sooner or later, come into its own.

II

After my experience of 1898, it was natural that a good deal of my early work should have been devoted to d'Indy. I was attracted not only by his music, but by the splendid work done by him in conjunction with Bordes. The appearance, in 1902, of his lyric drama *L'Etranger* provided me with a first opportunity to write on him at some length; and on this occasion I came into contact with him. I was greatly impressed by his restrained, forcible personality. Tall, grave, gentle in manner, he unfailingly produced this impression on all those who met him. As another composer, who neither liked him nor admired his music, once remarked to me, it was impossible, when speaking to him, not to use, instinctively, the respectful form of address, "Maître."

But another characteristic feature was a tranquil charm impossible to describe: the word "coldness" would almost unavoidably come into the description, conveying an altogether inaccurate impression—"steely" would perhaps be more suitable. I felt it very strongly, and am sure that I should have felt it even if his welcome to the unknown

IANCO BINENBAUM

A portrait of Charles Bordes

beginner I was had been less generous. As it was, I had the delight of discovering that he was interested in a piece of work which I had just completed—the French translation of Riemann's *Handbook of Harmony*. He very kindly promised to write an article on it; but unfortunately the translation was, after I had corrected the final proofs, so ruthlessly overhauled by Riemann that I had to insist upon it's not appearing under my signature; and of course I took no part in the sending out of review copies—so that d'Indy had no opportunity of carrying out his intention.

D'Indy did not like everything in my comments on *L'Etranger*. He was pleased with my assessment of the music, but regretted that I should have described the drama as coloured by pessimism. By way of conclusion to the talk we had on the subject of my essay, he presented me with the rough draft of *L'Etranger*—a most extraordinary manuscript, the staves of which are closely filled with tiny, almost gossamer notes faintly traced in pencil (but as legible as they are neat), with hardly an erasure from beginning to end.

III

Bordes, whose acquaintance I made the same year, was also a magnetic personality, but of an entirely different type—as bright and mercurial as d'Indy was grave and sedate. In appearance, with his old-fashioned ties and the even more old-fashioned cut of his hair—a fringe covering the top of his brows—he would have seemed to have stepped out of an old photograph album, but for the amazing vitality that animated him and radiated from him. He had infinite powers for both action and persuasion. No man has done so much to forward musical culture in France. His activities as an organizer, propagandist, and teacher, left him little time for composition—to the great regret of all those who knew him and remem-

D'Indy's second symphony

bered that César Franck used to consider him the most gifted of his pupils.

For a time, I used to see a good deal of him, and he seemed eager to find a way for me to help him in his work at the Schola Cantorum. Eventually he asked me to take charge of the small periodical issued by the School, *Les Tablettes de la Schola*. But I was utterly inexperienced in the matter of editorial work, and the printer whom I selected, who had promised that I could rely upon his help, let me down badly: so that after a brief inglorious attempt I had to give up the job.

Of course, haunting the Schola Cantorum, I found myself in more or less close contact with most of d'Indy's pupils, some of whom were far more uncompromising than their master, or perhaps simply lacked his gift for diplomacy. At the time when d'Indy had completed his Second Symphony, I was commissioned by the *Guide Musical* to write an article on this work. Accordingly, I asked d'Indy if he could let me see the manuscript score and give me whatever information he thought fit. He agreed; and, as his flat in Paris happened to be closed for the summer months, he said he would come to mine and asked whether a pupil of his, to whom he wished to show the symphony, might come too. This pupil arrived before d'Indy and started telling me things about the new work. A thing he told me was that of the two "cyclic" themes on which it was founded one was, as d'Indy himself had said, the "theme of good", and the other the "theme of evil". I remarked: "Yes: but that is hardly the sort of thing to bandy about." He did not reply a single word, but I saw that he was much annoyed: and the conversation languished until d'Indy appeared.

But I was not fated, on that occasion, to remain under a cloud: for, before beginning to play the symphony at the piano, d'Indy explained to us its structure; and one of his first remarks was: "I call the first theme the 'theme of good', and the second the 'theme of evil': but these designations represent merely the play of my mind, and are not intended for publication".

IV

D'Indy's gift for both analysis and synthesis struck me from the first as wonderful. His comments on musical works are extraordinarily illuminating even when the critical conclusions which he draws invite contradiction. Whenever I read his *Treatise of Composition*, I cannot help thinking how fascinating and illuminating it must have been for his pupils to attend his class.

The *Treatise* is very instructive with regard to d'Indy's personality, and anything that can cast light upon this matter is welcome to investigators. Whereas, for instance, there is no self-contradiction in Debussy or Ravel, there are, among the many aspects of d'Indy's nature, some which seem irreconcilable. It is almost impossible to understand how the same composer could have written, at four years' interval, the wonderfully sensuous, unconstrained *Symphonie sur un thème montagnard* and the austere, abstract First String Quartet. At times his conversations and certain of his writings conveyed to me the impression that he acknowledged the greatness of Liszt as a composer; at other times, however, it became clear that he took exception to it. Perhaps this was a case of feeling versus reason.

One day I had a definite opportunity of witnessing—or at least, so it appeared to me—the conflict between the two. Hearing him talk of Debussy's *Pelléas et Mélisande*, it occurred to me that what he was saying did not quite tally with the views expressed in an article of his on this work. I ventured to suggest as much, and he replied: "Oh! you see, two very different points of view are possible. The first time I heard *Pelléas et Mélisande* I listened to it as to 'music' in the ordinary sense of the

D'Indy's views on Debussy's 'Pelléas et Mélisande'

word, to 'music' as I conceive it. As such, it meant very little to me. Then, thinking matters over, I came to realize that I had been wrong, and ought to have listened to it as to something altogether different and new. So I went to hear it again, and in that new light I was able to admire it."

Now, a paragraph in d'Indy's article ran: "*Pelléas*, obviously, is neither an opera nor a lyric drama . . . it is both less and more: less, because music *per se* plays in it, most of the time, only a subordinate part—a part comparable to that of the illuminations in mediæval manuscripts, or of polychromy in mediæval sculpture; and more, because here it is the text that stands essential—the text whose musical setting constitutes a wonderful adaptation, bringing colour to the design, revealing the hidden meaning of the words, and intensifying their expressive power."

Here, I think, it is clear that d'Indy's reason rather than his feelings had led him to approve of *Pelléas et Mélisande*—the reverse of what I think was the case with regard to Liszt's music. But only his pupils, who heard him discuss, freely and at great length, works of all kinds, countries, and periods, could make certain points in his musical views clear.

V

In those days, he devoted fully two-thirds of the year to teaching, to administering the Schola, and to conducting its concerts. It was during the summer months only that he applied himself entirely to composing. He not only teemed with energy, but was splendidly equipped, both physically and mentally, for hard, continuous work.

The first time I saw him after the war, I had a striking instance of his grit. My wife and I had gone to hear his *Légende de Saint-Christophe* at the Opéra. He was conducting. As I longed to introduce my wife to him, and

A letter on Mussorgsky's "Boris Godunof"

we were leaving Paris the next day, we went round to talk to him at the end of the performance. He was quite fresh and fit, although he had just been doing three hours and a half of hard work at the desk—he was then well over seventy. After a few minutes, however, he asked to be excused, because he was rather tired, "having undergone a slight operation that morning."

In 1928, when the full genuine text of Mussorgsky's *Boris Godunof* appeared for the first time, I sent him a copy of the vocal score. He had attended one of the performances at the Opéra in 1908, and found much to praise in Mussorgsky's music. But—going, I suppose by Rimsky-Korsakof's rescoring of this music—he had quite unaccountably laid stress on Mussorgsky's "glittering orchestration, with muted trumpets and *glissandi* of the harp". I wanted him to become acquainted with the full, unadulterated *Boris Godunof*. I was well rewarded; for soon afterwards I received from him a letter in which he said: "The reconstitution of the genuine text is a splendid achievement. I have studied it with loving care. It was needful that such an edition should come, to reveal at last the genius of Mussorgsky in all its splendour, and that the task of preparing it should have been accomplished by genuine and scrupulous artists."

This was the last communication I received from him. When the news of his death came (December, 1931) I was very painfully surprised. Like all those who knew him, I was accustomed to think of him as of a man whose vitality would never be affected by the passing of years.

CHAPTER XIII

Claude Debussy—His sensitive and suspicious nature—An article of his commissioned and then rejected—A lampoon on Pelléas *circulated on the day of the Press rehearsal—A talk on contemporary music—Evils of premature discussion.*

I

Shortly after d'Indy had published the article on Debussy's *Pelléas et Mélisande* to which I have just referred, Debussy published one on d'Indy's *L'Etranger*, in which he in turn paid tribute, in liberal but well-weighed terms, to the achievement of a colleague who followed a path quite dissimilar—not to say antagonistic—to his own. He congratulated d'Indy for having partly shaken off "certain formulas as hard and cold as pieces of steel machinery", but deplored that he should not have shaken them off entirely. And, if d'Indy had remarked that in *Pelléas et Mélisande* the part played by the music was too subordinate, Debussy certainly got a bit of his own back by declaring that in *L'Etranger* there was too much music. "Why", he asked, "this continuous explaining and underlining which at times weighs down the finest things in the work?"

Of course, Debussy could no more approve of *L'Etranger* instinctively than d'Indy of *Pelléas*. But I had no opportunity of hearing him discuss the point. I never was on a footing approaching intimacy with him. Our acquaintance had not started under auspicious circumstances. At the end of 1902—that is at a time when he was still smarting under the unfair onslaughts on his *Pelléas*—he had been invited to contribute articles to *La Renaissance*

An article commissioned and then rejected

Latine. He accepted, and I was asked to write an article announcing the news (this article, entitled *Claude Debussy, Critique*, gave me a welcome opportunity to show again how much I regretted my obtuseness with regard to *Pelléas*). Then Debussy, who meanwhile had been offered, and had accepted, the post of musical critic of a daily paper, the *Gil Blas*, wrote to Binet-Valmer, the editor of *La Renaissance Latine*, that pressure of work would prevent his contributing to this periodical. Binet-Valmer, very much distressed, urged me to implore him to reconsider his decision. I, he said, as the musical critic of the *Renaissance*, was the only one to whom the task could be entrusted. Reluctantly, I accepted; and at last Debussy promised to do his best (a letter which he wrote to me on the matter is reproduced in Léon Vallas's book, *The Theories of Claude Debussy*, London, 1929). A few days later, he did send in an article—the one which is to be found under the title *Considérations sur la Musique de Plein Air* in his collected essays, *Monsieur Croche, Anti-Dilettante*, in which he suggested, among other things, that since *Pagliacci* was being given at the Opéra, it was high time to manufacture barrel-organs capable of playing Wagner's *Ring* in the streets.

The article was duly set in type, and lay waiting, when suddenly *La Renaissance Latine* changed hands. The new proprietor and editor, coming across it, gave it a glance, exclaimed: "Mais c'est idiot!" and decreed, despite my expostulations, that it was not to be published. I called at once upon Debussy to explain and apologize. He assured me that he quite realized my helplessness; but I am certain that the episode left in his mind as unpleasant a memory as it did in mine.

II

After that, I used to feel quite ill at ease whenever I met him. I knew him too little to be able to realize how

A lampoon on "Pelléas"

sensitive and shy he was. But, even so, I felt that he had excellent reasons for feeling suspicious and wishing to steer clear of all people who were not trusted friends of his—not because his music, and especially *Pelléas*, had been derided, but because of the usually unfair and often underhand methods to which his foes resorted. I shall not refer here to the many things that were said and done against *Pelléas*; but there was, in connection with the first performance, an incident which one or two biographers have mentioned, and which I should like to reduce to its true proportions.

On the day of the Press rehearsal (and in Paris the guests at a Press rehearsal comprise many hundreds of members of the general public) hawkers sold, outside the theatre, an analytical programme giving a clumsily jocular description of the play. As I probably am one of the very few people who have kept a copy of it as a document, I shall quote a few lines from it.

"Scène III: Pelléas, le frère de Golaud, se promène avec sa petite belle-sœur dans les jardins ombreux. Hé! Hé!

Scène VI: Mélisande file sa quenouille . . . et le parfait amour avec Pelléas; le petit Yniold, un enfant terrible, voit . . . et causera."

Naturally this pamphlet was regarded by many people as a deliberate manœuvre against Debussy. Those people, I think, were wrong. It is obvious enough that it was written by one of the hacks ordinarily employed to compile the unofficial programmes sold outside most Paris theatres—a hack who knew very little about the play which he purported to describe (for instance, in Scene III, Pelléas and Mélisande are not walking about the garden, and in Scene VI, Mélisande does not appear at the spinning wheel, nor is Yniold present)—and not, as was freely rumoured, by someone who knew it well and wished to wreck it for reasons of his own; or else the someone in question succeeded in covering his tracks with uncanny skill. But the very fact that the rumour did arise shows how electric the atmosphere was around Debussy.

III

After *Pelléas* had triumphed, he enjoyed a short respite, but a very little later he had again to suffer from the attacks of foes declared and undeclared. Almost every new work of his became a pretext for describing him as a composer who had but one or two tricks in his bag. Even one or two professed admirers of his started proclaiming that "these tricks were being exploited by his imitators far better than by himself"—which led one critic to remark that "many kinds of admiration were known to exist, but malevolent admiration was quite a new thing."

Others, while praising him, were obviously intent on writing "against" some other composer (as often as not, d'Indy or Ravel)—which must have annoyed him greatly and certainly helped to foster prejudice against him.

All this helps to account for the fact that years later, to a friend who had said to him: "Ecoute, Claude, les Debussystes m'agacent", he replied, "Et moi, ils me tuent." The friend was René Peter, who contributed interesting recollections to a special Debussy number of the Paris *Revue Musicale*.

Then, there were around him people who, playing upon his sensitive and suspicious nature, sought to estrange him from many of his friends—probably in order to monopolize him. They attempted to create ill feeling between him and Ravel, for instance; and, I understand, they succeeded so far as Debussy was concerned. Ravel was far too aloof and self-possessed to be affected, although surely it must have pained him on account of his great admiration for Debussy.

I suppose that I, on account of my friendship with

A talk on contemporary music

Ravel and my articles on his music, was an easy target for those people.

For several years I did not see Debussy. In 1908, I met him in Durand's music shop. I heard him ask one of the staff whether he knew anything about Rimsky-Korsakof's new opera *Le Coq d'Or*. I, who had just received advance copies of the vocal score of this, with my French translation, went to him and asked leave to send him one. He accepted; and a few days later I received from him a long letter congratulating me on "the skilful way in which I had dealt with the somewhat ponderous humour of the libretto"—which made me feel that far from deserving congratulations, I had achieved a translation which might convey wrong impressions. Anyhow, he had graciously accepted my diffidently offered olive-branch: and that was the main thing. To be quite candid, I do not know to this day whether there existed any reason for me to feel it needful to hold out an olive-branch to him: such was the atmosphere of Paris at that time.

IV

In 1913 I was asked by the editor of the Philadelphia *Etude* to interview him on modern musical developments, and on that occasion I had with him a long and interesting talk. All told, he asked me more questions than I was able to ask him: for, as he confessed, he had not followed recent events very closely "because he wished to concentrate and had made it a rule to hear as little music as possible." He did not know a single bar of Schönberg's music, which Ravel at that time had already begun to study eagerly, but he did know a few examples of Bartók's and Kodály's, and found these interesting in several respects. He praised Stravinsky's "keen, fervid curiosity", and remarked that "it was good for young artists to be alive to new possibilities and to cast about, but that no doubt Stravinsky would sober down in due

Evils of premature discussion

time". Then he started speaking feelingly of the evils of premature discussion of young composers. "I consider it", he said, "almost a crime. The former policy of allowing artists to ripen in peace was far sounder. It is unwise to unsettle young composers by making them the subjects of discussions that are, often, as shallow and prejudiced as they are premature. Hardly does a composer appear that people begin devoting essays to him and weighing his music down with ambitious definitions. They do far greater harm to young composers than even the fiercest detractors could do."

As I listened, I could not help regretting that these words of warning should not have been uttered some twenty years earlier, when they might have helped to scotch the growth of the practice. Then, perhaps, there might have been less of that pitting one composer against another which was soon to become disgraceful when it was not purely and simply ludicrous. By 1913, however, most people—including the leaders of the little cliques—had practically ceased wasting their energies in guerilla warfare. But for many years, starting from the moment when he first stepped into the limelight, Debussy himself had suffered at the hands of writers who did their utmost to deny him the peace for which he longed. And there was in the tone of his voice a wistfulness which made it clear that he was thinking of himself as much as of any of the younger composers he was referring to.

This was the last occasion on which I saw Debussy.

CHAPTER XIV

Erik Satie, composer, jester, and practical joker—He challenges the manager of the Paris Opéra to a duel—Pranks and stories—Significance and influence of his early works—Ballets with and without characters on the stage—Satie after the war.

I

It was, as I have said, Ravel who first introduced me to the music of Erik Satie and to Satie himself. At that time (I cannot remember the exact date) Satie's music was very little known. Only a small number of well-informed musicians were interested in it—for instance, Debussy, who had written an orchestral version of his *Gymnopédies;* Viñes, who played and replayed all his piano pieces then available; and Ravel, who loved those pieces so well that he would play them even to his flabbergasted comrades at the Conservatoire. He had spoken of them to me in the highest terms—not exaggerating their merits, but calling my attention especially to the innovations in the matter of idiom which they contained. These innovations, he said, had exercised no small influence upon the formation of Debussy's style, and of his own.

But if Satie was little known as a composer, he had acquired something of a reputation as a humorist, a practical joker, and a perturber of the common peace. When his name first came to public notice, in the 'nineties, it was by virtue of his connection with Péladan's noisily advertised *Rose + Croix*, which had been founded with the professed object of revolutionizing and regulating literature and the fine arts, as well as music, in the alleged

Pranks and stories

spirit of Wagner's æsthetics. Péladan had written a play, *Le Fils des Etoiles*, which bore the sub-title *Wagnérie Chaldéenne*, and Satie (who was, if I remember right, the group's "official" composer), had turned out incidental music for it. Then there were his encounters, verbal and pugilistic, with Gauthier-Villars, the one music critic who, at that time, had mentioned his name in print.

One day, the news came that he had offered a ballet to Bertrand, then the manager of the Opéra. The ballet was entitled *Uspude*, and its "cast" consisted of one character only. Bertrand had taken no notice of this offer—not even sent Satie the customary formal receipt for the manuscript: and Satie, electing to construe this piece of negligence as a personal insult, had challenged him to a duel.

This move was rather embarrassing for the unfortunate manager, because, in those days, when refusing to fight a duel, you had either to prove, to the satisfaction of a specially appointed *jury d'honneur*, that your challenger was "disqualified" (that is, unworthy), or, if you failed to prove it, become "disqualified" yourself. Fortunately Satie, mollified upon receiving formal notice that his ballet had been received, duly examined, and found unsuitable, magnanimously withdrew his challenge, and the knotty problem set to Bertrand was solved.

Another day, apparently, Satie had declared himself a candidate for a seat at the Institut, and gravely paid, according to custom, a preliminary visit to each of the members of that august body in order to canvass for his vote.

He would also tell stories as harmless as they were funny. One of these was about a faithful lobster, the pet of a family, which one day, its master's house having caught fire, heroically thrust a claw into the flames and then ran to warn the inmates of the house of their danger by showing the red-baked claw. Another—devised to get

Pranks and stories

even with an old lady who was always telling people of wonderful things done by her pets—was about a cat that drank boiling water.

"One day", Satie said, "I had a saucepan full of water on the gas ring. Just as it was about to boil, I was suddenly called away. When I came back, twenty minutes later, the saucepan was quite empty. Now, I had locked the door; the window was closed, and the room was empty except for the cat. So obviously it was the cat who drank the water."

As for the jokes in which he would indulge at the expense of complete strangers—stationmasters or café waiters for choice—some of them were funny, but a few, I understand, gave rise to trouble.

II

In short, he seemed to be a man whose chief concern in life was to think out and perpetrate jokes obviously intended for his own amusement rather than for that of others. To be prepared to take him seriously, and to break the silence observed by critics, with one accord, on the subject of his music, would have required a measure of courage but for the fact that musicians such as the three whom I have named were showing the way.

It would have been easy to imagine that all these mad pranks of his were devised merely as means of self-advertisement—and this is what most people thought. But as soon as you knew him, all possibility of entertaining the idea vanished. A single look at him, with his bald pate fringed with longish hair, his rosy cheeks and long, fair, pointed beard, his humorous eyes slyly twinkling behind glasses, and you felt him to be an altogether simple, likable fellow. He was unassuming and quiet in manner, and seemed highly amused with himself; but this (as with Fargue, mentioned in another chapter of this book) was obviously natural, and not at all a pose.

Significance and influence of Satie's early works

III

I soon found out that the few friends he had not only liked, but respected him. He was very poor, and bore his difficulties with a quiet dignity, never asking for help of any kind, and not even seeming to care whether his music would make headway or not. I too soon developed a genuine liking for him. At my request, he brought me his published pieces—not many, and at the time difficult to procure—and a good many others in manuscript, among which the three *Sarabandes* of 1887, the earliest of his really representative compositions.

Examining these works, I was able to see the truth of Ravel's appraisement. They were very simple in build and texture—often to the point of sketchiness—but teemed with attractive little melodies and pregnant, daring harmonies. In the Preludes to *Le Fils des Étoiles* (which were printed in red ink), there were, for instance, definite examples of the chords in fourths which were to become, much later, a prominent feature of Schönberg's music; and the *Sarabandes*, with their trains of ninths and distinctive melodic features, certainly foreshadowed the style of Debussy's maturity far more definitely (everybody knows this by now) than anything which Debussy had written by 1887.

The pieces in slow tempo in the *Morceaux en forme de poire* (which I was, a little later, to hear played by Viñes and Ravel) I found particularly delightful and touching. This title, Satie explained, had been given to them because Debussy had declared them shapeless: "So I called them 'pear-shaped'—and *that* ought to show him and everybody that they are *not* shapeless."

He also brought me the libretto—but, unfortunately, not the music—of his famous *Uspude*, a little pamphlet on the back cover of which appeared the truly wonderful announcement:

Ballets with and without characters
En Préparation:
Onotrotance, ballet en deux actes.
Irnebizolle, ballet en trois actes.
Corcleru, ballet en quatre actes.

This, he informed me, was not a joke: he actually carried in his head materials for all three ballets, and had indeed written parts of them down. I asked for particulars. I got them: "Let me see," he said: "*Onotrotance* . . . I haven't done much to that one yet, but it will be good, quite good. *Irnebizolle* . . . Oh! There's quite a lot of *that* done. It's a ballet in which no single person appears on the stage. As for *Corcleru*, it exists. . . . Oh, yes, it exists all right. There *are* people on the stage in it. It's difficult to explain, though. In the third act, there is a miraculous apparition. I'm rather pleased with *Corcleru*. . . ."

IV

As soon as we had become intimate enough to allow my doing so, I asked him how far all the queer stories current about him—stories so numerous that they could fill several chapters of this book—were true. He hesitated a while, and then said that about half of them were. He seemed rather shamefaced, and I could not tell whether he felt, now that people were showing signs of taking him in earnest, that these stories were too much of a good thing, or whether he regretted that truthfulness should compel him to confess that not all were true. "That's how I am," he added. "Supposing I had to appear in public as a pianist, I'd love to do so wearing a long red frock coat and a big fireman's helmet . . . for no particular reason, but I'd love to, really."

It was easy to realize that all these notions and pranks were intended for his own consumption. If you felt inclined to laugh with him, well and good; if you laughed at

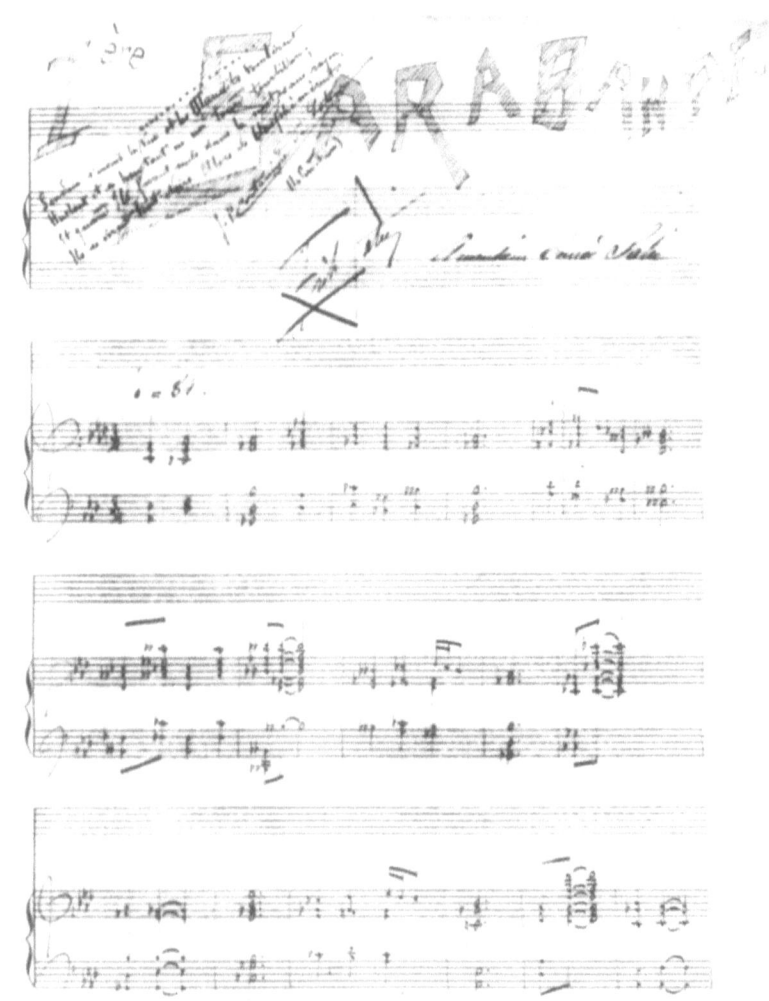

A "SARABANDE" BY SATIE, FIRST PAGE OF THE
AUTOGRAPH MANUSCRIPT

Satie after the war

him or betrayed bewilderment or irritation, you provided him with two jokes to enjoy instead of one. And I think that the remark also applies to the humorous (and often laboriously humorous) titles which he gave to certain of his compositions. I was not always prepared to laugh with him there; for, too often, pieces whose whimsical titles aroused expectations of pithy, original, and intrinsically humorous music turned out to be quite commonplace, to consist of mild, at times threadbare, musical jokes, or of parodies difficult to differentiate from the real thing poorly done—always a danger in attempts to write humorous music.

V

It was, however, with his merits from the purely musical point of view, and not with the quality of his musical humour, that I intended to deal when writing about him. My references to the jocular titles took the form of suggesting that there might lurk behind them a sound philosophic intention, that they constituted a sensitive musician's defence against smugness, a way he had found of proclaiming, "Odi profanum vulgus et arceo."

There must have been a measure of truth in the suggestion, for many others in turn have put it forward. But there have been, too, many writers who put quite another construction on these titles, alleging that they were intended as veiled, but malicious, thrusts at Debussy. This was at the time when, as I have said before, certain people were always trying to set composers against one another, while others were doing their best to estrange Debussy from various friends of his. The allegation was that Satie resented the fact that ideas of his, and actual innovations in his music, had served Debussy's purpose better than his own.

After the war, when he had become the leader of a small group of adoring disciples, it was hinted that the

Satie after the war

idea of setting Maeterlinck's *Pelléas et Mélisande* to music had occurred to Debussy directly after Satie had confided to him his ambition of setting to music another of Maeterlinck's plays; so that Debussy had stolen a march on him and effectually blocked his way. Debussy having started work on *Pelléas* as early as 1892, the rumour could hardly have spread close on thirty years later unless someone whose recollections harked back to the early 'nineties had talked; and, as all the members of the group around him belonged to a later generation, it is difficult to imagine who that someone could have been if not Satie himself.

Even so, of course, he may have spoken without malicious intention, relating what he considered a fact. Speaking to me in pre-war days, he never gave an indication of having against Debussy any grievance, real or imaginary. On the contrary, he appeared to be very much annoyed with the scandalmongers who were already at work. One day, in fact, he asked me to return to him the manuscripts of his *Sarabandes*, saying he wished to destroy them. I asked him why, and he replied: "Oh, because it is being said that I go about accusing Debussy of having cribbed from them; and the best way to stop this backbiting is to tear them up." I expostulated, and flatly refused to return the manuscripts—promising, however, that I would gladly hand them to any publisher with whom he might come to terms concerning them. He agreed, and the *Sarabandes* were published—after which he made me a present of the manuscripts.

VI

After the war I only saw Satie once—in 1924, I think. He had been proclaimed a *chef d'école*, and his disciples hailed him as the one man who had brought French music back to the path of simplicity. And Debussy, who twenty years earlier had been so generally extolled for having done precisely the same thing, they described, O marvel,

Satie after the war

as the very composer whose doings had rendered Satie's initiative needful.

I was listening to a rehearsal of his *Socrate*, which I had heard described as very beautiful, when I saw him enter the room. He had greatly changed in aspect. Gone were the humorous and sensitive character of his face and the twinkle in his eyes. He seemed to be taking himself in dead earnest, and to be intent on living up to his new dignity. He came to me and said: "Vous voyez, Calvocoressi, ce que j'ai voulu faire: l'originalité par la platitude." This may have been a piece of leg-pulling, but I doubt it. And, as it happened, the word "platitude" alone represented exactly what I felt with regard to *Socrate*.

It was, I must confess, with genuine regret that I found myself unable to speak one single word in praise of his late works. But then, I could find consolation in knowing that he no longer lacked supporters or opportunities to stand or fall on his merits (he had been taken up by Diaghilef among others), and that he probably would content himself with relegating me to the ranks of the uncomprehending, of whom he had once said: "Qu'ils avalent leurs barbes; qu'ils se dansent sur le ventre!"

On the whole Satie, who died in 1925, has had, I think, a fair innings; and I do not believe, as I do with regard to many of the lesser-known composers mentioned in this book, that there is much likelihood of his music becoming more generally known and finding more general favour. Due and, fortunately, not exaggerated tribute has been paid to his early works. And, after all, even if his later works have come in for a good deal of contemptuous criticism, they (including *Socrate*) have been praised by more than one excellent judge: so that the balance of opinion as it now stands should represent fairly well, so far as I can foresee, the attitude of posterity towards his music. As for Satie the man, I wonder whether anybody will ever be able to say what he really was.

CHAPTER XV

Gabriel Fauré—His great and beneficial influence on French music—Revolutionary innovations which official vigilance overlooked—The fate of his music outside France—Diaghilef tries to obtain a ballet from his pen—Bourgault-Ducoudray, a forgotten promoter of the modern renaissance of French music—Influence of his history class at the Conservatoire.

I

My reason for speaking here of Gabriel Fauré is not that I have many characteristic personal recollections to set down. From 1902 onwards I saw him fairly often: just enough to be able to appreciate that rare charm of his which all who knew him have praised, and also to feel that undefinable quality of authority which radiated from him despite his quiet, unassuming manner and his appearance of utter nonchalance. Both these idiosyncrasies contributed to make him, indeed, a prince among musicians. And this position was given him, too, for purely musical reasons, by his fellow countrymen in unanimous agreement. His music meant so much to us all in France—composers and writers on music and music lovers pure and simple—that no reference to musical France during the 'nineties and after would be adequate without some kind of comment on this fact; and I feel that I must explain here what he stood for to me as well as to many others.

This extreme importance of Fauré both as a creative artist and as an influence was acknowledged, for instance, by all French composers regardless—let this unusual

The fate of Fauré's music outside France

phenomenon be marked—of tendencies or party politics; by d'Indy and Debussy and Ravel as well as by most of the old-school die-hards and—later, and at the other extreme—by Darius Milhaud and Georges Auric. They all agreed not only in admiring and loving Fauré's music, but in emphasizing the capital part played by him in the modern evolution of French music generally, and in the liberation and extension of the musical vocabulary and syntax, by virtue of the new, most delicate and subtle order of sensitiveness and imagination which guided his inspiration. They felt that, in his unobtrusive restrained way, he was as bold an innovator as any of the more obviously progressive experimentalists.

This view was well expressed, despite a certain amount of picturesque exaggeration, by the French critic Vuillermoz, in a special Fauré number of the Paris *Revue Musicale*, proclaiming his wonderment that Fauré should not have been upbraided and denounced as a revolutionist and anarchist at the very outset of his career.

"Debussy and Ravel", he remarks, "had barely written three chords than all the policemen of æsthetics were after them. On the contrary, Fauré was appointed a professor of composition at the Conservatoire, and later the director of this establishment. And yet, the musical police might have discovered, among his credentials, far more subversive texts than those in the *dossiers* of Debussy and Ravel at the time of their first arraignment. The cautious and sparse audacities of Debussy's *Printemps* which scandalized the Institut, or of Ravel's *Pavane*, were little in comparison with the methodical, rational, irrevocable enfranchisement of Fauré's style."

II

Another equally strange phenomenon is that this music which meant, and still means, so much to France remains almost unrecognized abroad—altogether ignored in Ger-

The fate of Fauré's music outside France

many, disliked in Russia (I hardly ever encountered a Russian musician who had a good word to say for it), and held cheap in England after a short period of comparative popularity following, it seems to me, upon his visit to London in 1898, when Maeterlinck's *Pelléas et Mélisande* was given with his incidental music. What the position is in other European musical circles and in America I do not quite know: but I doubt whether it corresponds in any appreciable measure to the unanimous admiration of his fellow countrymen.

To account for this baffling discrepancy, it has often been said that Fauré's music is so utterly French as to be unable to cross the frontier. A few French critics have put the argument forward with a certain amount of patriotic pride, exactly as certain English critics resort to similar assertions with reference to the fact that the music of, say, Parry or Elgar makes little headway abroad. Obviously, to accept explanations of this kind is implicitly to acknowledge that the music of Fauré, of Parry, or of Elgar lacks certain of the essential qualities by virtue of which music, instead of appealing to one period or one country only, spreads and endures—which certainly is the last thing in the world that the users of the argument would wish to imply or be prepared to admit. What they are really driving at, consciously or unconsciously, is the assertion that the particular music they refer to is too good for any but excellent judges such as themselves. But, leaving aside this form of argument, it may be said that, when the whole of a vast and alert musical community such as France agrees in proclaiming the vital significance of Fauré's music, surely it is too late in the day for wise judges to admit that this music can be (as I have seen it described quite recently in English notices) "bloodless" or just "negatively delicate".

The fate of Fauré's music outside France

III

The truth is, I think, that—as indicated in Vuillermoz's comments—it is all too easy to dismiss it without a second thought. Even many of those who admire it tend simply to take it in their stride. It is not the kind of music that invites discussion, or seems, at first sight, to lend itself to comment. And indeed, the impression might easily be gained that in pre-war days, even France, although readily welcoming it, did not give it much thought—excepting, of course, the composers who eagerly studied it: for, whereas there cropped up a profusion of writings, critical and polemical, on other important composers such as d'Indy, Debussy, and Ravel, practically nothing except a few occasional articles and pamphlets appeared on the subject of Fauré. Everybody seemed to take him for granted, and there was no opposition to speak of.

This lack of literature on so important a topic was to continue until years after the war, although in 1913, at my suggestion, a pupil of mine started work on a book that was to cover both Fauré's biography and the whole of his musical output. I took him to see Fauré, who welcomed us very charmingly. This was the only occasion on which I saw him in the highly official setting of his directorial office at the Conservatoire; but, needless to add, the atmosphere and the tone of the interview were anything but official. He seemed mildly surprised, and also mildly delighted, that somebody should have thought of devoting a book to him and his work. He gave us a number of biographical particulars and reminiscences which at the time were invaluable, but by now have naturally become public property; and he invited us to come again whenever we should find it needful to ask further questions. We did not wish, however, to encroach upon his time more than we could help, and therefore deferred doing so until the preliminary work on the book should be finished. The outbreak of the war put an end to the scheme.

This was the second scheme of mine referring to Fauré which came to naught. In 1909, when Diaghilef and I were making plans for the near future, I had suggested that he be commissioned to write a ballet. Surely he would have turned out something wonderful either on a classical Greek theme or in a French eighteenth-century atmosphere. We approached him, and he agreed in principle. But he was leaving for Lugano, and asked that the discussion should be continued by correspondence. Diaghilef left Paris too, and the whole thing was allowed to drop.

After the war, on one of my first visits to France, I was able to see Fauré again. He was living at Auteuil, within a stone's throw of the house in which Albeniz had lived. I asked leave to call on him and to introduce my wife. His health was already failing, and he was cruelly tried, not only by bronchial trouble, but by the torture of steadily increasing deafness—an infirmity from which he had begun to suffer years before; yet his mellow and serene charm remained unaltered. He was at work on the string quartet which he just managed to finish, except for a bar or two, before death took him. He made a few allusions to past times, but spoke of himself very little. He made us a present of a manuscript page of his opera *Pénélope* which he inscribed to us jointly. This was the last occasion on which I saw him.

IV

A name that I wish to bring in close to Fauré's is that of the admirable and delightful Bourgault-Ducoudray, to whom France owes a heavy debt of gratitude for the unerring wisdom which led him to foresee the advantages that French composers might derive from the use, in art forms, of the free modes and rhythms of folk music and

Bourgault-Ducoudray

church music, and for the eagerness with which he threw himself into the task of bringing about a movement in that direction.

By his teachings and by the example of his own compositions, he played an all-important part in the modern revival of French music. He prepared the ground not only for men such as Bordes and d'Indy, but for the unexpected turn which was to take place with Debussy's advent, for the proper recognition of the Russian masters, with its far-reaching consequences, and, in fact, for nearly everything that took place in music until 1914.

A profession of faith such as that which he uttered as early as 1878, in the course of a lecture at the Paris Universal Exhibition, was of more than national importance, and its significance may be recognized even at the present time when a reaction against "national" elements in music is taking place. "No element of expression", he said, "to be found in any tune, however ancient or remote in origin, should be banished from our musical idiom. All that may help to rejuvenate this idiom should be welcome. The question is one not of giving up any previous conquests, but on the contrary of adding to them."

V

Looking backwards it is possible to see how right he was: musical art owes practically the whole of its progress during the last two decades of the nineteenth century and the first of the twentieth to two fertilizing influences: that of folk music, and that of poetic programmes. And even now that a new period of "pure" music has set in, all the conquests of that period play their part in the enrichment of the available resources, and remain an essential factor of evolution.

Bourgault-Ducoudray's own compositions show how deep and how sound was the influence exercised on him by the old music and exotic music which he studied so keenly.

Bourgault-Ducoudray

His fine *Carnaval d'Athènes* for orchestra, his opera *Thamara* are, in this respect, significant landmarks. But neither these, nor any other of his works, despite their genuine merits, ever enjoyed more than a *succès d'estime*. It may seem strange that a man who attracted so little notice as a composer, and who did not teach composition, should have exercised so great and so beneficent an influence. It all was done through his books and lectures on Greek music and folk music, and especially at his class of musical history at the Paris Conservatoire. To the students attending this class (attendance was not compulsory, nor rewarded by the possibility of winning any prize) from 1878 to 1909 he unfolded his views, patiently and lovingly giving invaluable advice, and sowing the good seed broadcast.

A considerable part of his output, including two operas entitled *Bretagne* and *Myrdhin*, remains unpublished. I was told that there were excellent things in both these operas, but this is all I know about them. There was a time when I saw Bourgault-Ducoudray fairly often; but at these meetings we never discussed his own music—they were devoted either to points relating to Greek folk music or to steps to be taken to propagate in France the works of Balakiref, whom he admired greatly.

I loved his simple and cheerful manner, his childlike faith and enthusiasms, his tranquil philosophy. He never seemed to care two pins whether he himself remained unhonoured, and his music practically unnoticed, so long as he could see that headway was being made in the very directions he had pointed out. Since then, I have often asked myself whether there still may be a future for his music or whether the oblivion into which it has sunk is final. One thing that may confidently be said is that his contributions to the art he loved so well have not been sufficiently tested, and remain unknown not only to the musical public at large, but also to specialists. Towards

Influence of his history class at the Conservatoire
the close of his life (he died in 1910, at the age of seventy), when he might have found less inadequate recognition, his own dislike for courting publicity and the lack of a small body of active supporters combined to keep his music in the background.

Among the works of his I know, many, were they heard to-day, would prove interesting and attractive. They do not lack freshness, nor poetic significance, and they deserve a place in the sun. But I doubt whether they would be found sufficiently exciting to create a movement in their favour after so many years of indifference.

But even so, it is none the less deplorable that not the slightest tribute should ever be paid to his work and influence by any of the writers who have dealt with the history of modern French music. Indeed, I cannot recall a single book or essay on this subject in which his name is even mentioned. Here, at least, it remains possible to remedy a positive injustice; and I sincerely hope that the record of the all-important part he played and the inestimable services he rendered will be rescued from oblivion.

CHAPTER XVI

Camille Erlanger—His Juif Polonais—*A glimpse of Victor Maurel and one of Caruso—Chaliapin in the 'nineties and after—The interpretation or the music?—Raoul Gunsbourg.*

I

Among the composers whose acquaintance I made during my pre-criticism days was Camille Erlanger, who died in 1919, at the age of fifty-six. One of my reasons for mentioning him, whose very name is probably unknown to most readers of this book, is that one at least of his works, the opera *Le Juif Polonais*, does not deserve, in my opinion, the oblivion into which it has fallen; and the same might be said, perhaps, of earlier works of his, among which the *Légende de Saint-Julien l'Hospitalier* and the opera *Kermaria*—both these, in their time, won praise from many competent judges.

Le Juif Polonais (which in this country would be named *The Bells*, like the well-known play on the same subject) was produced at the Opéra-Comique in 1900, and had a quite successful run. I was introduced to Erlanger during an interval of a performance. A quaint little figure he made: thin, sallow, with a small pointed beard, very much like a tame Mephistopheles in top hat and black frock coat with a crimson satin tie. Very soon we were on friendly terms, and for a time I saw a good deal of him. I attended several performances of *Le Juif Polonais*, and at each hearing liked it better. I was aware of certain defects in it. I specially disliked, in the prelude to the third act, an atrociously loud and cheap chorale for the brass alone, and wondered how he had come to write it. But with this

Chaliapin in the 'nineties and after

and a few other trifling exceptions, the music was unlaboured, well thought out, flowing, and effective. Of course, like *The Bells*, the work, as a whole, was very much a one-part affair, practically the whole burden resting on the principal character. It had been written, I believe, specially for Victor Maurel, who was admirable in it—all the more perhaps, because the part called for good acting and diction rather than for vocal brilliance.

Whether it was because no singer was found to take his place when his engagement at the Opéra-Comique came to an end that *Le Juif Polonais* did not run longer I do not know. But I think, even now, that if a suitable man could be found for the principal part, this work might prove a success in England and elsewhere.

Associated with it is one picturesque recollection of Maurel. After a performance, I was having supper with some friends at the Maison Dorée. In walked Maurel. He sat at a table not far from ours, and ordered three fried eggs, to be followed by "petites fraises des bois" (the delicious little wild strawberry which this country despises as too small to be worth troubling about). After disposing of his eggs, he proceeded to tackle the strawberries. These he poured from the basket in which they were brought to him into a soup plate until the plate would hold no more. Then he started pounding them with much castor sugar, adding water to the mixture until its consistency was quite to his liking. And then he ate them.

II

My memories of Chaliapin hark back to an even earlier date. I met him in 1898 during a stay of his—the first, I think—in Paris, at a boarding-house where I was calling to see some acquaintances. He was then twenty-five years of age, delightfully simple, and as irrepressible as he is now. He sang for us at the boarding-house. He came to

Chaliapin in the 'nineties and after

my house and sang for me alone, superbly regardless of the liberties I took with the accompaniments, songs of Schumann and Schubert and Mussorgsky's *Trepak*. I could not help thinking that with his stature, his strong, merry, delightfully naïve face, and his tumbled fair hair, he would have made, had he happened to be a tenor, an incomparable Siegfried. He knew practically no French. I knew no Russian, but we managed to get on swimmingly.

I saw him again during the Universal Exhibition of 1900. We spent an evening there, going round the shows. One of these consisted of a lady doing a Salome dance. We were in the front row of the stalls; and Chaliapin, whose French by that time had greatly improved, kept commenting upon the dancer's sumptuous and generously revealed proportions in a voice that was intended to be a whisper into my ears, but which caused ripples of laughter to run through the audience, while I plainly saw the object of the comments, not in the least offended by the frank tribute, bite her lips as she carried on with the dance.

We walked out of the Exhibition into the cool night. In the Avenue de l'Alma, Chaliapin, who was in high spirits (but let it be made clear that this was due to nothing stronger than the fun we had been having) started singing the popular Italian song whose burden is:

Ha, ha, ha, ha, tira mi la gamba, tira mi la gamba!
Ha, ha, ha, ha, tira mi la gamba, tira mi la ben!

Soon I began to fear that we might be run in for disturbing the peace. But the more I expostulated, the louder he sang. At last it occurred to me to say to him: "Hush, Feodor; look, we are passing by a church." And so I won my point. But we soon devised some other means of painting the town red: he was leaving Paris the next day, and this was our only meeting that year.

Chaliapin in the 'nineties and after

III

I had never heard him sing except in private (and, of course, in the Avenue de l'Alma). The first time I heard him on the concert platform was at Diaghilef's Russian Concerts in 1907, when he sang, among other things, excerpts from Mussorgsky's *Boris Godunof* and *Khovanshchina*. And the first time I saw him on the stage was the following year, when *Boris Godunof* was produced at the Opéra. So much has been written about the heights to which his interpretation of the part of Tsar Boris rises that I need not dwell on the point, and may rest content with saying that to me it was a wonderful experience—the most wonderful of the kind that I have ever had.

In 1909, his appearance as Tsar Ivan the Terrible in Rimsky-Korsakof's *The Maid of Pskof* (whose title Diaghilef considered not sensational enough and changed into *Ivan le Terrible*) was another thing to remember for ever. Even details such as his triumphant, yet watchful, scowl when on horseback he entered the captured city of Pskof, or his restless and bestial way of clutching and champing the bread and salt brought to him as tokens of submission, remain vivid in my memory to this day.

Two or three years later, I saw him at Monte Carlo in the title part in Massenet's *Don Quichotte*. He was so splendidly convincing that I was kept spellbound despite the insignificance, and indeed meretriciousness, of the music. And for the one and only time in my life I came near understanding how it can be that so many people, on the strength of a telling interpretation, come to credit certain works with merits of which they—as the same people would perhaps realize under other conditions—are intrinsically devoid. I am not alleging that Chaliapin alone could have made me feel thus. I am s mply stat ng that nobody else has. And even so, it must have been mainly the splendid acting that did it. Never did an inter-

A glimpse of Caruso

preter of instrumental music or of a song give me a similar feeling. In fact, the better they play or sing music which I find bad, the more irritated and disgusted I grow. It may be on account of a feeling of skill wasted on unworthy stuff, or it may be that for me, the fine interpretation brings out the weaknesses of the music instead of atoning for them. That not particularly experienced or naturally subtle people should be satisfied with music just because it is well sung or played I find quite natural. But when I hear really sensitive, experienced, and even fastidious judges aver that a fine interpretation of music not enjoyable in itself can be an enjoyable thing, I can but stand lost in amazement. But then I am, by nature utterly unable to enjoy, in matters of art, skill for skill's sake. Likewise, I am quite capable of enjoying a fine voice or tone, but only for a very short while unless they are used in the service of music I can enjoy. There may be to all this, as regards my own psychology, another moral; but I have not yet succeeded in discovering it.

For one who has had, one way and another, a good deal to do with opera, and vocal music generally, I have surprisingly few memories of singers. But one more, at least, I wish to record.

IV

Caruso I spoke to (or rather, was spoken to by) only once. It was in 1910. Raoul Gunsbourg, the manager of the Monte Carlo Opera, had asked me to help him in organizing a monster charity concert at the Trocadéro, at which the famous tenor was to appear. I owed this invitation, which was taking me very much more out of my own line of business than even my work with Diaghilef had done, to the fact that that work, as I shall presently relate, had brought me into contact with Gunsbourg, whom I liked and was wishful to oblige. I accepted all the more readily because the object was to succour the victims of a recent catastrophe—a flood, I think.

I did not see Caruso until the moment of the concert, when, while I was engaged in looking after things behind the scenes, a flustered attendant came to me and said: "Will you please come, sir? Mr. Caruso is outside. He says he won't come in. . . . He's very angry." I rushed out, and Caruso, without giving me time to open my mouth, bawled out: "Do you know that when I came there was nobody to meet me and show me to my dressing-room? Why was that? I've never seen such a thing in my life!" I tried to explain that there were many entrances to the Trocadéro, and that he would have found a porter and attendants in readiness at the stage-door; but he cut me short with: "That'll do! Not another word! Say another single word, and I'll leave the place. Have me taken to my room at once!" Needless to say I kept well clear of him during the concert. But when it was all over, as I was standing by the gateway, I saw him come out. He was in high feather. He came to me, beaming, and, with a perilous approach to digging me in the ribs, said: "Hello! Went well, didn't it? Got a cigarette?"

V

There could be no doubt that the concert had gone well. Gunsbourg had secured the help not only of Caruso and many other famous artists, but of the drums and fifes of the Garde Républicaine, whose contribution to the programme stands out above all others in my memory. They gave an amazing display of very old tattoos, calls, signals, and marching tunes, of which they alone have preserved the tradition, and which to my knowledge they do not perform in public once in ten years. All these are most attractive, and many are as picturesque and weird as anything that could be encountered in Tibet, Africa, or Australasia.

Raoul Gunsbourg

Painters and sculptors, too, had helped to make the concert a success by gifts of works, one of which was placed in each private box to become the property of the occupant, these gifts ranging from original drawings by Rodin to a caricature of Gunsbourg by a well-known cartoonist.

Gunsbourg, always as quiet as he was purposeful, taking everything in his stride and never showing a tithe of the strength in him, was a man who, whenever he pleased, could achieve the seemingly impossible. He was as kind as he was capable, and always ready to find work for singers or instrumentalists who stood in need of it; I have never met anyone who, having worked with or under him, had not learnt to like him. My first dealings with him were connected with Diaghilef's plans for a Russian ballet season at Monte Carlo; and soon afterwards it fell to my lot to have to ask him to help Diaghilef out of difficulties at the end of the 1909 Ballet season in Paris. Once, Diaghilef and I went to his house by appointment to discuss some important business; and he, who prided himself on his talents as a cook, received us in the kitchen where, with the help of two maids, he was engaged in preparing, among other things, a most complicated dish of lobster—his own recipe, he told us. It was a most picturesque affair, and I hugely enjoyed observing how nicely he held the balance between the various things simultaneously calling for his attention—discussion of dates, programmes, and fees, instructions to the two maids, and the skilful blending of seasonings, which he entrusted to no hands but his own.

We did not taste that wonderful lobster dish; but he invited us next day to a dinner which showed us that his pride in his cooking was fully justified.

One fine day it occurred to him to try his hand at turning out operas. He acknowledged frankly that he hadn't the faintest idea of the technique of composition; but he

Raoul Gunsbourg

declared that he had plenty of ideas in his head and only wanted them carried out. The method he adopted was to think out melodies and rhythms and hand these on to the conductor of the Monte Carlo Opera-house, who harmonized them and cast them into shape and scored them. Two operas thus composed were produced at Monte Carlo —one of them also at the Brussels Théâtre de la Monnaie.

After the war, I saw him again at Monte Carlo, where my wife and I stayed a while as his guests at the time when he produced *The Fair at Sorochintsi*, an opera left unfinished by Mussorgsky and completed by Tcherepnin. I found him as genial, as youthful, as expert in the art of conquering obstacles as ever. Long may he prosper!

CHAPTER XVII

Russian music—Balakiref's Islamey *and* Tamara*—Mussorgsky revealed by the d'Alheim couple—Russia's attitude to his music in the 'nineties—My early work on Russian music—An option on* Boris Godunof *disdained—My book of 1908 on Mussorgsky.*

I

I owe my earliest impressions of Russian music to Tchaikowsky's *Pathetic Symphony* and to Balakiref's *Tamara*, both of which I heard in the middle 'nineties; the symphony I loathed, and *Tamara* struck me as a thing of haunting beauty, never to be forgotten. For quite a long time I used to think of it daily, as I did of Wagner's music, always with a thrill and longing to hear it again. Borodin's *Steppes of Central Asia*, his *Polovtsian Dances*, and his first String Quartet also created deep and lasting impressions—his symphonies, at that time, were not played in France, and it was much later that I got to know them. Then came Rimsky-Korsakof's *Antar* and *Spanish Capriccio*. The former moved me deeply; but I regret to say that I did not enter into the spirit of the latter, and in fact was one of the few people who hissed at the end of its performance.

Balakiref's *Islamey*, which I heard played by Godowsky, provided another thrilling experience. While listening, I felt so excited and surprised by the novelty and joyful effervescence of it all that for a little I could have exclaimed, as the legendary Yankee seeing his first giraffe: "I don't believe it!"

Mussorgsky revealed

Then, last but not least, there came the sudden revelation of Mussorgsky's music, introduced to France by the admirable singer Marie Olénine d'Alheim and her husband, who lectured upon it with infectious enthusiasm. This was at a time when Russia paid very little attention to Mussorgsky's music, and other countries—including France, which knew rather more than was known elsewhere of Balakiref, Rimsky-Korsakof, and Borodin—were practically unaware even of its existence. The circumstances under which it came to pass that the first move in the campaign which was to call the whole musical world's attention to Mussorgsky's genius should be made in France are described in Robert Godet's book *En Marge de Boris Godunof* (London, 1926). A copy of the first edition of the vocal score of *Boris Godunof* fell into the hands of a French music-lover, named Jules de Brayer, in 1874. He studied it with ever-increasing admiration, and eventually communicated his enthusiasm to a small circle of friends, of whom Robert Godet was one. His efforts to interest performers and producers, however, proved vain until the moment when he met the d'Alheim people, who in 1896, having rented a small hall, gave a set of seven concerts with lectures, entirely devoted to Mussorgsky.

II

No worthier pioneers could have been found. Marie Olénine d'Alheim—who since then has made Mussorgsky's songs known throughout Europe—evinced from the first the keen musical intelligence, the perfect sense of style and proportion, the straightforwardness and pregnancy in interpretation that have won her a place entirely her own among singers. As for Pierre d'Alheim, he managed to speak of Mussorgsky and to describe his works relevantly and convincingly, speaking with childlike simplicity and faith. His lectures teemed with picturesque and vivid short cuts and images. He never attempted to indulge in purely musical considerations—which would have been, I believe, outside his experience—and yet made his audiences feel the significance of the music and long to grow familiar with it.

He was, I learnt, the descendant of a French family which had emigrated to Russia at the time of the French Revolution. He was born in France, to which country his father had returned. He was a journalist, a writer, and a poet. His lectures and his book on Mussorgsky (Paris, 1896) represent the whole of his activities in the domain of music, except for a number of articles on musical topics published later in a Russian periodical which he edited in conjunction with the activities of the Moscow *Maison du Lied*, founded by him and his wife. But he was also, apparently, a precursor in another respect: it was a book of his on the Ballet in Russia, entitled *Sur les Pointes*, that first gave Diaghilef the idea of launching the Russian Ballet in Western Europe.

In order fully to realize the importance of the initiative taken by the d'Alheims, it is necessary to know how shockingly Mussorgsky's music was neglected in Russia.

When the news reached Petrograd that concerts of Mussorgsky's works had been given in Paris and that they had taken French musical circles by storm, the editor of the *Russian Musical Gazette*, Professor Findeisen—one of Mussorgsky's few champions in Russia—availed himself of the opportunity to rebuke, in stinging terms, his indifferent fellow countrymen. Here is a quotation from the article he wrote:

"When telegrams from Paris acquainted Russian musical circles with the fact that Mussorgsky's music had been performed there with great success, great bewilderment arose; and it was thought most strange that even a few eccentric Frenchmen should have been found to evince interest in music which we Russians have cast aside as worthless. But meanwhile, those eccentric Frenchmen think it no less strange that we should neglect our own art, and even strive to obliterate it, while more progressive nations are striving to take it in and propagate it. Very probably, they compare us to those inhabitants of Laputa whom Swift describes as so absorbed in self-complacency, that they notice nothing around them until they are awakened by someone hitting them on the head with a bladder."

III

Since then, all writers, Russian or non-Russian, have acknowledged that France played a leading part in the vindication of Mussorgsky's genius. But for de Brayer, Godet, and the d'Alheims, this vindication might have begun far later. Nobody realized at the time how great a service the d'Alheims were rendering to the musical world at large; but almost everybody was moved to enthusiasm by the beauty of Mussorgsky's music, and Marie Olénine d'Alheim's Mussorgsky recitals became a welcome feature of the musical life of Paris. For my own part, I seldom missed one. A few years later, I got to know her and her husband. Him I found altogether delightful; lanky, loose-limbed, with straggly blond hair and beard, simple, expansive, ever ready to take to his heart anybody who shared his love for Mussorgsky. When I in turn started to write on Mussorgsky, he welcomed me as an ally; and when my own book on Mussorgsky appeared, I received from him a letter expressing warm approval and offering most interesting suggestions, of which I availed myself later.

She was more reserved in manner, and, so far as I can remember, spoke little as a rule. There was something enigmatic in her beautiful, pale, reposeful face, surrounded by a halo of golden hair. But the tremendous reserve of

Mussorgsky's music

force behind the tranquil aspect became manifest as soon as she began to sing.

I retain the memory of a curious little episode in connection with one of her recitals. I had just passed the ticket office when an attendant came to me and said: "Mrs. Olénine would like to speak to you." I went to the artists' room, and she asked me to turn the pages for her accompanist. Vainly did I seek to be excused—pointing out that I was wearing a lounge suit, and that I was attending the concert in my capacity as a critic, which made it doubly embarrassing for me to appear on the platform. She insisted, giving as a final reason that the accompanist and I were of the same size (which, by the by, was not quite accurate); and on the platform I had to go.

At one moment, I forgot that I was not in my own room, reading music with Ravel or Viñes, and I whispered a remark on some musical point or other into the accompanist's ear. Luckily, no catastrophe ensued. But, naturally, he was furious; and during the interval (when, being conscious of my guilt, I did not venture near him) I saw him expostulating with Mrs. d'Alheim on a subject which I could guess only too well.

The next day I received from Romain Rolland a letter thanking me for the tickets I had sent him for this recital and praising the singer's talent. "Je n'ai jamais entendu chanter avec autant d'intelligence," was one of the sentences in it. I wrote back saying that I had sent him no tickets, and so deserved no thanks. When next I met him, he said: "Seeing you on the platform, I naturally thought you had something to do with the concert." Since then, I have often wondered why I had been selected for the honour of turning those pages.

IV

Soon after having heard Mussorgsky's music for the first time, I tried to procure copies of his songs and operas.

My early work on Russian music

This was no easy task, but eventually I managed to secure a few, and others were lent to me. I experienced similar difficulties with the music of Balakiref, and for a long time had to rest content with the memory of what little I had heard of it, and the use of copies of *Tamara* and *Islamey* which belonged to Ravel. In those days I was far from suspecting that a time would come when I should delve deep into the output of both these composers, which seemed then so inaccessible. My real work on Mussorgsky's music began in 1904 or thereabouts. It is far from finished; and, so far as I can see, it will keep me busy to the end of my life. My work on Balakiref is still in its preliminary stage, and there seems to be very little likelihood of the documents which would enable me to carry it out (e.g., the whole of his correspondence with Stassof and Rimsky-Korsakof) being published in the near future.

Of the principal works of the other Russian composers from Glinka onwards I had acquired, by 1903, a fairly extensive knowledge. A good deal of that knowledge I owed to Ricardo Viñes, who was playing quantities of new music which no other pianist dreamt of touching. And of course, having started by then on my career as a critic, I had worked hard on the subject, which proved increasingly attractive to me.

V

Having become known, in a small way, as a specialist on the subject, I gained many facilities for increasing my knowledge of it, and for getting into touch with people. It was thus that I got acquainted with J. H. Zimmermann, of Berlin, who had become Balakiref's publisher and who commissioned me to translate a book of his songs, thus starting me on my career as a translator; and also with Bessel, of Petrograd, who (in 1905 I think) gave me an option on the copyright for France of Mussorgsky's *Boris Godunof*. With a vocal score of the 1874 edition under

My book of 1908 on Mussorgsky

my arm, I called upon one French publisher after another. But I was no luckier than Jules de Brayer had been thirty years before: not one of them would consider the matter. How sore they must have been when, three years later, *Boris* was given at the Paris Opéra by Diaghilef! The performing rights on these few performances amounted exactly to three quarters of the sum for which Bessel had been ready to sell the French copyright.

In 1906, when Diaghilef first came to Paris, to organize an exhibition of Russian paintings at the Salon d'Automne, I was introduced to him as one who might help him in his schemes for the diffusion of Russian music.

In 1907 I began to work with him, as will be related in a further chapter, and I wrote my book on Mussorgsky. This appeared in the spring of 1908, and was so favourably received, both in France and in Russia, that I could feel I had succeeded not only in helping to increase general interest in Mussorgsky, but in setting the ball rolling in the matter of the study of his musical idiom and style—a subject which, strange to say, nobody had yet thought of dealing with.

I do not allege that I had gone very far, or even proceeded on altogether right lines. Indeed I was to discover that having allowed myself to be influenced by what Russian musicians and critics had said of Mussorgsky's "stark realism" and "haphazard methods" I had not delved into things deeply enough. I had taken it for granted that there was in Mussorgsky's music a certain amount of disorder which had to be glossed over. I had even failed to mark, among other things, the wonderful structural and textural unity of *Boris Godunof*. But it was years later that I was able to measure the extent of my error.

VI

Apart from this inadequacy of my comments on Mus-

My book of 1908 on Mussorgsky

sorgsky's music, my book was fated soon to become out of date; for, during the two or three years that followed its publication, a quantity of new music by Mussorgsky and documents on his life and ideas cropped up—the score of his *Marriage-Broker*, a whole book of early songs, the manuscript of which was purchased by Charles Malherbe, the librarian of the Opéra, for the amazingly low sum of five hundred francs (£20). These songs were published after the war under the title *Years of Youth*. There were also his letters to Stassof and to Rimsky-Korsakof, to say nothing of a profusion of less important materials.

This, by the way, seems to be the fate in store for all books on Mussorgsky written outside Russia. No sooner do they appear than new information on his life or new music or letters from his pen are revealed; and so the books become inadequate almost as soon as published. Thus it has happened even with the books written a very few years ago in German by Von Riesemann and Von Wolfurt, and in French by Robert Godet.

By 1911 I had realized that a fresh book on Mussorgsky was called for, and I began to prepare one. In 1912 I was commissioned to write it by Serge Makowsky, the editor and publisher of a splendid Russian art periodical, *Apollon*, of which I was the Paris musical correspondent. The war prevented the carrying out of the scheme. After the war I reverted to it, very much encouraged by Kussewitsky, who as soon as he heard of my idea commissioned me to carry it out as quickly as possible. I am still at work on it; and when, by God's grace, it is finished, I wonder what unsuspected information on Mussorgsky will crop up as soon as it has gone through the press.

All those years I had been longing to go to Russia in order to meet Balakiref, with whom I had been corresponding since 1905, and to study the manuscripts of *Boris Godunof* preserved in the archives of the Imperial Theatres.

My book of 1908 on Mussorgsky

I wanted to examine the original full score, never published, and also to find out about the "unpublished portions" casually referred to by Mussorgsky's first Russian biographers. When writing my book, I had devoted an appendix to a comparison between the genuine *Boris*, as known in the form of the vocal score of 1874, and Rimsky-Korsakof's editions—a comparison very similar in the main to that which was made by Godet in his book of 1926, *En Marge de Boris Godunof*, except that I had not thought it needful to adopt an insulting tone when speaking of Rimsky-Korsakof's alterations. But as my agreement with the publisher stipulated that my book was not to exceed 250 printed pages, I found myself compelled not only to abridge portions of it but also to suppress the appendix, contenting myself with a footnote warning readers to shun all revised editions of Mussorgsky's masterpiece. But it was only in 1912 that I was able to go to Russia. By that time, Balakiref had been dead two years; and, as things turned out, I was unable to carry out my scheme of studying the manuscripts of *Boris Godunof*.

CHAPTER XVIII

Balakiref as seen from France—My correspondence with him—His isolation and the ingratitude of his fellow countrymen—His plans for a Rhapsody on Greek folk-tunes—His tone-poem In Bohemia*—His views on modern French music—Celebrating Chopin's centenary.*

I

At the time when I began to develop an interest in Russian music, Balakiref, to all of us in France, was surrounded by an aura of legend as Glinka's heir, the leader of the modern Russian school, the man to whom Mussorgsky and Borodin and Rimsky-Korsakof had gone for tuition. And in another way too he seemed to be a figure of legend, because so little could be known about him and his musical output. Apparently, nobody could tell where he lived and whether he was still composing, and where his works other than *Tamara* and *Islamey* could be procured. Bourgault-Ducoudray, the French composer and scholar, a great admirer of his, had corresponded with him in the early 'nineties; so had, a little later, Charles Malherbe, when preparing with Weingärtner the collected edition of the works of Berlioz (on which Balakiref was an authority), but nothing of that had become public. More fortunate than Balakiref's French admirers, Mrs. Rosa Newmarch, the English specialist on Russian music, had met him in Petrograd in 1901; but whatever she may have published on that occasion had not reached France. Nor had Balakiref been invited to join the group of Russian composers who, in 1889 and 1900, came to Paris for the Russian concerts at the Universal Exhibitions. In

My correspondence with Balakiref

short, most of us (not that we were many to evince an interest in the matter) were in complete ignorance, and could but wonder why everything concerning him seemed doomed to remain shrouded in mystery.

II

None of us knew that for various reasons—not all of them quite clear even nowadays—he was living in almost absolute seclusion, estranged from most of his quondam pupils and friends, ignored and practically forgotten by the greater part of the musical world of Russia, suspicious, and embittered. Since then, the tale of the ingratitude of his fellow countrymen has been partly told, and we are able to see that his own uncompromising and autocratic disposition had something to do with it: but surely his love of his art, his eagerness for disinterested service, his achievements as teacher, composer, and propagator of Russian music deserved a better reward.

It was in 1904 only that I got into touch with him. I met at the house of some friends of mine, Babaian by name (one of the family was Marguerite, the singer, who gave me invaluable help in my investigations of Russian music and provided many fine illustrations to my lectures —shortly afterwards, she was to be the first to sing in Paris a number of Balakiref's songs), Theodore Akimenko, the composer, who had been a pupil of Balakiref. He told me that Balakiref was living in Petrograd and actually was able to give me his address. My excitement knew no bounds. I promptly wrote to Balakiref, and thus a correspondence was started which continued to the end of his life.

His first letter gave me all the information I required as to his works published and unpublished, so that I was able to start preparing the articles I was longing to write. But one of his very first concerns, after that, was to call my attention to the music of Liapunof. "This fine music",

Isolation, and ingratitude of his fellow countrymen
he wrote, "is probably unknown to you, as it is, unfortunately, to everybody except a few German specialists, who hold it in high esteem." Following this suggestion, I procured the music (Zimmermann, the publisher, had just arranged for an agency in Paris) and soon after I was corresponding with Liapunof too.

Balakiref sent to Viñes, whom I had mentioned to him as a peerless interpreter of Russian music, a copy of Liapunof's piano concerto and was very wishful that this concerto should be played in Paris. On my suggestion Bourgault-Ducoudray—who had brought about the first Paris performance of *Tamara*—was asked to set his shoulder to the wheel, and did so readily, but nothing came out of it: no conductor would consider the concerto.

I was more fortunate with Balakiref's own works, beginning with the cantata which he had written for the celebration of Glinka's centenary. I suggested to Georges Marty, the conductor of the Concerts du Conservatoire, that a performance of the cantata would be an excellent way of commemorating the centenary in Paris; he gave his assent and, as the celebration in Petrograd happened to be delayed, the cantata was given in Paris before being given in Russia.

Balakiref was delighted. He had so set his heart upon the commemoration that no performance, in Paris or elsewhere, of any other work of his would have given him half as much satisfaction. A few years later, he was to display the same eagerness with regard to the celebration of the centenary of Chopin's birth. Commemoration of that kind was a great feature of the musical life of Russia. But alas, in 1907, the fiftieth anniversary of Balakiref's own début as pianist and composer was to pass unmarked —not even one of his former pupils thought of organizing (as was done, as a matter of course, for all musicians of any standing) some kind of concert or ceremony befitting the occasion.

His plans for a Rhapsody on Greek folk-tunes

III

At the beginning of 1906, the correspondence between Balakiref and myself, so far restricted to musical topics, took a far more personal and intimate character. He had asked me for particulars about myself, and was delighted to hear that I was of Greek origin, and belonged to the Orthodox persuasion.

"This", he wrote, "creates so strong a bond between us two that our relations must become even more cordial than they have been so far. You are one of *us*, and I impatiently await the moment when you will know Russian well enough to enable me to write to you in that language instead of resorting to the help of friends in order to send you letters written in French."

I asked him to start writing in Russian forthwith. But, although his handwriting was beautifully clear, for a long time I had to ask my Russian friends to help me read it.

As, in reply to a question of his, I had praised the beauty of Greek folk-tunes, he wrote to me: "If, as you say, there are no Greek composers to find worthy inspiration in those beautiful folk-songs, it is for us Russians to render honour to them. Could you give me the titles of the best collections, or have them sent to me, including, of course, the fine one by Bourgault-Ducoudray, which I once had but have lost? Already Glazunof has written two overtures on tunes from that collection. I am so old that I can hardly hope to compose a work of a kind that calls for a very special disposition of mind; but Liapunof, who is younger, might certainly do it."

I was thrilled by the notion that perhaps he would write such a work after all. I arranged for him to receive the collections by Bourgault-Ducoudray and Pachticos, and also Pernot's *Songs of Chio*. I especially hoped that the lovely tunes in the last-named would attract and tempt him. And indeed, for a while, he entertained the idea of

BALAKIREF, WITH A FEW BARS
FROM HIS "TAMARA"

Balakiref's tone-poem "In Bohemia"

writing a Rhapsody on Greek tunes. In March, 1906, he wrote to me:

"I cannot start composing it at once, because I am hard at work on my piano concerto. But while doing this, I shall prepare materials for it, if only my health permits my so doing."

IV

In 1907 his tone-poem *In Bohemia* was performed at the Paris Concerts Lamoureux, Paul Vidal conducting. Bourgault-Ducoudray had helped me to arrange for this performance. Again Balakiref was particularly pleased, because it was his love for the Czech nation that had moved him to compose this work. In March, 1906, he had written to me:

"With all my heart I long for the French to learn to love the tunes of the Czech people, and so develop, perhaps, an increased interest in that lovable little nation which is so energetically resisting the attempts of the Germans to absorb it. When in my youth I was studying history, I used to think that no event was more appalling than the taking of Constantinople by the Turks. And yet, Mahomet II eventually allowed the Greeks to practise their religion. But when the Germans took Prague, the Jesuits were with them and caused all the ritual books to be burnt in public, and soldiers were sent to persecute the people until they promised to embrace the Roman faith."

Other letters of his covered a wide range of topics, referring not only to his own music, but to his likes and dislikes. They gave many inklings of that complex, uncompromising, umbrageous nature of his which even those who knew him best found so difficult to fathom and describe. They contained, now and then brief, bitter allusions to the Russian composers who were no longer his friends, but, in the main, showed that he was not interested in what Russia thought of his music. The Russian critics

Balakiref's views on modern French music
especially he had given up as hopeless; but he was eager to know what was being thought of his works abroad.

V

When writing my book on Mussorgsky, I asked him to help me with information, and he did so readily; but the information was not very useful. In fact, he shared the current Russian opinion that Mussorgsky had taken unforgivable liberties with the grammar of music; and he did not remember much about Mussorgsky's early unpublished works, on which I was eager to secure particulars. But it was mainly his reservations as to the quality of Mussorgsky's music that I found disappointing.

Another surprise of the same kind was in store for me. He had expressed curiosity as to the new French music which he had seen mentioned in articles of mine. I sent him a few of the works I thought most likely to interest him. Alas! Not one of them found grace in his eyes. Ravel's music, he declared, showed genuine talent, but he found "the harmonic cynicism of it unbearable". Nothing else of what I had sent was worth the paper it was printed on. He wound up his denunciation of the whole contents of the parcel with the words: "I advise you, in all friendliness, to cease boosting this stuff."

On a modern symphony which I had indirectly helped to bring to his notice he wrote: "I think the composer must have been unfortunate in his choice of a teacher. Advise him to study Beethoven's symphonies, Schumann's, Schubert's in C major, and Berlioz's *Symphonie Fantastique* and *Harold en Italie*. Then he may acquire what he lacks." All this, of course, was Balakiref all over. But what a disappointment to find him, who had opened to music wide horizons, so hostile to new developments!

In the spring of 1909 I received from him a letter saying: "My health is failing fast, but my doctor says that if we have a warm summer, I may live until the autumn.

Celebrating Chopin's centenary

Since you are planning to come to Russia, do it soon, or I shall not be there to see you." He was, however, to live another twelve months, and to take part in the celebration of the centenary of his beloved Chopin.

This was, at the time, his chief preoccupation. In September, 1909, he wrote to me: "It is very kind of you to take steps towards having my second symphony performed in Paris: but just now, it would be better to leave this scheme aside and turn your attention to another. 22 February, 1910, will be the centenary of the birth of Frédéric Chopin. As France was Chopin's adopted country, Paris ought to celebrate this anniversary with due solemnity, beginning with a short service on his tomb at the Père Lachaise, and ending with a grand concert of his works and of works composed in honour of the occasion."

Balakiref (who, needless to say, greatly overrated my influence in matters Parisian) had arranged into an orchestral suite, in view of the centenary, four pieces by Chopin, and Liapunof had composed a short tone-poem, based on Polish folk-tunes and on the theme of Chopin's *Berceuse*. These two works were performed both at Petrograd and at Warsaw. I do not exactly remember what kind of official celebrations took place in Paris. Viñes gave a piano recital of Chopin's works, and I contributed an introductory lecture; we were invited to repeat this programme at a *Soirée Chopin* organized by a French daily paper in cooperation with a Society of Alsaciens-Lorrains. That was all, but it enabled me to inform Balakiref that I had done my poor best.

On 20 April, 1910, he wrote to say how glad he was to hear that his first Symphony had been played in Paris, at the Philharmonic concerts—Ravel and I had arranged for that. He also eagerly asked whether it would be possible to arrange for a performance of Liapunof's symphony, and as I had told him that his own Second Symphony was to be played at the Concerts Lamoureux, he

Celebrating Chopin's centenary
suggested that the performance be deferred until the autumn rather than take place at the end of the season. And it was deferred until the following November. But Balakiref died on May 29th—that letter was the last one I received from him. Liapunof sent me a penholder he had used, and a photograph of him on his deathbed.

CHAPTER XIX

Diaghilef in 1907 and after—His ideas—His advisers and helpers—Their wonderful team-work—His catholicity and mutability of outlook—My opinion of his production of a Tamara ballet.

I

The description of Diaghilef which I am about to give differs in an appreciable measure from those which other people have given. The reason is that I worked with him not during the early period of his activities in Russia, nor after the first years of his career abroad, but only from 1907 to 1910 inclusive—that is, during the first four years of this career, the years that saw the actual launching of Russian opera and the Russian Ballet (which should be called, more rightly, the Diaghilef Ballet) outside Russia.

At that time, enterprise was comparatively easy for him. He was able to borrow, for his short seasons abroad, all the artists and experts he required from the companies and staff of the Russian Imperial Theatres—a very different thing from having to maintain, as was the case later, a company of his own permanently. He was in great favour with the Grand Duke Vladimir, and, when organizing an exhibition or season, had only to ask for the subsidy he needed.

The Grand Duke died in 1909, and his widow was, I think, hostile to Diaghilef, so that he could no longer hope for help from that quarter. The 1909 season, although a great artistic success, had been disastrous from the financial point of view. For a time, indeed, I feared that

Diaghilef's advisers and helpers

Diaghilef might go under. I did not know him well enough to realize that he was the kind of man who never goes under—his resourcefulness was infinite, and his powers of persuasion (backed, as they were, by a record of splendid artistic achievement) were and remained adequate to the task of always finding support in time of need.

From the time when, besides having acquired experience (and a great variety of it) of both the Western world and the business of producing works and running a company, he had to fight for survival, he may have changed a great deal. I can only speak of him as I knew him.

From the first, I found him to be a man endowed with a good deal of taste, but a taste so catholic and mutable as to be most disconcerting until one remembered that he was the type *par excellence* of the cosmopolitan Russian—very cosmopolitan and very, very Russian. But he was endowed with both the will to do things and an extraordinary capacity for doing them. He had an almost uncanny genius for finding the right people to help him, for bringing their ideas out and carrying them to materialization.

II

Looking back after all these years, I still doubt whether, left to himself, he would ever have determined upon and followed a steady and original artistic policy. When he started his campaign in Paris, he was assisted by a really wonderful general staff. As regards music, he had in Walter Nouvel and Alfred Nourok (whom I mentioned in my chapter on Ravel) two invaluable advisers. They remained very much in the background, but were really most useful and active collaborators. Once, in 1907, I asked them if there was, among the younger Russian composers unknown outside their own country, someone who really mattered. The reply was: "Yes, one or two;

Diaghilef's advisers and helpers

especially one, whom we are keeping back for the present *de peur qu'on ne nous le gâte.*" Three years later, I found out that the composer in question was Stravinsky.

Then, in the matter of stage settings and costumes, there were Bakst and Benois—to say nothing of other fine painters, who however were not, like those two, always with us and always at work. Benois's erudition, in matters of art, was as extensive as his taste was refined, subtle, and imaginative. There is no trace in his work of the remorseless deliberation which now and then characterized that of Bakst. One could not help feeling, at times, that Bakst sacrificed almost everything to effect, and that there was more "back thought" in the methods of Benois.

Diaghilef's stage producer, for opera, was Sanin, also a genius at his job. I have never seen—and I hardly hope to see again—anything comparable to the Revolution scene in *Boris Godunof* as produced by him in 1908. It is true that he had, in the splendidly trained and ever-willing Moscow choristers, matchless material to work on. And if I select this one instance of his achievements for special mention, it is because it stands out in my mind among many others equally fine.

For the ballet, there was Fokin, teeming with ideas, and brimful with energy. The way in which, like Sanin, but with the additional difficulties of ballet conditions, he could handle masses and make them not merely "hold the stage", but actually live their parts, rendered him incomparable and irreplaceable.

III

Diaghilef's genius consisted for a great part in his ability not only to enlist such a wonderful staff, but to bring about their eager cooperation and to get out of them, continuously and invariably, the best they were capable of giving.

His catholicity and mutability of outlook

It is impossible adequately to describe the closeness and efficiency of the cooperation which Diaghilef received from these men, and from others too, among whom was Charles Waltz, the stage engineer-in-chief of the Imperial Theatres, then a veteran with nearly fifty years' service, surprisingly youthful, and a splendid fellow all round. Only by attending rehearsals, and the numerous councils of war that took place in between these, could one have formed a true idea of it. And as soon as one considers results, and remembers that Diaghilef alone brought this superb organization into being, it will become clear, I trust, that by attempting to describe him exactly as I saw him I am not in the least trying to belittle him.

As soon as I began to work with him, I had ample proof of his extreme catholicity of outlook, and of the speed with which he could assimilate and expand new ideas.

When we two were discussing the plan of the 1908 Opera season in Paris, he thought of producing, besides *Boris Godunof*, at least one opera by Tchaikowsky, and he wished, in due time, to produce several. I was aware that there existed in Paris very little taste for Tchaikowsky's music; and, in musical circles, a definite distaste. I foresaw, accordingly, that this was not the way to score a big success and arouse a keen, lasting interest in the *Russian Seasons*. Had I been as enthusiastic an admirer of Tchaikowsky as I was of Mussorgsky, Borodin, and Rimsky-Korsakof, I might have agreed and said: "All right, let us work for a victory in the teeth of opposition!" As it was, I had, rightly or wrongly, a poor opinion of Tchaikowsky's operas; so that without the slightest compunction I strove to dissuade him. I was met, at first, with arguments such as: "Ah! but you don't know, Calvo, how delightful a thing *Eugen Oneghin* is with Sobinof (a famous Russian tenor) in the title part. A dream! Nobody could resist it!" He did not seem to realize in the least that *Boris Godunof* stood in a class by itself in Russian opera, and

His catholicity and mutability of outlook
indeed, as people are now beginning to realize, in the world's repertory. I honestly believe that, if he was planning to produce it, the main reason was the recent success it had scored in Russia when Chaliapin first appeared in it. Even at that comparatively recent period, very few people in Russia seemed to recognize the significance of *Boris Godunof*. I remember discussing the matter with Nouvel and Nourok, and being amazed at their lukewarmness. If I remember right, they even told me, to my further amazement, that they preferred Mussorgsky's other opera, *Khovanshchina*—a preference which may be a mere matter of taste, but which is nowadays, and was already at that time, rather unusual.

IV

Diaghilef was thinking, also, of giving Rimsky-Korsakof's *Sadko*; and there, of course, I heartily concurred in principle. But, considering that this first "Opera Season" was to be a very short one, I did my utmost to persuade him to stake his all on *Boris Godunof*. And at last—with Ravel's help, as recorded in a previous chapter—I succeeded.

Let it be said, incidentally, that events proved my advice to have been good: we found that we could have filled, with *Boris Godunof*, twice as many houses, had a longer run been possible. In 1911, a "Russian Opera Season" was organized by another Russian impresario, whose train of reasoning must have been: "If the Paris public give so fervid a welcome to *Boris Godunof*, what will they not do when they hear, performed by our best singers, the operas which we Russians really love?" Accordingly, he gave pride of place to operas by Tchaikowsky; and, as it happened, his season was cut short by financial disaster. I understand, too, that when Diaghilef, reverting, after the war, to his old faith in Tchaikowsky, produced the ballet *The Sleeping Beauty*, he received very

My opinion of his production of a "Tamara" ballet
little support from either the Paris or the London public.

Later I had a striking instance of his mutability. He and I once talked of Balakiref's *Tamara*, and he said: "My dear Calvo, this enthusiasm of yours is really excessive. How can you think that *Tamara* is something unique and wonderful? It is just one average good example of Russian music, but nothing to rave about: there are many finer things in the Russian repertory." I jumped up, and gave him a piece of my mind on the Russians who were incapable of assessing their musical treasures at their true value. This did not seem to impress him much; but the following year, one fine day, he produced a piano arrangement of *Tamara*, began to play bits of it, and said: "How lovely it all is! None of you non-Russians will ever know all that this music means to *us*."

V

How far our talks on *Tamara* may have contributed to his notion of using it for a ballet, as he did Rimsky-Korsakof's *Shéhérazade*, I cannot tell. If they did at all, I deeply regret it. This ballet was, in my opinion, an unpardonable error. The significance of the music of *Tamara* resides in its character of spaciousness, remoteness, and mystery, in its sombre grandeur and deep undercurrents of passion into which bitterness and disenchantment gradually creep. I do not know whether it would have been possible to convey something at least of all this on the stage. Probably the remoteness and mystery could have been partly suggested by appropriate light and colour schemes. But in the Diaghilef production, nothing of the kind was achieved or even attempted. The matter-of-fact, and at times very gaudy, display not only ignored, but actually counteracted the suggestions of the music.

I remember telling Fokin how strongly I objected to what he and Bakst had done to *Tamara*. His reply was: "I see why you don't like it: it's because for the purposes

My opinion of his production of a "Tamara" ballet of dancing, much of the music has to be taken in too quick a tempo." I explained to him that there were other reasons as well, but that this one fact should have warned him that he had not succeeded in devising the requisite kind of dancing. I did not have the opportunity to discuss the matter with Bakst: when *Tamara* was produced, I had long ceased to work with Diaghilef; and, so far as I can remember, I did not see Bakst again until after the war.

Nothing of what I have written is intended to convey that Diaghilef, however mutable and interested in new ideas he may have been by nature, was at all easy to sway. In order to take effect on him, the right suggestion had to come at the right moment and from the right people; and he had a wonderful flair for knowing whether such was the case or not. For instance, the only time I talked music with him after I had broken with him in 1910 was after the war, when I suggested to him that he should produce Bartók's ballet *The Wooden Prince*, of which I gave him a score. This may have been the right suggestion, artistically speaking. It may have come at the right moment (it was shortly before he produced Tchaikowsky's *Sleeping Beauty* and Stravinsky's *Mavra*). But certainly, from his point of view, it did not come from the right person. It did not correspond to any marked trend of opinion among the musical public at large, but expressed the feeling of a very small minority, and would probably have found no echo among the people who were advising him at the time. The reason he gave me a few days later, for his refusal, was certainly remarkable—and I suspect, inspired: "Non, Calvo, ça ne me va pas: faux modernisme!"

CHAPTER XX

The Russian concerts of 1907—Russian composers in Paris —Rimsky-Korsakof on Boris Godunof, *on French music, and on his own opera* Sadko—*Felix Blumenfeld—Glazunof —A French critic's blunder—A glimpse of Scriabin—I become Diaghilef's second-in-command—He decides to produce* Boris Godunof—*Impossibility of producing it in its genuine form.*

I

Such was the man with whom I started, in 1907, a campaign of work which fascinated me greatly— partly because its object was the diffusion of the Russian music I loved so well, and partly because it was as exciting as it was different from my usual work at the writing-desk.

It all began simply enough. When he was preparing the Russian Concerts which he gave in 1907 at the Paris Opéra, he asked me to help him by providing a few French translations of excerpts to be performed, and by preparing, jointly with Nouvel, programme notices founded on materials supplied by the Russian critic Alexander Ossowsky. He also invited me to attend rehearsals; so that I was not long in becoming acquainted with the Russian composers and artists who had come to take part in the concerts. I was particularly delighted to meet Rimsky-Korsakof—with whom I had corresponded, a year or two before, on the subject of my French translations of Mussorgsky's songs, published under his editorship—and Glazunof.

Rimsky-Korsakof on "Boris Godunof"

Rimsky-Korsakof I found most genial, simple and lovable. He had come with his wife, his two sons, Andrei and Vladimir, and his daughter, and they all seemed heartily to enjoy their stay in Paris. They were very kind to me, and made much of my humble activities on behalf of Russian music.

Rimsky-Korsakof and I had several talks on musical subjects. I must confess that once I had the audacity to pit my views on Mussorgsky's music against his, and to express my preference for the unrevised *Boris Godunof*. He was not offended in the least. He merely smiled, shook his head, and said: "You young people in France go picking out in Mussorgsky's music just the specks of dirt; and then you put them all on an altar and worship them." He was alluding, I think, not only to the fact that a few people in France had already started a campaign in favour of the genuine *Boris*, but also to certain particularities of idiom and methods in the music of Debussy and Ravel, which certainly seem to be due to Mussorgsky's influence. He asked me many questions about French music, but I do not remember his ever expressing an opinion on any example of it in my presence. Other people have recorded that he went to hear Debussy's *Pelléas et Mélisande* at the Opéra-Comique, and said: "I will have nothing further to do with this music, lest by misfortune I should develop a liking for it." A couple of years before, in a letter to a friend (quoted in the Preface to the third [Russian] edition of his *Memoirs of my Musical Life*), he had named Debussy's music as an example of the "unintelligible developments" which were taking place in music, and he had tarred the music of d'Indy and Strauss with the same brush.

II

French composers, and especially the younger ones, liked his music far better than he liked theirs. The

Rimsky-Korsakof on his own opera "Sadko"

majority of his orchestral compositions were, by then, fairly well known in Paris—*Antar* and *Shéhérazade* enjoying special favour. Not so, however, his operas, of which no single one had been performed outside Russia. Excerpts of three of these conducted by him—the fantastic scenes in *Mlada*, the underseas act in *Sadko*, and the orchestral suite from *Tsar Saltan*—were among the main novelties on Diaghilef's programmes; and, together with the second act of *Boris Godunof*, they took Paris by storm. The last-named especially stands vivid in my memory. Not that it is finer than the others in any way: but the *Mlada* and *Sadko* scenes are forcible and high-coloured enough to come off comparatively easily; whereas I have never heard another performance equal in brilliancy and point of the more subtle, more restrained, and more formalized music of *Tsar Saltan*. The orchestra, stimulated by his presence at the desk, did wonders.

Rimsky-Korsakof was particularly pleased with what he had achieved in *Sadko*. There, he used to explain, he had really gone in for working-out; and he had found it a most fascinating task to develop the themes used by him, long before, in his tone-poem of the same title, first composed in 1867 and remodelled later. He asked me if I knew the reasons why there seemed to be difficulties in the way of *Sadko* being done at the Paris Opéra. I could give no definite reply, but suggested that perhaps it was because of the great length of the work. He then said: "Yes, it is long, I know: but if it is found too long for one evening, why not give it in two halves—the first one evening, and the second the next!" I could but stare in blank amazement; but he meant every word of it. He, who in his 1896 edition of *Boris Godunof* had sanctioned the appalling cuts by which producers were wont to disfigure Mussorgsky's masterpiece, could not admit that a single bar of his own music should ever be cut. There are declarations to that effect in the prefaces to several of his

Felix Blumenfeld

operas. I cannot remember whether, eventually, I did explain to him that no theatre in France was likely to consider the notion of devoting two evenings to the performance of one opera on the instalment plan.

When the Rimsky-Korsakof family left Paris, Diaghilef and I saw them off—I little dreaming that I should never meet Rimsky-Korsakof again. The news of his death came towards the end of the following Russian season. It was I who, having read it in the morning paper, broke it to Diaghilef. We had not even heard of his last illness. That day we bitterly regretted not having included his *Sadko* in the season's doings.

III

Another Russian who evinced curiosity as to new developments in French music was Felix Blumenfeld, the conductor and composer. Soon after his arrival, he and I had become great friends. One day he asked me: "Well, what about all this French stuff you speak so highly of?" I suggested that he should come to my house and see for himself. He came, and I placed in front of him a number of things by Ravel, d'Indy, Debussy, Fauré, Sévérac, Schmitt, Ladmirault, and others. He sat at the piano and began playing. He was a splendid reader: I remember, in particular, being amazed at his renderings, at sight, of Debussy's *Reflets dans l'Eau* and Ravel's *Alborada*. After each piece—and often while playing—he gave vent to sundry grunts and other expressions of disapproval. At length—but not before having exhausted the pile—he took his leave, declaring that he did not think much of my taste in French music. But when he came back to Paris to conduct *Boris Godunof*, he seized the very first opportunity to ask me, almost sheepishly, whether he might come and have another look at all the nasty stuff I had shown him the year before.

Glazunof—A glimpse of Scriabin

For Glazunof, burly, quiet, sometimes taciturn but always affable, I developed a great liking. No opportunity arose of talking music with him. I was most disappointed when the announcement came that his Second Symphony (in my mind, one of his finest) was to be replaced on the programmes by a later and less important Orchestral Suite of his. Had I known that no opportunity of hearing it (nor, I may add, the third and fourth, which I also consider very fine) would ever be given to me, my disappointment would have been even greater.

This change of programme, by the way, did not prevent one French musical periodical from expatiating, in the notice it gave of Diaghilef's concerts, not only on the merits and demerits—and chiefly the demerits—of the symphony in question, but on the effect it had produced upon the audience. If Glazunof saw the notice, he must have been vastly amused.

I feel sure that if I had been able to see more of him at the time, I should have heard from him many things worth hearing. I did when I saw him in Russia five years later, and again after the war in Paris. As things are, I have nothing more to record with regard to our meetings in 1907 but the following little story.

Jules Ecorcheville, then the president of the French section of the International Music Society, gave a dinner in honour of the Russian composers. At that dinner I sat between Glazunof and Scriabin. The talk veered round to Scriabin's Second Symphony, which had been played the day before. Scriabin said to me, casually, "It is a very mediocre work." As this represented my own opinion, I felt very much embarrassed and contented myself with some kind of non-committal mumble. A moment later, Glazunof whispered into my ear, with perfect gravity: "You have offended him: he expected to be contradicted."

RIMSKY-KORSAKOF, WITH A QUOTATION FROM HIS OPERA "TSAR SALTAN"

I become Diaghilef's second-in-command

IV

One of the most interesting features of the concerts was a performance of nearly the whole first act of Glinka's *Russlan and Liudmila*; though, for some reason or other, this lovely music appealed but slightly to the audience. In point of fact, French lovers of Russian music incline, as a rule, to pay little attention to Glinka. Even specialists seem to think of him as a name and influence, but hardly more. I must add that it was conducted by Nikisch, who, in my opinion did not in the least do justice to it.

I have, apart from the delight which I experienced while listening, a special reason for remembering that performance. In a notice written for *La Grande Revue*, I devoted a few lines to the wonderful originality of Glinka's music, pointing out that in 1842 (the year in which *Russlan and Liudmila* was first performed) Wagner had only just finished the *Flying Dutchman*, and Meyerbeer was engaged in composing *Le Prophète*. A line of type fell out during the process of printing, and when my article appeared, I was horrified to read in it: "En 1842, Wagner était en train de composer *Le Prophète*."

When the concerts were over, Diaghilef asked me what he owed me for my work (which I had been called upon to extend far beyond the limits originally foreseen). I named a sum, and he handed it to me. When I thanked him, he asked: "You are satisfied?" I assented. "Quite satisfied?" I assented again. "Well, you are the only one. Oh! How sick I am of it all!" Then, suddenly: "Now look here: I want to do an opera festival next year. But this time, things will have to be on very different lines. Will you be my second-in-command?" I accepted, and then and there we started discussing plans, as recorded in the foregoing chapter.

After we had decided to do *Boris Godunof* only, I remarked: "Of course, you will do the genuine *Boris* and

Impossibility of producing "Boris" in genuine form
not the Rimsky-Korsakof arrangement?" He replied that this was out of the question. The soloists and the choir all knew their parts in the remodelled version, and would be not only unwilling, but positively unable to learn the genuine text even if time could be found for study. I realized only too well that, alas, he was right. To this day, indeed, I feel sure that a singer who has studied the one version would find it well-nigh impossible to be at home in the other. The pitfalls are too many: Rimsky-Korsakof tampered with keys and time-signatures and harmonies and modulations, and even, though more seldom, with melodies. Diaghilef's argument was unanswerable.

V

In my heart of hearts, I believed that the production of the Rimsky-Korsakof arrangement would pave the way for an early production of the genuine *Boris* (as then known; that is, in the 1874 edition of the vocal score—I was unaware at that time that even this did not represent the whole of *Boris* as written by Mussorgsky). Diaghilef did not tell me that no full score and parts of the genuine *Boris* were available even in Russia. Probably he neither knew nor cared. Perhaps, like all Russians at the time, he preferred Rimsky-Korsakof's revision to the original. I learnt, later, that it was he who asked Rimsky-Korsakof to lengthen the Coronation scene in view of the Paris production, so as to provide more opportunity for display on the stage. In that scene Mussorgsky, as people began to realize when the 1928 edition appeared, is more concerned with suggesting the sullen character of the officially enforced rejoicings, and the atmosphere of strain, depression and gloom which spreads over the whole ceremony, than with mere pageantry.

Nor did Diaghilef tell me that there was no prospect of the genuine score ever being put on the market, and that the only manuscript of it in existence lay buried in the

Impossibility of producing "Boris" in genuine form

archives of the Imperial Theatres. So that there was nothing to warn me that every step taken to propagate the revised version of *Boris* would have the twofold and contradictory effect of increasing public interest in Mussorgsky and creating fresh obstacles in the way of a return to the genuine form of his masterpiece; that obviously most people would be encouraged to think: "Since the revised version is doing well, why bother about the other and inaccessible one?"

Had I known this, it would probably have made little difference. I suppose that I should have helped Diaghilef as wholeheartedly, on the principle that half a loaf is better than no bread. Since then, many people have said that but for the performances of Rimsky-Korsakof's version, the awakening of the general public's interest in *Boris Godunof* might have taken place far later, and perhaps this is true. To wonder what might have happened if in 1908 the genuine *Boris*, and not the revised, had been revealed in Paris would be idle speculation.

As things turned out, however, by harping on the subject of the genuine *Boris*, I had done the best I could towards the end I had in view, and far more than I hoped for. To my surprise and delight Diaghilef, on one of his visits to Paris during the winter, brought with him a number of copies of the 1874 edition and instructed me to distribute them to French critics as I thought fit. The result was that when noticing *Boris Godunof* as performed at the Paris Opéra, a number of critics inveighed severely —and in some cases violently—against Rimsky-Korsakof and clamoured loudly for the genuine text. I was sorry that indignation should have led a few of them to speak of Rimsky-Korsakof in most insulting terms, completely overlooking the fact that the revision had been carried out in accordance not merely with his own views, but with what the whole of musical Russia felt on the matter. Apart from that, of course, I was pleased. It was only a

Impossibility of producing "Boris" in genuine form
moral victory; but at least a current of opinion had been created, far stronger and more definite than had existed previously. In time, it was to grow stronger; and, small as it was, it may have exercised a measure of influence even on far-away, obstinate Russia, who was so heartily ashamed of Mussorgsky's "ungrammatical idiom and haphazard methods".

CHAPTER XXI

Boris Godunof *at the Paris Opéra—Ruthless excisions— A stuffed parrot as compensation for a suppressed episode—I prevent the cutting out of the Revolution scene—Rehearsing under difficulties—A Press rehearsal of an unusual kind— Impromptu scene-shifters—An angry editor—Triumph rewards our efforts.*

I

Russian incomprehension had led to *Boris Godunof* being reduced, in performance, to a curious selection of "elegant extracts" arranged in a variable, but invariably wrong, order—as shown by Rimsky-Korsakof's edition of 1896 (now withdrawn from the market) and by the analysis which Mrs. Rosa Newmarch gives in her book, *Russian Opera*, of 1913. It should be added, in all fairness, that many of the cuts had been made before the first Russian performance (1874) for fear of incurring the State censorship's wrath, and also of displeasing the opera-goers of the time.

It was, likewise, almost in the form of "elegant extracts" that Diaghilef had planned to give the work in Paris. I endeavoured to save as much as I could from his pruning-knife, and succeeded in persuading him not to leave out all the portions usually omitted. One of the passages thus rescued was, in the second act, the Tsarewitch Feodor repeating his geography lesson. When the first rehearsal took place, Blumenfeld stared at the restored pages of the score, turned round, and grumbled: "You leave this in? Ah! It's obvious enough that Mister Calvocoressi is in this show."

A stuffed parrot as compensation

I was not so fortunate in other points. No insistence of mine could dissuade Diaghilef from cutting out, in the same Act, the lovely humorous episode of the escaped parrot. In order to mitigate my disappointment, he (or perhaps it was Bakst or Benois) informed me that to atone for the suppression the stage properties would include a stuffed parrot in a cage. If this had been a mere piece of leg-pulling, it would have been funny enough. But what is even funnier is that the properties did comprise one—a multicoloured parakeet from Australia, which nobody could see from the auditorium because the cage was of gilt wood in fretwork patterns, and placed in a dark corner of the stage.

II

On one point I had to fight a battle royal. It was in the winter, at one of the preliminary meetings of the acting committee. The attendance consisted of Messager and Broussan (the managers of the Paris Opéra), Diaghilef, myself, and one or two others. The agenda was, how much (or rather, how little) of *Boris Godunof* should be performed. Diaghilef declared that in order to avoid making the performance too long for the audience, it was imperative to cut out the scene at the inn and the Revolution scene—both of which are of vital importance. I raised my voice in loud protest. If anything must go, I said, let it be the Polish act, which has nothing to do with the main issue of the drama. They all jumped up, and in turn protested: "That would be madness! What about the prima donna, and the first tenor, and the dances, and the love-duets?"

Here was history repeating itself with a vengeance. When first submitted to the committee of the Imperial Theatres, *Boris* had been rejected, one of the reasons given being that it did not give the customary prominence to tenor and prima donna, and contained no dances (and,

I prevent the cutting of the Revolution scene

indeed, Marina did not appear at all, and Dimitri appeared in the first act only). Mussorgsky added the Polish act in order to meet the objection. I was not intent upon persuading them to do away with this act or even parts of it, but I felt sure that if *Boris* had to be curtailed for fear that audiences could not endure the whole of it, the Polish act was the only one which could be abridged or suppressed without serious detriment to the drama as a whole. And there was our committee, forty years after the committee of the Russian theatres, taking the same short-sighted view and devoting more attention to accessories than to essentials.

After a while, I succeeded in persuading them to go deeper into the matter. By careful timing it was found that there would be no need to suppress both the scenes. The question that remained was, which of the two should go. They all said that it should be the Revolution scene. Again, their view was founded on purely conventional considerations. They pointed out that the revolution scene was almost entirely choral, and for this reason alone would bewilder and bore the public, whereas the scene at the inn was excellent comedy, rich in incidents and contrasts, and contributed directly to the progress of the plot. I assured them that I was not blind to the merits of this scene, and that I agreed it would be a shame to cut it. "But", I continued, "since you will not rest content unless you cut out one scene of vital importance, better cut this than the revolution scene, the very climax of *Boris Godunof*." They remained obdurate, so I burnt my boats and started shouting (deliberately overdoing the whole thing, in the best Russian style, so as to produce the desired effect): "You must not suppress the Revolution scene! You must not! If you dare suppress it, I shall resign and explain why in letters to the whole Press!" I repeated this again and again. At length, out of sheer weariness, they yielded, but with bad grace. One French member of

Rehearsing under difficulties

the committee said to me: "All right, Calvocoressi, but it will wreck *Boris*. On your head be the responsibility!" "I gladly accept it," I retorted. When, at the first performance, the curtain fell at the end of the Revolution scene, the whole auditorium burst into frantic cheers, and the choristers had to take eight calls—an event unexampled in the annals of opera in France and, I believe, in most other countries. Not even Chaliapin, the peerless Tsar Boris, not even the poignant death scene, created a deeper impression. I rushed behind the scenes, impatient to enjoy my little triumph at the expense of my colleagues of the acting committee. But the first one I encountered was precisely he who had predicted that my pigheadedness would lead to disaster. He was waving his arms about in glee and yelled to me: "What a triumph! Didn't I tell you so?"

III

Boris Godunof was prepared with incredible difficulties, and under adverse circumstances. To begin with, the only time that the managers of the Opéra had granted us for rehearsals was the amount left free by the ordinary duties of the Opéra—which comprised four performances a week and rehearsals on certain other nights. And we also had to take into account the usual trade-union restrictions and the fact that, under the terms of their agreement, the orchestral players were not bound to rehearse in the daytime. By a deplorable coincidence, the month selected for our performances of *Boris Godunof* was also selected for the production of Rameau's *Hippolyte et Aricie*. In consequence, the "ordinary duties" of the Opéra took up far more time than was usual, and the stage-carpenters and hands were very much overworked. Diaghilef and his technical staff came to Paris rather late—nearly at the end of April. The date fixed for the first performance was May 19th. The choir was even later, having temporarily

Rehearsing under difficulties

lost, between Moscow and the Russian frontier, the guide in charge of the party and the tickets—an accident which gave rise to many frantic telegrams from and to Moscow, and from bewildered stationmasters along the line.

Apart from the paucity of time available for rehearsals, there was the tiredness of the stage-hands to consider. The Opéra stage is a huge one, with no single labour-saving appliance. Everything had to be done by hand and by sheer force of muscle. To raise or lower the back-cloth you did not press a button and let electricity do the rest: you sent fifteen men or so up to the flies (to which they climbed by means of rope-ladders) and they manipulated the cloth almost as sailors would a sail. The job took nearly a quarter of an hour every time. So that, between the rigging up of the settings for *Hippolyte et Aricie* and the manœuvring of the settings of the operas played in the ordinary course of business, the men were working full time, and overtime, seven days a week. We waited and waited in vain for them to tackle the settings of *Boris Godunof*. The tension grew, and rumours of an impending strike arose. Diaghilef, for some reason or other, feared that a deliberate attempt might be made to incite the men to strike in order to wreck our plans—and to change the dates fixed for the performances was out of the question.

There was against us, here and there, a certain amount of hostility, probably due in part to our having freely broadcast the announcement that Diaghilef was about to achieve wonders, and that the forthcoming production was going to be an object lesson and to deal the death blow to many obsolete conventions. Of this hostility we were conscious—even exaggeratedly conscious. Being over-wrought, we became suspicious and inclined to see foes and plots everywhere. For instance, when we started preparing the setting for the Revolution scene—a clearing in a snow-clad forest, the trees being represented by painted canvas whose cut-out patterns had to be supported by netting—it turned out that the only netting available was black. "Impossible!" Diaghilef declared. "This will rob our setting of half the whiteness on which the effectiveness depends." But the Opéra could not, or would not, supply white netting. So, after hastily consulting a trades directory, I jumped into a taxi and eventually obtained from a net factory the requisite amount of white netting. For this feat I was heartily patted on the back and given to understand that I had helped to frustrate another deliberate plot against the Russian season. Later on, however, the stage carpenter-in-chief of the Opéra assured me that black netting would not have affected the whiteness in the least.

IV

The stage walkers available at the Opéra were a very independent corporation. A few years before, when Saint-Saëns's opera *Les Barbares* was produced, they had made history by refusing, one and all, to shave their beards or moustaches, so that the producer had had to resign himself to showing on the stage bearded Roman senators and soldiers. To us they gave no trouble, except that they proved most reluctant to forgo the innocent privilege of chatting with their favourite friends while on the stage, and therefore persisted in trying to form groups regardless of the line and colour schemes carefully calculated by Sanin, Bakst, and Benois. Every night, before the Coronation scene, we had to marshal them and sternly warn them to keep their appointed places. The women, moreover, evinced a deplorable tendency to allow kiss curls to peep under their headgear—a thoroughly un-Russian practice which had to be crushed afresh every night.

Among them were six girls (aged about fourteen) borrowed from the Opéra dancing-class for the special purpose of wearing certain crimson costumes with green

Rehearsing under difficulties

shawls. Somebody or other had had the bright idea of teaching one of them to utter, parrot-wise, a few chosen words of Russian. Proud of the knowledge, she grasped, during a pause at rehearsal, the opportunity to show it off. She went from one Russian to another and spoke. Some of them smiled, others scowled. Then, all of a sudden, Sanin's voice rose in anger, calling to the French stage manager: "Monsieur Domengie! Monsieur Domengie! Il faut punir cette demoiselle. Elle est très grossière. Savez-vous ce qu'elle m'a demandé? Elle m'a demandé si je voulais faire l'amour avec elle!" The girl was fined five francs. Later, her companions came to me and implored me to get her off. I appealed to Domengie, who, biting his lip, gravely remitted the fine. Even if she had known the exact purport of the words, she would have deserved to be let off: for she had provided, unwittingly, the one moment of comic relief which occurred during those anxious days. We were on tenterhooks all the time.

I remember spending the whole time of the Press rehearsal of *Hippolyte et Aricie* getting hold of one stage carpenter after another, questioning them, and trying to find out how far we could rely on them. I found that they were not ill disposed towards us, but tired out and longing for a rest. The schedule of work for the week allowed no time for the rigging up of our settings. We had arranged to give our Press rehearsal on Sunday, May 17th, and all the invitations had been dispatched. This meant that the men would have to work the whole of Sunday rigging up the settings, and again on the Sunday night manœuvring them. Well, their spokesman declared, they were not going to do it (although I offered them a pound apiece over their usual rate of pay): they hadn't had a day's rest for six weeks, and they were going to take one on the 17th. On Monday, the 18th, all their time would be taken up by their ordinary duties, but on

Rehearsing under difficulties

the 19th, they would start work at 7 a.m., carry on uninterruptedly, and all would be ready for the performance that night at 8 p.m.

I could quite see their reasons, but from our point of view it all seemed preposterous, impossible. I turned to their chief, Pétremand, and his foreman, Loiseau (I shall never forget how loyally these two stood by us, then and after), who did their best to reassure me. "If the men want to do it," they told me, "they can." And with this assurance I had to rest content.

After the performance of *Hippolyte et Aricie*, Diaghilef, Sanin, Nouvel, Waltz, and I went to the Restaurant Larue for a council of war over supper. To this day I can remember how we devoured duck in aspic while we reviewed the situation. Things looked almost desperate. We knew that quite a lot of people were waiting to see the collapse of the handful of foolish amateurs who proclaimed themselves so far superior to everybody else. Well, it seemed that these people were not going to be denied the pleasure of seeing their hopes fulfilled. The Press rehearsal would have to go overboard; and this alone seemed sure to bring disaster in its wake. The seats for the 19th were nearly sold out, so that there would be no possibility of accommodating that night the Press and the hundreds of influential people who had been invited for the 17th—let alone accommodating them so as not to offend their susceptibilities. We felt that to postpone the Press rehearsal to the 19th and alter the dates of the public performances would spell financial disaster by inconveniencing the people who had bought seats, and shaking confidence in us.

V

After a long debate, we decided that on the Sunday a semi-private rehearsal would take place, with the company in costumes, but without settings. All the pressmen and

An angry editor

a few of our friends would be invited. Then, relying on the stage carpenters' promise, we would give our first performance on the Tuesday, and do our best to accommodate, on that or following nights, the other people whom we had asked to attend the Press rehearsal. The result, we felt sure, could never be worse than would ensue from a postponement.

And so, at 3 a.m., we parted company, after having dispatched an announcement to the Press. The next thing was to stop the sale of tickets for the 19th and see what could be done with the few seats and boxes still available. It was very much like trying to pack an outfit for a world tour into a week-end suitcase; but, by dint of hard work, some kind of arrangement was devised.

Remained to persuade the critics and editors and pressmen of all kinds whom it is customary to invite to Paris "répétitions générales" to accept this arrangement. Most of them, understanding our quandary, did so with good grace. Others were very hurt and angry. The editor of one important daily—short, pompous, bald, and very much bewhiskered—expressed his feelings in the following terms: "You say you can't give me a box and you offer me two dress-circle stalls instead? What do you mean by that, sir? The dress-circle is for pretty women. Look at me! Am I a pretty woman? You can keep your stalls. For over thirty years I have had a *baignoire* (ground-floor box) at every Press rehearsal in Paris, and I will have that or nothing. Keep your stalls, sir. But have no fear: My Paper will continue to support the Russian season." Then, majestically: "That is how My Paper understands revenge!"

VI

The rehearsal was an amazing affair. The settings and props were represented by extemporized landmarks: two chairs for a door, another for a pillar, a crate for the Tsar's

Rehearsing under Difficulties

throne, and so on. All these were put into place and moved about by a staff of stage hands consisting of Bakst, Benois, Pétremand, and Loiseau (who had come in protest against the defection of their men), Diaghilef, his secretary, his valet, and myself—all of us in our shirtsleeves, and very grimy. In the auditorium, a hundred spectators or so could enjoy the sight of every one of our movements, for there was nobody to raise or drop the curtain.

In this hideous setting the company rehearsed in splendid costumes. The situation was serious for them all: the settings to come were all new and unknown to them, so that on the Tuesday they would have to move among surroundings of which they had no experience. It was particularly grave for the choristers, who in the Revolution scene have to rush about briskly, so as to create an impression of tumult, amid and around the slender strips of painted canvas representing tree trunks. No arrangement of chairs, or chalk-marks on the floor, could enable them to rehearse those difficult evolutions usefully. But they went through the farce with gusto, and on the first night, O wonder, they rushed and whirled about as if they had been thoroughly used to the setting.

On the fateful Tuesday, the stage carpenters began work early, as promised. But at 1.30 p.m. only two of the seven settings had been dealt with. We began to shudder again. At 6.45 all seven were ready and the lighting regulated. I rushed away, swallowed a few sandwiches and many glasses of mineral water while dressing, and at 7.15 was back to stand by, in case of unforeseen complications, at the opening of the gates, to check the booking-sheets (I had no idea how to do this, but the kind *contrôleur en chef* showed me) and to rush back behind the stage, where a hundred and one things were still waiting to be done.

Another of Diaghilef's anxieties with regard to that fateful night was that the Grand Duke Vladimir and the Grand Duchess having promised to attend the performance, a Nihilist outrage was feared. He told me that he had received from the leaders of the party a letter assuring him that they would not dream of doing anything that might jeopardize the success of this first production abroad of a Russian masterpiece particularly dear to their hearts. Nevertheless, all possible precautions were taken—quite wisely, since it was clear that the party's promise did not exclude the possibility of an isolated attempt. On the day of the performance, all parts of the building accessible to the public were carefully searched; and during the performance a hundred and ten detectives—so I was told—were on duty in the auditorium and corridors.

A few days later, the Moscow Choir gave a concert of its own. The Grand Duke and Grand Duchess attended, but unofficially. I do not know whether special police precautions were taken, but a few of us were asked to stand by close to the box they occupied.

VII

So great was the success of *Boris Godunof* that we considered the possibility of giving a few extra performances. The managers of the Opéra were willing to let us have the theatre, but there were other difficulties in the way—especially the risk created by the coming of the hot weather and the "end of the season". So we left well alone, although those extra performances would probably have made all the difference from the financial point of view.

As it was, the financial result was a deficit slightly smaller than the subsidy (a huge one) which Diaghilef had received from the Imperial purse—a highly satisfactory result, considering the cost of bringing from Russia, for seven performances only, the soloists and choir and technical staff, and all the costumes, props, and settings; and moreover, that to fight our way through the difficulties that had constantly been arising, we had been compelled to spend money like water.

Triumph rewards our efforts

Diaghilef had also been lavish in the matter of costumes. In the Coronation scene, all the women choristers and most of the stage walkers wore silk shawls, some of them ancient and valuable, and genuine old Russian bonnets with seed-pearl trimmings, which would have delighted a collector. The boyars' cloaks were of splendid brocade with collars and cuffs of real fur. As for Chaliapin's robe of gold cloth for that scene, its weight was no less amazing than its splendour.

Far less had been spent on the settings, except in fees to the painters. They consisted mainly of painted canvas, with practically no built-up pieces. This was an innovation which greatly surprised the technical staff of the Opéra and was sharply criticized in certain of the Press notices—some of these suggesting, of all things in the world, that this had been done in order to save money.

Fortunately, painters and other specialists of standing were not tardy in doing justice to Diaghilef's initiative in this matter. They expressed their delight at seeing at last, on the stage, settings that were really paintings and not clumsily realistic reproductions. They praised the effective simplicity, the absence of superfluous details, the beauty of the colour schemes, and the suggestive power of the ensemble in which settings and costumes cooperated. But all this, of course, is ancient history.

When all was over, a rain of rewards came from Russia. The managers of the Opéra were made Knights Commander of the Imperial Order of Saint Anne, and I a Knight of the same order. Chaliapin received from the French Government the Cross of the Legion of Honour; Waltz and Blumenfeld too; and I am glad to say that my faithful friends in need, Pétremand and Loiseau, were not forgotten.

According to the terms of Diaghilef's agreement with the managers of the Opéra, the settings and costumes were to become their property, so as to enable them to add

Triumph rewards our efforts

Boris Godunof to their current repertory. This, it seemed, would have been the normal thing for them to do at once. Yet, years were to elapse before they did so. For a time they remained unwilling, I suppose, to run the risk unavoidably entailed by comparisons not only between Chaliapin and any one of the singers they could afford to have for the title part, but also between the wonderful Moscow choir and their own. And in a way they were right: Diaghilef himself never gave us again a *Boris* comparable to that of 1908.

VIII

So ended a thrilling, altogether mad period—a period of living at an incredible pace, with hardly time in which to act, and no time at all to think at moments when hard thinking was most needful. The maddest of it all was that, apart from the stage end of the venture, which had been perfectly organized in Russia, we seemed to have no organization at all. We did not even have an office. The management of the Opéra had not thought of providing one for us in the building (they were to be more considerate in 1910), and it had not occurred to either of us to ask for one. All the office work was done in Diaghilef's rather cramped hotel quarters; and, before his arrival, at my own flat. Diaghilef's private secretary was in charge of all the accounts, except for a few special ones which had to be in my own hands. And in conjunction with this, I remember one little episode of a particularly Russian flavour.

A Russian who lived in Paris, plying the trade, I think, of antique broker or furniture dealer—a delightful old man who in his time had been in close touch with musical Russia, and had actually known Mussorgsky, about whom he used to tell curious but perhaps not altogether accurate stories—had done some work for Diaghilef. He turned up at the hotel for payment. Apparently, he had applied

Triumph rewards our efforts

several times already and been referred to me, although to settle his account was none of my business. I did not even know what work he had actually done, or what terms had been agreed to. So I told him I would consult Diaghilef and do my best, but that anyhow I could not pay him until the evening. I had no money in hand, but knew that at six o'clock I could impound a portion of the day's takings before these were diverted into other channels. He walked out, looking rather disconsolate. A little later, having nothing to do at the time, I went for a short stroll in the Avenue de l'Opéra, to look at the shop-windows. I was admiring a delightful piece of Copenhagen china—representing wild ducks in flight—when suddenly I found my Russian friend at my elbow. We started chatting. I pointed at the ducks and said: "Look, isn't this lovely?" He looked, but not for long. After one glance he turned back to me and said, brightly: "Look here: get me paid to-night, and I'll buy it for you." I do not know who was more surprised: I at hearing the proposal, or he at the dressing-down which he received then and there for having made it. Poor fellow! He had thought, quite honestly, that he was only following my lead in an old game very popular in Russia. I ought to have remembered Gogol's *The Inspector*. Later, I learnt not to waste steam on such trifles. I heard since that it had been said of me that "if I did not make two thousand on the sly every Russian season I was a b—— fool." Remembering many things, I have since come to the conclusion that maybe I had been one.

CHAPTER XXII

Relaxations during the Russian season—At the Louvre with Bakst—The Bal des Quat'z-Arts—*A memory of Mata-Hari—Scenes and costumes at the* Bal des Quat'z-Arts.

I

From the day of Diaghilef's arrival until the day when we saw the Russian choristers safe into their train, I had only two opportunities for a little recreation. The first occurred unexpectedly one afternoon, when Diaghilef, Bakst, and I, discovered that we actually had a couple of hours free. It was raining, so Bakst suggested going to the Louvre together. To look at pictures in his company proved to be a rare delight. He made long stays in front of paintings by Veronese and Titian, commenting on their beauties lovingly. Giorgione's *Concert Champêtre*, he said, was his favourite picture in the whole Louvre. Then he took us to see a tiny painting by Fra Angelico, the *Decollation of John the Baptist*, and said: "Tenez, voilà l'idéal des décorateurs russes." And, looking at the wonderfully simple and effective composition —for setting just a curtain, pillars, a table, and an arch opening on a courtyard behind; the scheme consisting mainly of crimson and vermilion, with strong relief introduced by other pure colours, among which a lovely apple green—it was quite easy to see that he spoke the truth.

II

The other relaxation I had was to go to the *Bal des Quat'z-Arts*—invitations to which were greatly coveted and practically impossible to obtain unless one belonged

Relaxations during the Russian season

to the set responsible for organizing this famous function.

The *Bal des Quat'z-Arts* began by being a purely private affair, the students of the École des Beaux-Arts renting, once a year, a large hall in which to disport themselves freely. It was not very generally known to exist—or at any rate attracted very little notice—until one year, in the early 'nineties, a complaint was lodged by the *Ligue contre la licence des rues* (founded and presided over by Senator Bérenger, now remembered chiefly as the promoter of the French First Offenders' Act, *La Loi Bérenger*). Several participants were prosecuted for indecent exhibition, including one model—an American girl, Sarah Brown by name—who was sentenced (without benefiting by the said *Loi Bérenger*) to a fairly long term of imprisonment. Some little time after being released, she died—from consumption, it was said, contracted or aggravated in prison; and there was, on that account, much indignation against the Ligue. After that, the police authorities, to whom it had been represented that the *Bal* was an entirely private affair, agreed to its continuing to take place as usual, but on condition that it should be kept rigorously private, nobody but the students and their *bonafide* guests being allowed access to it. I do not know when policemen began to picket the *Bal*, exactly as if it was a public function. By the time I went, this was done as a matter of course, plenty of men (both *gardes municipaux* in splendid uniforms and *sergents de ville* in sober black) standing about, not in order to keep watch over the revellers' attire, or the moral turn of the assembly, but simply to maintain, if need arose, the common peace as understood under the circumstances.

The Ligue tried several times to institute fresh proceedings, but without success. It was, in those days, ever instituting proceedings against somebody or other, or trying to. And the police, stimulated by its influence, kept a vigilant watch over things in general (other than the *Bal*

A memory of Mata-Hari

des Quat'z-Arts). More than once in Paris, circus or music-hall posters representing lady acrobats in tights, after being displayed for a day or two, would be covered by other posters of the same design, but with a big blank in the middle, across which were printed, in bold type, the words: *Cette partie du dessin a été interdite.*

A few years later, however, posters of a very different kind were to be seen in Paris. I never forgot one advertising a music-hall revue, which read: *Ce soir, Vendredi Saint, soirée de gala. Nu esthétique. Danses lascives.* To appreciate the true inwardness of this announcement, it should be known that, on Good Friday, State-aided theatres were bound to remain closed, and other theatres spontaneously followed suit: but not so music-halls, which accordingly did their utmost to advertise the fact and attract big audiences.

By the time this poster and other similar ones appeared, the Ligue had long given up its activities in despair, and "le nu" was gradually invading the music-hall. The first woman to dance *in puris naturalibus* (but only at private parties) was the famous Mata-Hari. She had appeared in Paris in 1905, out of the blue, giving out that she was half Dutch, half Javanese, had been educated in a convent or school for sacred dancers on the banks of the Ganges, initiated there in all the mysteries and taught the ritual dances for which nudity was compulsory. She was married, she said, to a British officer; and she styled herself Lady McLeod Mata-Hari. It leaked out later that she had indeed married an officer named McLeod, but he was a Dutchman.

A grand matinée (private, of course) was organized at the Musée Guimet, by Guimet himself. Expert orientalists and ambassadors, society people and critics, were invited. Everybody was taken in. Not even the experts suspected that she had never learnt to dance in India (or, indeed, elsewhere), and that all she did was her own in-

The "Bal des Quat'z-Arts"

vention. Grave periodicals, some of which—Combarieu's *Revue Musicale*, for instance—did not often run to illustrations, published long articles, with reproductions of photographs of her "sacred nakedness".

She danced entirely naked, except for metal breastplates. She told a journalist who was interviewing her a horrible story of cruelty to account for her wearing these. Later, to another journalist, she complained bitterly that other women had started dancing naked, which she alone had the right to do, and declared that henceforth she would dance in long robes. She continued in demand a while for private entertainments. Then she appeared on the music-hall stage; but as her dancing consisted almost entirely of posturing, and her beauty was not particularly striking, she was a failure. As a dancer, she was forgotten long before the outbreak of the war.

III

To revert to the *Bal des Quat'z-Arts*, the Sarah Brown case had advertised it sensationally, and thenceforth many people did their utmost to secure admittance. Students, tempted by the big prices offered (at times, I heard, £10 and more) would sometimes sell their own tickets to outsiders, who, arriving at the hall, had to run the gauntlet of the *massiers* (senior students, captains of each *atelier* or class) assembled at the entrance. And they, bewildering intruders with a cross-fire of sharp questions, soon detected them for what they were and shoved them out through a side door. The organizers well knew that should it be proved that a single ticket had been sold to a member of the public, or any unauthorized person admitted, there would be fresh proceedings, and this would mean the withdrawal of the permission to hold the *Bal*. Only the committee had the right to issue invitations to non-students.

I had never tried to get one. I knew there was practic-

Scenes and costumes at the "Bal des Quat'z-Arts"

ally no chance of success. Then, thanks to the Russian opera season, the chance came.

One day, I was doing some work or other in connection with the settings or costumes for *Boris Godunof* with Pinchon, the principal designer of the Opéra, and he expressed the hope that I would not keep him late that night, because he was going to the *Bal des Quat'z-Arts*.

"Lucky dog!" I exclaimed. He asked: "Would you like to come?"—and upon my replying: "Oh, shouldn't I!" rang up the *grand-massier* (the head of the committee) and asked him to invite the *secrétaire-général* (such was my official title) of the Russian opera committee. The reply was favourable, and an hour later the invitation card arrived, duly stamped with the magic words *Comité, entrée spéciale*.

I found that I did not require Pinchon's services very late that night—at least, not at the Opéra. He took me to his own studio and began to hunt up things for my costume. The period, that year, was ancient Egypt. He found a narrow strip of some soft stuff, white with gold embroideries, several yards in length, and wound it around me so as to simulate an Egyptian tunic reaching from neck to ankles. One end was draped over my head hoodwise, as there was no time to manufacture a headdress. The whole thing was very effective, but as suitable for moving about as the tightest of hobbled skirts might have been. Anyhow, it was the best that could be done, and eventually I managed to adjust my gait to conditions. Most excellent Pinchon! At the end of the season, he was awarded the Cross of Saint Stanislaus of Russia: he thoroughly deserved it!

From that time on, the committee of the *Bal* were kind enough always to invite me. In 1909 they offered, through me, a collective invitation for the artists of the Russian ballet to attend, forming a pageant of their own. The girls, when warned of the character of the *Bal*, refused

Scenes and costumes at the "Bal des Quat'z-Arts"
indignantly, and the scheme fell through. But I fear more than one of them attended the *Bal* unofficially.

IV

I have read, in English and other books, descriptions of the *Bal* which do not tally in the least with my own experiences of it—which, accordingly, may be worth recording. The published excerpts of Arnold Bennett's journal include the notes he made of some of the things I told him in 1908, but there is far more to tell. I understand that of late the character of the *Bal* has changed not a little. Here are a few of the things which I observed between 1908 and 1914—the last year I attended the *Bal*.

To begin with, it certainly was free, and more than free. About half the women, and a good proportion of the men, were quite naked or almost. But the atmosphere was not in the least one of promiscuity; far rather that of a country where to go about without clothes was quite natural. People, as a rule, behaved very much in the same way as at an ordinary, but very lively, public fancy-dress ball. Ninety per cent of the revellers were students and models and other girls, and knew one another; whatever liberties were taken between them were taken *en connaissance de cause*. Nobody would have thought of annoying, or even addressing, a stranger, no matter how few clothes she happened to be wearing; and it would have fared ill with any outsider who, having managed to elude the vigilance of the watchers at the entrance, would make himself conspicuous by infringing this unwritten law. I overheard a rebuke which I thought very characteristic; a man who was trying to force his attentions upon a girl was asked by one of her companions, "Dis donc, s——, est-ce que tu te crois au bal de l'Opéra?"

The hall was splendidly decorated, each *atelier* erecting and adorning its own stand or loggia besides contributing to the carrying out of the general scheme. And some of

Scenes and costumes at the "Bal des Quat'z-Arts"
the decorations were as startlingly graphic as anything at Pompeii or in the secret room of the Naples museum; but this in a hearty, thoroughly Rabelaisian spirit, not one of leering pruriency.

Great ingenuity and taste were expended on the costumes, which had to be in keeping with the period. People were specially warned not to be casual in the matter of footwear. If I remember rightly, the warning, in 1908, read: *Les porteurs de croquenots ou godasses* (slang for shapeless or battered shoes) *devront les laisser au vestiaire*. I wish I could remember all the costumes which struck me. In 1908, one man had got himself up as an Egyptian statue. He wore nothing but a huge oval headgear and a necklet, but had painted his whole body green—the green of old bronze, with a few touches of bronze paint here and there. The result was most effective. Then, in 1912 (the finest *Bal des Quat'z-Arts* I have seen—the period was the Arabian Nights), there were some truly wonderful Arab warriors in coats of mail made of the metal caps of champagne corks, their helmets (quite impressive) consisting of tin colanders—the kind that stands on three feet, which in the circumstances did duty for quoits.

But the most beautiful invention of all, to my mind, was one I saw in 1914, the period being the Trojan war: a young man and woman got up as Greek vases (though not exactly vases of the Trojan period). Their bodies were painted ochre with black designs. Above the knees, a bulging tulip-shaped arrangement of wired black cloth suggested the calyx at the base of the body of the vase; and out of this a curved strip arose, representing the handle, its upper end being fixed to a funnel-shaped headdress with rim and beak.

The night began with a good deal of romping about, extemporized shows of dancing and athletics—some of them really splendid—and the like. As the night wore on,

Scenes and costumes at the "Bal des Quat'z-Arts"

many of the people who had started wearing clothes discarded them. The members of the band had been provided with coloured overalls so as not to clash with their surroundings. One of them, a tubby little fellow with a very pink face and a sandy beard, who played the big drum, availed himself of a pause to jerk off his overall and then the rest of his clothes, to the cheering of all those who noticed him doing so. He was but one of the many people who would have been better advised to remain clothed. I saw, another year, a disgracefully ill-built and more than middle-aged woman dancing and posturing on a high stand. She too was cheered, and wildly. And as she carried on, she beamed on the grinning crowd. I have always wondered whether she had entered the spirit of the thing and was exhibiting her ugliness in a spirit of fun or defiance, or whether she misinterpreted the ironical clamours. The latter, probably. She was an absolute nightmare. But, after all, did not Rodin sculpt a statue of *La Belle qui fut heaulmière?*

At two a.m. or so, the floor was cleared for the pageant. Each *atelier* contributed a chariot and retinue, most beautifully devised and carried out. On the chariots the best models posed, and many more danced around. Afterwards there was more romping about until supper time, when the stopping of the music and loud calls from the men in charge of the buffet made it known that the moment had come to rush the bar, purchase, after much elbowing, the required number of suppers (consisting of hard-boiled eggs, cold meat, cheese and fruit, ready packed in brown-paper carriers) and bottles of wine, and then, return to one's companions and—unless one had the privilege of access to a loggia—find room to unpack and eat it, if one was lucky, on the steps, or otherwise on the base of a pillar, or on the floor.

I remember once, at supper time, an amazing sight: three or four naked girls clustered around the base of a

Scenes and costumes at the "Bal des Quat'z-Arts"

pillar against which stood a *garde municipal*, very erect, splendid in his uniform of blue, white and red with shining sword and spurs all complete, and plying him with cup after cup of champagne. But, as a rule, the policemen on duty made it a point of honour not to unbend, and to remain as stolidly indifferent as if they were attending a fruit and vegetable show—or rather more so: some of them might perhaps have seen their way to relaxing, without loss of dignity, at the sight of some unusually opulent marrow.

During supper, a *concours de beauté* took place. All the models, and any other girls who chose, posed alone or in pairs on a platform under the beams of searchlights.

After supper, things grew more riotous. Supper-plates flew across the hall—luckily they were made of cardboard. But, although there was a certain amount of horseplay, the atmosphere remained, as a rule, the same as before. Only once (in 1914) did I witness an unspeakable scene, enacted in the middle of the hall; and that year, as luck would have it, I had with me a Russian lady doctor whom I knew very little, but had taken at her pressing request through a common friend. We happened to be in the midst of a thick crowd and the only thing to do was to take a leaf out of the policemen's book and stand by with perfect unconcern.

In 1908 I did not stay till the end of the ball. I had to resume work at 8 a.m., so left at about four. As I walked out, I saw, in the middle of the carriage drive in front of the hall—which was separated from the road only by iron railings—a girl who, wishing to enjoy a cigarette in the cool of the lovely May night, had walked out all pink as she was except for a pair of scarlet dancing slippers, and stood under the glare of strong electric lamps, calmly puffing away in full sight of a big crowd of chauffeurs, milkmen and passers-by who watched her in anything but silence.

Scenes and costumes at the "Bal des Quat'z-Arts"

But, since then, I joined more than once the general exit, at 5 a.m. or so—a scene as strange and picturesque as the *Bal*, and in strong contrast with the decorous arrival, a few hours earlier, when everybody wore the usual amount of clothing, or, at least, full-size cloaks. The police extended, to the processional return to the Ecole des Beaux-Arts, the privileges allowed at the *Bal* itself. Naked men and girls rushed along the streets, shouting and dancing. Many of them climbed on to the top of the vegetable carts going to the central market, there to strike attitudes on pedestals of carrots or turnips. Some bathed in the ornamental fountains in public squares. Indeed, Senator Bérenger's *Ligue contre la licence des rues* had been definitely vanquished!

Once, as I was preparing to leave the *Bal*, I witnessed a strange scene. In the men's cloakroom—just a big unscreened alcove, with rows of pegs, on one side of the entrance hall, a man, a finely built American of thirty or so, with strong hawklike features, grey eyes, and raven-black hair, had collected from the pegs a score or so of overcoats, arranged them into a heap in the middle of the floor, and was lying upon them naked, blind drunk, gazing very sternly at a quartet of *sergents de ville* who, greatly embarrassed and wishful not to excite or manhandle him, were trying to coax him to move along, so that people might regain possession of their overcoats. How the affair ended I do not know. Of course, drunken people occasionally caused trouble there, as they will anywhere: but on the whole the *Bals des Quat'z-Arts* which I attended were orgies of riotousness, not of vice.

CHAPTER XXIII

*The début in Paris of Diaghilef's Ballet—Fokin at work—
Scarcity of suitable music and how it was overcome—The
Igor dances and Cleopatra—First Act of Glinka's Russlan
and Liudmila - Rimsky-Korsakof's Maid of Pskof produced
under a new name—Nijinsky, Pavlova, Karsavina—Memories of Caran d'Ache—Our plans for a London Season and
a visit to London—My first break with Diaghilef.*

I

Of the 1909 season at the Théâtre de Châtelet, the first one in which Diaghilef's Ballet appeared, I have many memories—most of them picturesque, but not all of them pleasant. Diaghilef had not stuck to his resolve of 1907, and so conditions had become such as to render certain of my duties difficult and unpalatable.

This, however, is by the way. The Ballet itself was, of course, a delight pure and simple, and most of the old friends—Bakst and Benois and Sanin and Waltz among others—were there again. Two new conductors had come: Tcherepnin and Cooper, the former being also the composer of the ballet with which the season opened, *Le Pavillon d'Armide*. Then there was Fokin, the ballet master. It was especially he who aroused my enthusiasm. To watch him at rehearsal was as great a treat as it was to watch Sanin. Amazingly lithe and springy, cheerful and patient even when he might have had the best reason for losing his temper, he danced and rushed all round the stage, watching and stimulating every one of his dancers. He seemed to have a hundred eyes in his head. At an incredible speed, he would go round each line or group

Scarcity of suitable music and how it was overcome
in turn, showing one dancer how to perform a step, correcting another one's attitude, helping a third to understand the rhythm and phrasing of the music. He had an unerring sense of construction as well as of colour and motion. I doubt whether, without him, Diaghilef's Ballet could have come into being.

Nobody realized then—Diaghilef did not advertise the fact; he never attempted to advertise himself, but on the contrary strove to keep as much as possible in the background, getting things done—that the "Russian Ballet" revealed in 1909 was not something that existed in Russia and had simply been exported, with perhaps, as in the case of *Boris Godunof*, a few innovations in the matter of production; that it had been created entirely by Diaghilef's will and under Diaghilef. Since then, of course, many writers have said and repeated it, rendering justice to his colossal achievement.

II

At the time there existed practically no repertory of ballets suitable for the furtherance of Fokin's schemes. The programme of the 1909 season included only two works originally written for the purposes of dancing and given in the actual shape intended by their authors: Tcherepnin's *Pavillon d'Armide* and the admirable *Polovtsian Dances* from Borodin's *Prince Igor*. *Le Festin* consisted of a set of separate dance-numbers to music by various composers, with the Finale of Tchaikowsky's Second Symphony by way of conclusion; *Les Sylphides* —Pavlova's first triumph in Paris—of pieces by Chopin scored (not always very felicitously) and loosely strung together. As for *Cléopâtre*—which shared with the *Polovtsian Dances* the honours of this first season—it was, musically speaking, a weird and wonderful concoction in which entered, among other things, the *Turkish Dance* from Glinka's *Russlan and Liudmila*, the *Persian Dances*

CHALIAPIN AS IVAN THE TERRIBLE, 1909
FROM AN ORIGINAL PRINT BY DE LOSQUES

Rimsky-Korsakof's "Maid of Pskof"
from Mussorgsky's *Khovanshchina*, the *Bacchanal* from Glazunof's *Les Saisons*, excerpts from Rimsky-Korsakof's *Mlada*, and, it should be acknowledged, a few bits from Arensky's ballet *Cleopatra*, from which the idea of the new *Cléopâtre* had sprung. But the whole thing had been done so cleverly, and the ballet, in its setting by Bakst, was so impressively beautiful that one hardly thought of keeping watch for discrepancies of style in the music.

III

The season was not entirely devoted to the Ballet. Diaghilef also gave the first act of Glinka's *Russlan and Liudmila* and Rimsky-Korsakof's *The Maid of Pskof*—renamed, as I have said, *Ivan le Terrible*.

This was beautifully produced. Among the extraordinary effects devised by Bakst, I remember a setting in which a combination of three reds—the scarlet canvas of the tent, the deep red brocade of Chaliapin's costume, and the cherry red of Lydia Lipkowska's dress—was something never to be forgotten. The loveliness of it sank into you deeply. It rivalled, in sheer beauty, the setting of the *Igor* dances—a masterpiece of Roerich's in which the sulphurous sky, the low hemispheric tents, and the few thin columns of smoke rising from the camp conveyed an indescribable impression of space, emptiness, and desolation.

Ivan le Terrible scored a very great success, although not a triumph comparable with that of *Boris Godunof* the previous year. As for the first act of *Russlan and Liudmila*, again it passed almost unnoticed, despite the splendid way in which it was performed, Cooper conducting.

One rehearsal of *Russlan* gave me the opportunity of witnessing an incident the like of which occurs often enough in comic literature, but which I never dreamt could happen in real life. The cast comprises two baritones, who impersonate very chivalrous and courteous

A rehearsal of "Russlan"

knights. At the appointed time, one of them was missing. Inquiries revealed that he had quarrelled with the other and gone away in dudgeon. I jumped into a taxi, and found him at his hotel, comfortably in bed (at two in the afternoon) with a pile of newspapers and a supply of cigarettes close at hand. With difficulty I persuaded him not to leave us all in the lurch. He dressed and followed me sulkily, but during the whole of the rehearsal I had to stand between him and the other baritone, lest they should come to blows; and they availed themselves of every pause in their parts to hurl at one another choice insults and dire threats that strangely contrasted with the declarations of mutual admiration and amity which they had to sing.

IV

Happenings behind the scenes, at rehearsals and other times, were now and then as picturesque and unexpected as the show itself. The dancers were quiet and disciplined enough, and so were the women choristers, but no one else seemed to be. Once I asked Nouvel why some of the Russians took no notice of my instructions. He replied that it probably was because I spoke to them politely. I took the hint, and from that moment on had no more trouble with them—at least in that respect.

There was bad blood between the Russian stage carpenters and their French colleagues. One day a free fight took place. One side was intrenched behind a pile of settings, and the others were trying to get at them with the property halberds used in *Ivan le Terrible*. The racket was increased by the business manager, who stood yelling: "Fetch the police! Fetch the police!" I grasped him by the shoulder and said: "Go and fetch them yourself!" And I stepped in the midst of the fray at the imminent risk of having my top-hat scratched. It was a tradition in those days always to wear a top-hat on the stage during intervals. One night (but this was in 1908, at the Opéra)

NIJINSKY IN "SHEHERAZADE"
[*Photo. Bert, Paris*]

Behind the Scenes

I wanted to take Arnold Bennett behind the scenes. He, who had come specially for the occasion from Fontainebleau where he lived, was not wearing a top-hat. The usher in charge of the door leading from the auditorium to the stage insisted on stopping him, and I had to use my most official and authoritative tone of voice to overcome his resistance. And even so, Bennett had to leave his hat behind and go bareheaded at his own risk (there were risks of sorts: the top-hat afforded protection against anything that might fall from the flies, from cockroaches upwards).

Another time, an attendant appeared, very much out of breath: "Sir," he panted, "what is to be done? Two of those Russian choristers have arrived blind drunk. Ils se sont mis tout nus, ils sont sur le toit, et ils p—— sur les passants." An inspiration prompted me to tell him to fetch the fireman, who succeeded in subduing the culprits.

One night, a few minutes before the *Igor* dances were due to begin, I was informed that the top-boots worn by the girls in these dances were not to be found. Forgetting a strict order which I myself had issued, I rushed into the corridor on which the girls' dressing-rooms opened. At the end of the corridor there was a tap. I caught a fleeting vision of nymphs in nature's garb awaiting their turn to fill their water-jugs. Shrieks arose, jugs were dropped in the scurry, and a second or two later, from behind safely closed doors, a chorus of reproachful voices wailed: "Oh, Mikhal Dimitrievitch, how *could* you do it?" And meanwhile, somebody else had found those confounded top-boots!

V

Of Nijinsky I have few recollections to set down. All that I could say by way of tribute to his supremacy as a dancer has been said, and well said, by others. I found him to be pleasant, rather quiet, and endowed with the

Nijinsky

mentality of a young child—not at all the kind of man whom by any effort of imagination one might expect to develop into a ballet master, as he did a few years later. But Diaghilef was urging him forward with all his might, and had already resolved, I feel sure, that he should ascend all possible heights in turn. Nijinsky having fallen ill (nothing very serious) was conveyed to the hotel at which Diaghilef was staying, and so I began to see a good deal of him when with Diaghilef. One day, he started discussing with us the technique of his famous leap sideways in *Le Pavillon d'Armide*—a leap which enabled him to stay in the air, it was said, longer than any dancer had ever done before. He gave us a demonstration, and offered to teach us both how to do it. Diaghilef refused, but I accepted. Following instructions, I placed my feet, bent my knees, swung my arms limply to the right, and then violently to the left, hurling myself into the air in the same direction. I did it time after time, Nijinsky gravely rectifying mistakes and Diaghilef splitting his sides with laughter. Since then I have often boasted of having actually received a private lesson in ballet dancing from the great Nijinsky.

Nijinsky was to go to Venice with Diaghilef after the season. As he had no French, I was asked to help him buy his bathing-kit. In the choice of a bathing-suit, he showed himself as exacting as if it had been a stage costume. He had to be taken into a fitting-room, and tried several on before finding a fit which satisfied him. The attendant's reminders that the fabric would shrink when wet were so much waste of breath. I had to continue my interpreting in the fitting-room, and was amazed to see how powerful and harmonious Nijinsky was in build. Although his muscles were on the big side, his body suggested that of a Greek athlete, reposeful as well as strong, and in sharp contrast with the mobile, monkeyish face. It had none of the almost feminine grace which he so often showed when appearing in stage costume—in *Armide*, for instance, and later in *Le Spectre de la Rose*.

VI

Of Pavlova I have nothing to record for the simple reason that after a few performances she left Diaghilef and went to dance in London—perhaps with the feeling that she had not been adequately "starred" nor properly appreciated. In the latter respect, at any rate, she was mistaken: people, very rightly, were extolling her to the skies, together with Nijinsky and Fokin and Karsavina. But there can be no doubt that her wonderful talent did not fit in with Diaghilef and Fokin's schemes, except so far as these included the production of ballets on the traditional, classical style, such as *Les Sylphides*. She was, first and last, a *prima ballerina* of the old school, and not very adaptable. She must have disliked the part of the principal slave which she was given in *Cléopâtre*, not only because it did not stand out in the same way as *prima-ballerina* parts usually do, but because as dancing it was not quite within her province—although of course she filled it splendidly. So to London she went, and the Russian "balletomaniacs" (experts who, among other things, knew who had taken any part in any ballet old or new, anywhere, and at any time, and who could do thirty-two *fouettés* in succession and who couldn't, and who could do thirty-nine and how long, to a split second, it took her to do them) shook their heads, and had premonitions of disaster for Diaghilef until Karsavina had taken up the Pavlova parts as well as those which had been given to her from the outset, and proved altogether admirable. Throughout the remainder of the season, she had to do double the normal amount (already heavy) of work; and she proved as eager and cheerful about it as she was gifted and versatile, unselfishly interested in the general purpose of the Ballet, always a help in the furtherance of the common cause.

Dancers and Corps-de-ballet

VII

The company as a whole, and every solo dancer individually, forthwith carried the day. But it was especially the male dancers and the *corps de ballet* who amazed Paris. To register this fact (which was obvious from the outset and became more obvious as the season advanced) is not in the least derogatory to Pavlova, Karsavina, or the other female soloists—among whom I especially remember Sophia Feodorova, a little cricket of a thing, endowed with intense vitality, and splendid in character-dancing and national dances. It simply means that to see first-rate *ballerines* was no surprise for the Parisian connoisseurs. Between the dancing of Pavlova or Karsavina and that of Adeline Genée or Carlotta Zambelli there was no striking difference of standard—even the Russian experts readily granted as much. But never within living memory —even leaving aside the peerless Nijinsky—had such male dancers been seen as the Russian Ballet had to show. They could dance with classical grace and polish, and they could be athletic or acrobatic; and above all, to see them dancing never created an impression of incongruity, so thoroughly did they seem to be in their natural element (this alone was a new experience for most of us). Fokin —who appeared in many parts, and was capable of taking any at a moment's notice—Bolm as the chief archer in the *Igor* dances, Rosay and his partners as the jesters in *Armide*, Mordkin in classical steps, could hold the stage as perfectly as the greatest of *ballerine*.

Then, as regards the *corps de ballet*, the same thing happened as with the Moscow choir. They had as great a personal success as any of the soloists. Such splendid team-work as theirs had never been seen in Paris—where, indeed, the *corps de ballet* had always been a weak point, especially at the Opéra. Later, I was not in the least surprised to hear that when Diaghilef found it impossible to

LOPOKHOVA IN THE "IGOR" DANCES, 1910

The "Igor" dances and "Cleopatra"

recruit dancers in Russia, he turned at once to England—a country which was reputed for the efficiency and discipline of its group-dancers even in musical comedy and on the music-hall stage.

It was in the *Igor* dances (which include practically no solo dancing) that the *corps de ballet* first scored. A second triumph came a few days later, with *Cléopâtre*, in which most of its evolutions centred in Ida Rubinstein, tall, slim, supple, and indolent, her face very white under a powder-blue wig. A wonderful moment was when the dancers, circling, unrolled the long strands of silken fabrics in which she was swathed like a mummy—whether this corresponded to any historical reality I am unable to say, but it was most effective. Then came a Bacchanal, at the end of which she and Fokin collapsed on to a couch around which the slaves held up a curtain. At that climax one could always feel a thrill running through the auditorium. A Frenchwoman said to me one day: "Last night, I had a seat right at the side in the dress-circle. I was glad of that, because from there I could see Rubinstein and Fokin behind the curtain. I had always longed to. I expected to see them continuing their love-making. Pas du tout: ils buvaient de la bière!"

VIII

I have one very pathetic memory of that time. It was during an interval one night that I met for the last time, in a corridor of the Châtelet, Caran d'Ache, the famous French cartoonist. Ten years or so before, I used to see a lot of him. I had been particularly glad to make his acquaintance, because, like everybody in France, I had revelled in his cartoons from the days of my childhood; and I had found him to be hospitable, attractive, and amusing (it was at his house, by the way, that I enjoyed my first experiences of Russian cookery.) He was the son of a French father and a Russian mother—his real

Memories of Caran d'Ache

name was Poiré, or Poiret—tall, well built, with twinkling blue-grey eyes and a long drooping blond moustache; a trifle smooth and suave, but not unpleasantly so; and no end of a fop. He had the biggest wardrobe I have ever seen, and the strangest. And he took great joy in exhibiting and explaining it all to his friends. He had a mania for egregious clothes. He would wear bell-shaped raglans the bottom of which, he told me proudly, measured over six yards round. "This putty-coloured one for going to the races is nearly seven yards round. This gives particularly nice folds at the sides. And these patterns in stitching across the shoulders and round the edges are there lest the cloth might appear too monotonously smooth." He owned waistcoats whose many-hued splendour was rivalled only by that of their buttons. Whenever he saw a piece of material which he liked, and which gave him an idea for a garment, he would buy it, whether it was suiting for ladies, or a travelling rug, or a bath-towel —he actually had a waistcoat made out of one of these, honey-coloured with a blue pattern.

Materials which were too showy even for him served as linings. He showed me a double-breasted lounge suit of thick blue serge lined with warm vicuna cloth. This, he said, enabled him to take constitutionals in the Avenue du Bois in the coldest weather, without wearing an overcoat. "Pendant que les autres grelottent sous leurs pardessus fourrés, moi je me ballade tranquillement en pet-en-l'air!"

All this sounds very peculiar, I know. And yet, somehow or other, quite unaccountably, he managed to carry it off. However egregious his get-up, he never looked a bounder—scarcely even on the boundary line. He was as irrepressible and irresponsible as a child; and also a great philanderer. Every now and then he would run away from home and wife (she was a nice, rather quiet Frenchwoman) to reappear a month or two later and find ever-ready forgiveness. At last he ran away for good. When I had last seen him, he was established in a bachelor studio, with a very pretty, very youthful, lady secretary.

And that night, all of a sudden, I saw him in front of me, looking very ill, his face a waxen yellow, hardly able to walk with the help of two sticks, and speaking with great difficulty. The saddest of all was that he seemed terribly conscious of his plight. He inquired could he be taken round to see Chaliapin. And when I had said: "Certainly", he asked diffidently whether he might take my arm, and would I also bring him back afterwards. I led him to Chaliapin's dressing-room and waited outside while they talked. He refused to be introduced to any other member of the company. He died a year or two later.

IX

That season, work, although as hard as ever, was not so pressing as to exclude all possibility of relaxation, as in 1908. Fresh air, however, was practically out of the question except at night after the rehearsals or shows, when those of us whose taste did not run to more stuffiness in restaurants would jump into taxis and go for long rides outside town. My usual companions on these expeditions were three girls from the *corps de ballet*, all three very jolly and simple, but far better at pulling my leg as to my Russian than at helping me to improve it.

One blessed Saturday the news came that the morrow would be free. I offered to take the girls to Versailles, which they were longing to see. They demurred a while, then asked whether one of their colleagues, with whom they had promised to make a party that day, could come too. I assented. The colleague was a particularly prim person and happened to know a little French—why I record these two points will presently appear.

We started the day by lunching at an English tavern

Diaghilef's plans for a London Season

near the Gare Saint-Lazare, famous since the days when Huysmans, in his novel *A Rebours*, had extolled its typically English atmosphere and bill of fare—he had made his hero, des Esseintes, have a meal there on his way to London, where a sudden whim was driving him, and, the meal finished, decide that London could give him nothing more English, and forthwith return to the seclusion of his own country home.

We duly enjoyed the pickled salmon, the steak and kidney pudding, the raspberry tart and the stout. Then we took a taxi. As the girls were entering it, the head waiter (not an Englishman), who was holding the door open, said to me: "Monsieur, pourquoi vous en aller? Nous avons en haut une bonne chambre où vous serez très bien avec vos petites amies." I couldn't believe my ears. I gasped, entered the taxi, and strove to preserve my composure. I failed. The idea was too stupendous. I had to explode. I rocked with laughter. The three girls who understood no French stared at me in amazement, and also at the fourth, who was sitting very rigid, eyes sparkling with anger, her face a rich crimson. The three demanded an explanation. I said, quite truthfully, that I was unable to explain in Russian what had made me laugh, and left it to the one who had understood to satisfy their curiosity later if she cared to do so.

X

Towards the end of the season, Diaghilef and I paid a flying visit to London in order to prepare the ground for a Russian season there. He had received the offer of an engagement at a big music-hall. We went to see a show at this hall and, while watching proceedings on the stage, Diaghilef kept indignantly repeating: "The Russian Ballet sandwiched between performing dogs and a fat lady playing a silver-plated trombone! Never! Never!" Nijinsky at his side nodded approval the while. After the war,

My first break with Diaghilef

however, the Russian Ballet was to appear on that very stage—but, I hasten to add, not thus sandwiched.

Diaghilef decided to rent Drury Lane Theatre; and Collins, the lessee, met him readily. An agreement for the following year was arrived at, to come into force on the payment, within a fortnight, of a £500 earnest.

The Paris season ended as triumphantly as it had begun; but financially it was, despite big takings, a disaster. The Grand Duke Vladimir had just died, and Diaghilef could hope for no further help from Russia. He was unable to pay the stipulated £500, and so the scheme for a London season in 1910 collapsed. How he extricated himself from his difficulties I do not know. I stayed by him and helped him to the best of my ability until he was clear and ready to start for his holiday in his beloved Venice. But then, I told him that I would never work with him again. I was particularly annoyed with him for having disregarded the repeated warnings I had given him. I felt—rightly or wrongly—that had he listened to me there would not have been so terrible a mess to clear up at the end. We did not part bad friends: there was no reason to. But in my mind, it was a parting for good and all. He thought so too. Not long before, he had said to me: "You are a funny chap, Calvo. With some people one quarrels, and then one makes it up again. But with you it is different." "It is", I retorted. But this was not a quarrel. I simply was as "sick of it all" as he had been at the end of the 1907 season. And, as it happens, I did change my mind in that matter a few months later.

CHAPTER XXIV

Differences adjusted—The 1910 Ballet Season at the Opéra —Stravinsky's Fire-Bird - *Shéhérazade—Revival of Adolphe Adam's* Giselle—*My final break with Diaghilef and a memory of an earlier quarrel—The first performance of Stravinsky's* Rite of Spring—*The Diaghilef version of* Khovanshchina—*Diaghilef on possessions.*

I

Towards the end of the following winter, Nouvel came to Paris, bringing with him Baron Dimitri de Gunzburg, Diaghilef's new backer. They urged me to reconsider my resignation and assured me that if I was willing to take charge of the coming season, none of the conditions to which I had objected would recur. I hesitated. I had just promised to help Raoul Gunsbourg to organize the monster charity concert to which I have referred in a previous chapter, and did not feel like assuming more heavy work and responsibilities, and being kept away from my writing-table again. But they insisted so much that I relented—especially after having heard that the programme was to include the first performance of Stravinsky's *Fire-Bird*. I made cast-iron terms so as to guard against all unpleasant contingencies; they were accepted, and so, when Diaghilef arrived, there I was, ready once again to fall into step with him.

The 1910 season, which took place at the Opéra, was a triumph from all points of view and went smoothly from beginning to end. Besides Stravinsky's *Fire-Bird* the most sensational novelty was *Shéhérazade*, to the music of Rimsky-Korsakof's long-known symphonic suite. I thor-

Shéhérazade

oughly enjoyed it. Like everybody who saw it, I considered it purely and simply amazing. Bakst's setting was a glory of green with enhancing touches of red, and in the costumes yellow, orange, and purple predominated in marvellously calculated blends or contrasts. And the dancing too was glorious on the part of both soloists and ensembles. The *corps de ballet* once again covered itself with glory, and Nijinsky showed for the first time—at least in France—that he was as superb a mime as he was a dancer.

In principle, I know, my critical sense ought to have made me feel that it was absolutely wrong to use a symphonic work, intended for the concert-platform only, for the purposes of a ballet—and especially a ballet whose subject had nothing to do with the composer's avowed poetic and descriptive intentions (for instance, as one French critic indignantly pointed out, a massacre of negro slaves in a harem took place to music inspired by the notion of a tempest at sea and the wrecking of Sindbad's ship). I could see that Rimsky-Korsakof's widow and eldest son had very good reasons for angrily protesting against the travesty in both the French and the Russian Press. And I myself, deeply loving the music of *Shéhérazade*, ought to have felt that there must be something wrong somewhere. But what I actually did feel was that stage atmosphere, stage action, and music were never at cross purposes—perhaps because there are in *Shéhérazade* no deep undercurrents such as characterize, for instance, *Tamara*; and that what Diaghilef was giving his public was a picturesque, lively, and versi-colour spectacle to music which was essentially picturesque, lively, and versi-colour without ever pretending to be more than that.

Of course, neither *Shéhérazade* nor *Tamara* follows a definite programme: so that the question whether there are incompatibilities between the music and the arbitrarily superimposed stage action can be answered only accord-

Revival of Adolphe Adam's "Giselle"

ing to feeling. As I have said in another chapter, I was to feel very strongly on the subject of Diaghilef's choreographic adaptation of *Tamara*. If this is inconsequence, I plead guilty.

II

Diaghilef also revived Adolphe Adam's *Giselle*, a ballet long forgotten in its native France but still popular in Russia. Everybody in Paris was surprised at the idea, and foresaw that the artistic result would be paltry and the success poor. But, by a freak, so to speak, of spiritual atavism, the oldtime Russian "balletomaniac" was cropping up in Diaghilef, prompting him to produce a ballet of the very kind against which he and his group had been striving so hard to react, and would not be gainsaid.

We had a lot of trouble in securing permission to give *Giselle*, because it was still copyright in France, and we did not know in whom the copyright was vested. Eventually we discovered the assignee, a music-publisher who lived in a side street at Versailles. We went to see him. I believe he had quite forgotten the very existence of *Giselle*. He gave us the required permission with glee, and prepared for the novel experience of pocketing the performing fees that were falling to him from the skies.

Great trouble was taken, too, with the production. I can still see Benois at the eleventh hour retouching the settings with pastels to secure additional high lights here and there, and all the old-fashioned routine of the *corps de ballet's* evolutions being gone through with as much care as if it was one of Fokin's most original and complicated creations. But nothing availed. *Giselle* was received with polite approval and withdrawn, I seem to remember, after two performances. One critic wrote that the revival "had taught us nothing new." It is, I am sure, the one and only time that such a thing could be said of a Diaghilef production.

GRIGORIEF AND BOULGAKOF
IN "THE FIRE-BIRD"
[*Photo. Bert, Paris*]

My final break with Diaghilef

III

Of Stravinsky I have little to record beyond the fact that he was forthwith welcomed as the heir presumptive of the great Russians whom we loved so well. This, I know, was not quite the right perspective in which to see him, even at that early period of his career. But it does not mean that anybody failed to realize the originality, in both conception and execution, that characterizes the music of the *Fire-Bird*.

I did not see much of him during the season. I was kept too busy to be able to see much of anybody. I met him the following winter at Beaulieu, near Nice, and had the pleasure of hearing him play, at the piano, parts of his *Petrushka*. In due course, the task befell me of translating into French, or English, or both, most of his early vocal works, from the first songs to the opera *The Nightingale*.

Nor did I see much of the other dancers appearing in Paris for the first time that year—among whom the ballerina Catherine Gheltzer and the altogether delightful Lydia Lopokhova, then a very youthful débutante but already a general favourite, whom all connoisseurs hailed as a rising star.

At the end of the season I discovered that Diaghilef had decided not to adhere, in the future, to the terms made with me on his behalf by Gunzburg and Nouvel. Then I made up my mind for good and all; and on the very day when my work was finished, I resigned, treating him to a grand scene *à la Diaghilef*. I must have imitated his own way of expressing fury quite well: for he never retorted a word except: "And I who was going to ask you to take charge of my London seasons!" My reply to this need not be recorded—especially as, besides being unprintable, it did not in the least represent my real feelings.

A memory of an earlier quarrel

IV

Since then, I have heard a good deal about his "Tsarist" methods. All I can say is that I never had the slightest evidence of anything of the sort. On the contrary, I had many opportunities of realizing that he could be kind even to the humblest member of his company. I can remember only one occasion on which a quarrel arose between him and me. It was a trifling one. When I submitted to him the accounts for *Boris Godunof* he objected to one item (amounting to a very few pounds) which he declared he had not authorized, whereas I was convinced he had. After sticking to my guns a while, I stopped the argument with: "All right: since I was mistaken, I'll pay it out of my own pocket." He gasped, glared at me, and snapped: "Nothing of the kind! Let's carry on." Obviously what he had looked forward to was a protracted argument in Russian fashion, ending in my duly eating humble pie, after which he would graciously concede the point. Half an hour later, he queried another item. Without arguing, I said: "Well, if you think I'm wrong, I shall pay for it." He exclaimed angrily: "You'll . . . you'll . . .! Look here, Calvo, I'm feeling hot. I must go and get a whisky and soda." He grasped his hat and stick and walked out of the room. I waited in vain for his return, and after a long while went home. The next morning I turned up at the usual time, we greeted one another as usual, and finished going over the accounts without further trouble.

A year or two after, I came to imagine (quite mistakenly) on the strength of an announcement he made, that he had appropriated an idea which I had submitted to him. I was so angry that, meeting him at the rehearsal of *L'Après-Midi d'un Faune*, I foolishly showed my anger instead of seeking for an explanation. He naturally was offended; and a duel would have ensued had I not, after consulting Ravel and one or two other friends, acknow-

Stravinsky's "Rite of Spring"

ledged myself in the wrong. His attitude, on that occasion, was irreproachable.

In those days duels, although still fairly common in France, were rare in the musical world. I remember only two in my time. Vincent d'Indy fought one with a journalist, following upon a quarrel as to whether he had promised or not to set to music a libretto by the said journalist. This was fought with pistols, and ended in the not infrequent "deux balles échangées sans résultat". The other took place between a critic and a publisher. It was attended by operators of a cinema gazette, and the cinema company presented both combatants with a set of enlarged photos of the duel. I saw one of these sets framed and hung in the sitting-room of one of the parties.

V

From 1911 onwards, having resumed my ordinary position as a critic, I might have found myself, now and then, in a quandary with regard to Diaghilef's productions. Fortunately, my connection with the Press remained almost entirely that of a free-lance contributor, so that I never was compelled to deal with his seasons, and was free to do so or not according to my inclination.

It was only when he produced *Tamara* that, in deference to Cicero's axiom, "Nihil est turpius quam cum eo bellum gerere quocum familiariter vixeris", I had to curb a strong impulse to protest publicly. Once or twice I wrote special articles on things done by Diaghilef which aroused my admiration. For instance, I simply had to write in praise of Stravinsky's *Petrushka*; and, later, of his *Rite of Spring*, whose production in 1913 under Nijinsky, with settings by Roerich, I remember as something rather wonderful—in my opinion miles above the "abstract" production of later years.

Only twice in my life have I seen really disorderly audiences: at *Pelléas* in 1902 and at the *Rite* in 1913. The

The Diaghilef version of "Khovanshchina"
uproar at the Schönberg Concerts in Berlin and Vienna, in 1908, and after, had I been present, might have provided me with further objects of comparison. But, speaking only of these two, I must say that although far more noisy than at *Pelléas*—and indeed so noisy at times that you could not hear the music—the disturbances at the *Rite* were far less loathsome. People were really roused, not merely bewildered and scandalized. They protested angrily, not prudishly and in shocked "Oh-Oh-Oh's!" Nor was there in their demonstrations anything of the note of personal hostility to the composer which was so definitely discernible in 1902. No: the *Rite* was simply too much for part of the audiences. Stravinsky's French biographer, André Schaeffner, has said that the disturbances were simply the "counterproof of the work's novelty and daring."

It was obvious that the dancing had caused as much irritation as the music. The evolutions of the dancers had been made as constrained, gawky, and heavy as possible, in order to evoke the primitive, apprehensive mentality of the men and women of the stone age, struggling against the awesome forces of nature arrayed against them. The idea was excellent, but not successfully carried out. Nijinsky's choreography stopped half-way, taking into account all the rhythmic suggestions of the music separately, but not coordinating them into a whole. The results were, now and then, almost caricatural. Most of his other schemes suffered from the same defect. After having seen the choreography devised by him for *Jeux* (also produced in 1913), Debussy wrote to a friend (the letter was published years later): "Cet homme regarde passer la musique d'un œil mauvais . . . c'est vilain; c'est même Dalcrozien."

And yet, how beautiful most of the *Rite* was! Nobody who witnessed the 1913 production will ever forget the wonderfully impressive entry of the warriors clad in eland

DANCERS IN "THE RITE OF SPRING", 1913
[Photo. Gerschell, Paris]

The Diaghilef version of "Khovanshchina"

skins and wearing eland skulls on their heads, nor the strangely inhuman, hysterical dance of the maiden before the sacrifice.

Maybe a few of us overpraised the *Rite;* but this, I think, was mainly in order to stem the tide of opposition.

VI

When Diaghilef was about to produce Mussorgsky's *Khovanshchina* and the announcement came that Stravinsky, with the help of Ravel, was restoring to their original form certain portions of the score which Rimsky-Korsakof had altered, and writing a new final scene in place of the one provided by Rimsky-Korsakof (Mussorgsky left the score unfinished), I took a hand in the discussion which followed, beginning with protests in the Russian Press.

Believing the position to be the same as with regard to *Boris Godunof* (for at that time little was known as to the true state of Mussorgsky's manuscripts of *Khovanshchina*), I joined the small minority of those who were proclaiming that it was high time for the musical world at large to know the genuine text of this second and last of Mussorgsky's operas. Could I, who years before had been at such pains to persuade Diaghilef to do the genuine *Boris*, fail to support him at the moment when he proclaimed that he was preparing to do the genuine *Khovanshchina*?

From Russia, however, Andrei Rimsky-Korsakof gave us all a hard and well-deserved rap on the knuckles, simply by pointing out that, however much a fresh edition of *Khovanshchina* might be desirable, this should be carried out straight from Mussorgsky's manuscripts and not—as Stravinsky had done—partly on the basis of Rimsky-Korsakof's edition.

It is only in 1931, when the genuine text of *Khovanshchina* was published at last in Russia, that I was able to see: firstly, that, unlike *Boris*, *Khovanshchina* (apart from being unfinished) was too long and loosely built to be

Diaghilef on possessions

able to hold its own on the stage without curtailments; and secondly, that although Stravinsky and Ravel had unquestionably restored certain portions of the general harmonic and melodic texture, Diaghilef, in producing *Khovanshschina*, had taken greater liberties than Rimsky-Korsakof would ever have dreamt of taking—cutting out episodes, or inverting their order, with utter ruthlessness.

VII

A trait of character which Diaghilef revealed in the course of a talk is, I think, worth recording. He had been describing some very beautiful objects—pictures or antiques—he had come across, and I asked him had he bought them. He replied: "No. I did not want to own them. I have no possessions and wish for none. To own things is cumbersome and tedious. A couple of trunkfuls of personal effects is all I have in the world."

Was this a pose? I cannot tell. I think that at the time he had no fixed home, which would help to account for this feeling. From his obituaries I learnt that eventually he had developed a great taste for books, and built up a fine library.

That, although capable of planning well ahead, he lived very much from day to day was shown by the fact that he died, apparently, without having made any arrangements for the transfer of his settings, costumes, and performing rights. But, even if he had, I doubt whether anybody could have carried on. The Russian Ballet, which he brought into being and kept going through thick and thin, even (a truly amazing achievement) during the war years, was bound to disappear with him.

CHAPTER XXV

I start on a journey to Petrograd—A visit to Schönberg in Berlin—His views on the use and misuse of modern devices—His paintings—Schönberg amid his pupils—His Handbook of Harmony—The Russian customs.

I

Early in 1912 I started on my journey to Petrograd, where I spent a whole delightful month meeting musicians and collecting materials for further work on Russian music. On the way, I spent a couple of days in Berlin for the special purpose of meeting Arnold Schönberg.

What I had heard and read about him and his music had greatly stimulated my curiosity. No notices of the first performance in 1905 of his symphonic poem *Pelléas und Mélisande* had reached me; but in 1907 I had read in German periodicals the startling information that at a concert given in Vienna by the Rosé Quartet, members of the audience had very nearly come to blows, the cause of the trouble being the first performance of a string quartet by him, which had roused a few listeners to enthusiasm, and a great many more to disgust and fury. A little later, there had been an even greater uproar on the occasion of the first performance of his Chamber Symphony—another performance of that work in 1913 was to end with a battle royal in the concert-hall.

Then there had been the publication, in 1911, of his famous piano pieces Op. 11—I remember Ravel and Stravinsky looking at them at my house; Stravinsky was particularly excited about certain things in them, and Ravel,

A visit to Schönberg in Berlin

although colder, was greatly interested. I was merely amazed and disconcerted, but I felt that the questions stirred by the sudden disclosure of this strange music were worth looking into with care.

This feeling was confirmed by my meeting in Paris Egon Wellesz, a pupil of Schönberg. He spoke with enthusiasm of Schönberg's personality, music, and teaching. He told me how a number of young composers had clustered around him, not only because they found him a peerless teacher, but because his work was the very embodiment of something for which they had been longing and more or less consciously groping. (A testimony of what the revelation had meant to them all is the book *Arnold Schönberg*, by eleven of his pupils and friends, which appeared at Munich in 1912.) I developed a strong desire to introduce Schönberg's music to my students at the Ecole des Hautes Etudes Sociales as soon as possible. At my request, Wellesz very kindly arranged for me to meet Schönberg in Berlin.

II

He was then living at Zehlendorf, where I called upon him on a bright, crisp, bitterly cold winter morning. I had a long, most instructive and enjoyable talk with him. He explained that he did not consider himself, and disliked being considered, a revolutionist. He could not see how the part played by tradition in his own formation could be overlooked. He had been very much under the influence of Brahms, and even more under that of Mahler, of whom he spoke in enthusiastic terms. He had also been influenced, in a measure, by Debussy, and had noticed with interest, in Bartók's early piano pieces—the only works of this composer which he then knew—features of idiom not dissimilar to devices which he himself was putting to use.

Novel devices, he continued, generally represent short

Schönberg amid his pupils

cuts aiming at sharpness and terseness of expression, but therein lurks a danger: a short cut is not always the best way to reach the goal. Generally speaking, no composer should resort to such devices unless he feels that they are the only possible means of uttering something which an inner necessity compels him to utter.

In his house I saw his paintings, too—some of them weird, nightmarish visions of monstrous faces, others, such as his portraits of himself, and a portrait of a lady, straightforward enough examples of methods not dissimilar to those of the so-called post-impressionists, but representing, at best, a moderate level of technique. One of the portraits of himself, by the way, was a back view of him taking a walk.

III

He invited me to attend the rehearsal of a chamber concert of his works on the next afternoon. To see him at work with the players and surrounded by his pupils, quiet, keen, and deferential, was a most interesting experience. The day after, I attended the concert, which took place at noon in a small hall. I heard for the first time his enigmatic little piano pieces Op. 19, his song-set *Das Buch der hängenden Gärten*, and the arrangement for double piano duet of three of the orchestral pieces that were to be played the same year in London. I listened carefully, but the music appealed to my mind rather than to my imagination; so that I was left perplexed. I did not feel irritated and bored as I did, years later, when listening for instance to his Quintet for wind instruments. Nor was I fascinated, as happened when I heard the same orchestral pieces played in their real form. But I felt no inclination to dismiss those works light heartedly. On the contrary, I promised myself to study them as soon as possible and with all possible care. At that concert I was introduced to

The Russian customs

Busoni, who sat in the auditorium. He told me that he was greatly interested in Schönberg's experiments.

Schönberg gave me a copy of his recently published *Handbook of Harmony*. I began reading this in the train between Berlin and Petrograd, and was so deeply fascinated (not by the technicalities, but by the philosophy of it—for it is besprinkled with considerations on music generally) that I started then and there scribbling an article which I finished in Petrograd, and which, translated into Russian, appeared soon after in the *Apollon*. And not long after returning to Paris, I delivered a first lecture on the result of my investigations of both Schönberg's admirable book and his, alas, very baffling music.

IV

On account of my projected short stay in Berlin, I had booked my trunk straight from Paris to Petrograd, expecting, in my innocence, to find it awaiting me at the station there. But not at all. It had been taken to the central customs depot. When I mentioned the fact to the friends I saw on my arrival, they shook their heads and seemed very sorry for me. However, to the depot I went—there was nothing else to be done. I explained my case to the porter at the gate. He pocketed his tip and called a man who took me to the proper department. I tipped him and handed my voucher to the man in charge (third tip). Presently an official came, took my voucher, led me to a warehouse, and left me there a while; then he reappeared followed by two porters carrying my trunk, and a magnificent officer in imposing uniform. I gave my key. At a sign from the officer, the official opened my trunk. At another sign, the trays were lifted and the contents inspected. A third sign, and the trays were replaced and the trunk closed. I tipped the porters and the official. They vanished. The officer did not. I looked at him, doubtfully raising a hand towards my waistcoat pocket.

The Russian customs

He remained erect and impassive, but, ever so slightly, crooked his hand. All risk of misunderstanding thus removed, more small silver passed. It was not a big tip—rather, maybe, an inadequate one considering his probable rank. It would hardly have paid for polish for all his braid and buttons. But he seemed perfectly satisfied, and bid me a kind good-bye. And there was nobody else to tip except a couple of men who appeared in time to carry my trunk to my sleigh. The whole affair, drive included, did not last much more than two hours and a half, and was carried out at a total cost of about five roubles, that is, half a guinea or so.

CHAPTER XXVI

Petrograd—A visit to Glazunof—César Cui—Ziloti—Gretchaninof, Liapunof, and a surfeit of pancakes—A manuscript of Mussorgsky revised by Balakiref—The home of the Rimsky-Korsakofs—Wonderful hospitality—Karatyghin and Mussorgsky's Salammbô—*Findeisen—Importance of his work as critic, historian, and editor—Young Russian composers—I am arraigned for my opinions on Tchaikowsky—Vain attempt to examine the* Boris Godunof *manuscripts—Street dialogues.*

I

At Petrograd I met with an extraordinarily cordial welcome from the people I knew, from those to whom I had letters of introduction, and from a great many others whom I just met. I cannot even attempt to mention them all, but the memory of their kindness and eagerness to give me a good time and assist me in fulfilling the purpose of my journey remains warm in my heart.

Glazunof, to whom I paid at the Conservatoire a call which I expected to be a simple visit of courtesy, lasting about five minutes, greeted me very quietly, but after a moment rose from his chair and said: "Now come and see the place." He took me round the whole building, had the Glinka Museum opened for me and the treasures in it displayed. And when at last I took leave, he invited me to attend in his company a concert conducted by Ziloti the same night.

At that concert I heard for the first time Ziloti play the piano. He played little preludes by Bach in a way that made me thirst to hear him every day in my life.

A visit to Glazunof

In the audience I saw a smart, erect, active-looking man with a grey beard, wearing a military uniform. I thought that he resembled the portraits I had seen of César Cui. But it could not be Cui, I told myself, because I knew that Cui was seventy-seven years old, and the man I was looking at appeared to be a full fifteen years younger. I asked Glazunof, who said, "Oh, it's Cui all right: come and be introduced," Cui cordially invited me to call on him the next morning.

During the interval, Glazunof, who had said he was going to take me round to Ziloti, was so beset by people that I had to go round alone and introduce myself. I sent in my card, and after greeting me Ziloti, peering at the card and at me alternately, asked me what he could do for me. I said that I should be grateful if he could grant me an appointment at his convenience to talk various things over (I had undertaken to call his attention to certain new French works not yet known in Russia). He replied: "I am very sorry: I'm terribly busy just now, and fear that I cannot find one free moment." So I bowed and took my leave.

II

The next morning I was called on the phone, and the following conversation took place:

"Is that Mr. Calvocoressi?"

"Yes."

"Ziloti speaking. I say, I'm terribly sorry. Last night I never realized you were *you*. Glazunof told me afterwards. I thought you were one of your pupils introducing himself with a card of yours. You see, when we Russians think of Mr. Calvocoressi, we always imagine him to be an elderly man with spectacles and a white beard. Now do come to see me. When you are free? Can you come to lunch? Can you come even earlier?"

And to lunch I came. Before the meal, we began talking of music—Russian and French. The conversation veered round to Scriabin's works, and he sharply rebuked me for my contemptuous attitude towards them. He produced a full score of *Prometheus* and said: "Now, here's an absolute masterpiece. Look at this, and this, and this. How can you say it's not all splendid? Here, read the score awhile and think things over. You'll get no lunch until you recant." Thereupon, asking to be excused a while, he walked out of the room and I started perusing the score. After a few minutes, all of a sudden I felt an affectionate kiss fall upon the baldest spot of my occiput. I gasped, rose, turned round, and found myself confronting a perfectly unknown female, who uttered a loud shriek of dismay. It was Ziloti's sister-in-law, who, seeing a bald crown above the back of his desk chair, had never imagined that the chair could be occupied by an intruder. The excitement created by the incident enabled me to get my lunch without having to prevaricate.

After a bout of chaff in which the whole family took part, there was more talk about music. Ziloti told me many things about Liszt, and could not believe me when I told him how neglected many of Liszt's finest works were in France and in England. Among contemporary French composers, Debussy, Ravel, and Roger-Ducasse interested him most. Like the majority of Russians, he did not seem to care for d'Indy and Fauré. Before I left, another meeting was arranged for; and many and pleasant were the hours which I spent in his home.

III

Another delightful host was Gretchaninof, some of whose songs I had been translating. It being the week preceding Lent, he invited me "na blin"—that is to say, to eat, according to custom, "blinyi". For the sake of the uninformed, let me explain that "blinyi" are small, thick buckwheat pancakes, served very hot. You spread one

Liapunof and a surfeit of pancakes

on your plate, put a pat of caviare on it, pour sour cream and melted butter over the caviare, roll the pancake up, eat it, swallow a mouthful of vodka, and then start afresh.

I thoroughly enjoyed the "blinyi", yielded without reluctance to my host's pressing invitations to eat plenty of them; and we sat at table, eating and chatting, until about half-past two, when, having an appointment with Liapunof at three, I rose, took my leave, and tumbled into a sleigh, hoping that the cold air would revive me a little. I arrived safely at Liapunof's house, was introduced to his wife and children, and five minutes later found myself shepherded into the dining-room where, to my amazement, the table was laid with a big dish of "blinyi" steaming in the centre. Vainly I tried to apologize, explaining what the position was. "Oh, but it is *maslenitsa* (carnival, literally 'butter week') and you *must* eat 'blinyi' with us!" they all cried. And I had to join them; but they were much distressed at my lack of appetite, and I had to gasp for mercy before they ceased plying me with good things.

Liapunof was an attractive man, grave and kind of mien, rather priestlike in aspect, with a bald head, a flowing black beard, a pale complexion and beautiful blue-grey eyes. He had much to tell me about the last years of Balakiref's life, his almost complete isolation in Russia, and the joy it had been for him to know that in other countries there were at least a few people interested in him and his music. He showed me some precious manuscripts, which he pulled unconcernedly out of a wooden chest beside the piano: some of Balakiref's, then a draft full score of Mussorgsky's *Night on the Bare Mountain*. I do not know which of the three versions of this tone-poem which Mussorgsky wrote at different times it was. The manuscript, a fairly thick book in black boards, was covered with notes in blue pencil, with erasures and alterations of all sorts in Balakiref's hand: "bad"; "suppress";

Dimitri Stassof

"needs rewriting"; "carry back to previous section" were among the remarks I read. So that had this version appeared with Balakiref's emendations, we should have had another "official" text of the *Night on the Bare Mountain* as widely different from Mussorgsky's actual composition as the version long current, which was a revision by Rimsky-Korsakof. I longed to study the manuscript then and there, but there was no time that day, and no other opportunity arose. Now that the genuine text of the tone-poem is published (in Professor Lamm's edition, at Moscow) everybody can see how little of it was known until 1932.

IV

The following Sunday, Liapunof took me to hear some fine church-singing, and afterwards to the Alexandre-Nevsky cemetery to see Balakiref's tomb. There was no monument on it yet. I heard later that Liapunof and Alexandre Tanéief, another composer friend of the departed master, had had great trouble in collecting, by means of a subscription, the needful funds for the erection of one. On the bare earth a canvas tent was spread, protecting a little mound covered with green boughs of fir. A few steps farther stood the graves of Glinka, Mussorgsky, and Borodin. They were covered deep with snow; but of the earth on Balakiref's grave I brought back a few particles.

The same evening Liapunof took me to the house of Dimitri Stassof, the brother of the famous critic Vladimir Stassof, and he himself a keen and well-informed music-lover. We arrived late and, hearing that music was being played, remained waiting at the door of the flat until the piece—a piano arrangement of Liszt's *Hamlet*—was finished. As soon as the greetings were over, Stassof shouted to me: "You heard what was being played? Wasn't it fine? Do you know what it was? It was something by

My visit to César Cui

Tchaikowsky, the Tchaikowsky you so dislike!" I did not like having to spoil his little joke, but I felt I had to assure him that I knew Liszt's *Hamlet* well enough to recognize it even from behind a closed door. "Molodetz!" he exclaimed (the Russian equivalent of "good egg"); and the conversation veered round to other topics. But this was only a foretaste of the onslaughts, playful or earnest, that were to be made on me during my stay on account of my disparaging attitude to Tchaikowsky's music.

V

My visit to César Cui was marked by an amusing incident, when, after inviting me to take a seat, he offered me a cigarette, which I accepted and lit. I had barely drawn a couple of puffs when at the far end of the big room in which we were a door opened and an angry male voice yelled: "Who in hell is smoking?" Whereupon the door closed with a bang. Of course, Cui and I carried on as if nothing had happened, but, surmising that tobacco smoke might be bad for him, I took the hint so gently given by the anonymous voice and disposed of my cigarette surreptitiously.

On music generally, and on his colleagues in the heroic days of the past, Cui had little of interest to say. He was full of a musical lampoon he had just composed. "I've been writing a parody of Debussy's music," he told me. "I've entitled it *l'après-midi d'un faune . . . qui lit son journal*. Funny, isn't it? *Qui lit son journal!*" All I could do was to utter, by way of reply, some monosyllabic grunt or other; fortunately, he was enjoying his own joke so heartily that he did not notice my lack of enthusiasm. And while he went on laughing, I remembered that long before he had acquired notoriety of a kind by writing a lampoon on Wagner entitled *Lohengrin, or Curiosity Punished*.

I was no great admirer of Cui's music, nor of the part

Findeisen

played by him in the history of the group (usually, and very inappropriately, called the "Five") around Balakiref —the group of which Rimsky-Korsakof had been the youngest member. And yet I felt that I ought to have been thrilled by this meeting with a man who had known Balakiref, Borodin, and Mussorgsky in their youth and after, had closely followed their early activities, and had championed them lustily, although in an erratic, prejudiced, and unreliable way. I did not know, then, how badly he had treated Mussorgsky in his articles on *Boris Godunof*. I especially hoped that he would be able to tell me things about Mussorgsky; but in this respect I was disappointed. Indeed, of all the people I met who had known Mussorgsky, not one contributed a typical recollection to my slender stock of information on the composer about whom I was so wishful to know more.

VI

Liadof I was unable to meet, because he was at that time too ill to receive visitors.

At the Rimsky-Korsakofs' house I found a particularly delightful welcome. There I met Findeisen, Karatyghin, and Ossowsky, the critics; Bielsky, the librettist of Rimsky-Korsakof's *Golden Cockerel*, and many other interesting people. A chain of invitations ensued. People would come to me and say: "Mr. Calvocoressi, to-morrow you are lunching with X—— and dining with Y——; on Wednesday you are lunching with Z—— and attending such-and-such a concert in the evening; but we believe that on Thursday you are free, and we should be glad if you can come to our place." Everybody seemed to know exactly what my future movements were to be, and to have calculated to a nicety the time for an invitation which I should be able to accept. I felt absolutely overwhelmed by all this kindness.

Karatyghin, a critic whose work on Mussorgsky and

Importance of his work as critic, historian and editor
other Russian composers had won him a deserved reputation, had just finished setting in order all that Mussorgsky had written of his early lyric drama *Salammbô*. I heard several scenes of this at his house, he playing the piano and an excellent singer, Mrs. Sakhnovskaya, singing the title-part. I was at last learning something really new about Mussorgsky's early achievements—for of *Salammbô* little was known except by hearsay. But, as the result of Karatyghin's labour was shortly to be published, I did not think it worth while to take any notes then and there. I regretted it afterwards, for, on account of the war, the publication was cut short after only one scene had appeared. Karatyghin died a few years later; and to this day the whole of what exists of *Salammbô* is not available for study.

VII

My meetings with Findeisen, the editor of the *Russian Musical Gazette*, resulted in a piece of exceptionally good fortune for me. The work, and even the name, of this very erudite and industrious scholar and journalist are not sufficiently known outside Russia. For years his *Gazette* was the only Russian periodical to keep pace with musical developments in Russia and abroad and to provide, besides useful information, stimulating comments on the life and work of many composers. A complete file of it, were it procurable, would be worth its weight in gold to students of Russian music; and his books and collected editions of the correspondence of Glinka and of Dargomyjsky, compiled many years ago, remain to this day indispensable as works of reference.

I called on him, we talked music, exchanged information, and compared notes. I told him that one of my objects was to collect documents on Russian music, and asked him for a few suggestions as to what to procure and where to find it. "I'll think it over," he replied. "Come back in a couple of days' time." When I came back, he said: "I think I've found the way to help you: *only don't thank me*". And, pointing to a huge pile of books and papers in a corner of the room, he explained: "These may be of use to you. They're just a few duplicates I found in my library, and I shall be very glad if you will accept them."

The "few duplicates" even at first glance proved to be a priceless miscellany of books and periodicals and cuttings, old and recent; it included several years of the *Russian Musical Gazette*, and many other things that would have been practically impossible to trace, let alone procure, elsewhere. I was so taken aback that I very nearly complied with his preliminary injunction.

From that time on I kept in close touch with him: and now and then I was able to make some small return in kind—supplying him with documents and music from France. After the war, our relations were resumed. At my suggestion, he wrote the articles on Tchaikowsky's chamber music and on early Russian chamber music which are among the finest in Cobbett's *Encyclopedic Survey*; and, on the other hand, he continued to supply me with invaluable documents and information. His last book, a big history of Russian music, transcends by far any other work on the subject. It was barely published when the news came of his death, which distressed me deeply.

VIII

Among the younger composers whom I met at Petrograd were Steinberg, Senilof, and Prokofief. The former two were pupils of Rimsky-Korsakof, but beyond that had little in common. Steinberg, who lacked neither temperament nor individuality, was in the main moderate in tendency, and classically inclined. In his second Symphony, which he showed me, I found much that I liked. He told me that he was at work on an oratorio, *Heaven*

Young Russian composers

and Earth, on a poem by Bielsky which Rimsky-Korsakof had intended to set—actually writing down nothing but a few themes which Steinberg was now using. The score was completed in 1916, but I have heard nothing of it since.

Senilof, who had studied in Germany before studying under Rimsky-Korsakof, was a shy and quiet man, thirty-seven years old, of whom a few people thought highly. He had written, besides many songs and minor instrumental works, three big tone-poems entitled *The Wild Geese*, *Pan*, and *The Scythians*. The first two of them had been played, but not so the third. None was ever published. Karatyghin informed me that they showed genuine dramatic qualities and a fine sense of structure, polyphony and orchestral colour. I found many of the songs insignificant, but one which I saw in manuscript, *The Bear-Cub's Lullaby* (it was published in 1913), struck me as instinct with rare originality and beauty. All told, I feel sure that those who knew his music best were right in thinking that he was only just finding himself after a long period of indecision, and that his progress would be well worth watching. But he was destined never to become better known. During the following years he composed little, and in 1920 he died. I cannot remember whether his *Scythians* was ever performed in Russia. Perhaps if the manuscript of this work, which I heard generally described as his best, still exists, it may help, some day, to rescue his name from oblivion.

Prokofief, in February, 1912, was a very cheerful and unassuming young fellow, nearing his twenty-first birthday. All the people around him felt that a bright future lay in store for him. He had not yet published anything of importance; but I heard, played on two pianos, his First Concerto, with which he had won the Rubinstein Prize in 1910; and I liked it for its brilliancy and raciness. At that time he, and also, let it be recorded, Steinberg, had

I am arraigned for my opinions on Tchaikowsky
already been marked by Diaghilef, Nouvel, and Nourok. But it is only in 1916 that a work by Steinberg (the ballet *The Metamorphoses*) and in 1921 that one by Prokofief (the ballet *Chout*) was added to Diaghilef's repertory.

IX

The last meeting to which I shall refer here was a rather amusing one, arranged to take place, if I remember right, at Bielsky's house with the special object of arraigning me for my wrong-headed attitude towards Tchaikowsky's music. I had been asked whether I would consent to sit in the dock, and of course had agreed to do so. Our host, Ossowsky, the Rimsky-Korsakofs, and others—a round dozen of them in all—were judges and jury, and I, alone against all, began to state my case. I explained that, with a very few exceptions, I did not like Tchaikowsky's music, but that I was quite ready to acknowledge that in my writings I might have made far less capital out of my reasons—good or bad—for disliking it had I not felt that its popularity stood in the way of due recognition of other Russian masters; many people, in Russia and abroad, seemed to think that his music was not only the finest Russian music but the only Russian music worth bothering about.

They partly conceded the point, and went into my reasons for holding Tchaikowsky's music cheap. And there, needless to say, I was found guilty by unanimous agreement. But it was after court and culprit had adjourned for refreshments that the really amusing part of the affair began. One of my quondam opponents drew me apart and said: "If you mean Tchaikowsky's operas, I incline to agree with you: but his symphonies, my dear fellow—his symphonies!" Then another came to me and said, in a low voice: "You may be more or less right as regards the symphonies—but what of his songs and chamber music?" A third confessed that he did not care for the

Attempt to examine "Boris Godunof" manuscripts

symphonies but proclaimed his love for the operas—and in the end I found myself getting back on the swings nearly all that I had lost on the roundabouts. Of course, my way of brushing aside Tchaikowsky's music *en bloc*, or very nearly, had been, as I acknowledged on that memorable occasion, far too summary. But even now, twenty years later, my feelings on the matter remain unchanged.

X

Remains to speak of my one big disappointment. All my efforts to gain access to the original full score of *Boris Godunof*, preserved in manuscript in the archives of the Imperial Theatres, remained fruitless. Either the building was temporarily closed for repairs, or the custodian absent —I do not quite remember what excuse was given.

I know by now that even if I had been allowed to study that manuscript, I should not have found out all about the genuine *Boris*, because many of the unpublished portions had been torn out of it and were, at the time, in the hands of various owners or in files on the shelves of other libraries. Nothing short of the alert ingenuity displayed, and the tremendous labour carried out, in later days, by Professor Lamm, could have solved the enigma of the genuine *Boris*. But at least I should have seen what Mussorgsky's much-decried scoring was like, and a few other things besides.

My disappointment was a little lessened by the hope I had of returning to Russia soon. The conviction that I should be able to do this was so strong that I did not even try to include Moscow in my itinerary; and of Petrograd, where I stayed the whole time of my visit, I saw comparatively little. I was so taken up by my meetings with musicians that I hardly visited the galleries and museums, and I saw nothing of the lighter—or, rather, more hectic —side of life in Petrograd. I did not even see "the Is-

Street dialogues

lands" with their famous night-restaurants, the Montmartre of the Russian capital.

For these and other reasons I shall not attempt to give any general impressions of Petrograd, although of course I carried away many. I doubt if any of them was in the least original. Certainly it was impossible not to feel that disaster was bound to come soon. You cannot, for instance, see an elderly, benevolent-looking gentleman break his walking stick on his sleigh-driver's back at three o'clock in the afternoon in the middle of the Nevsky Prospekt (the Bond Street of Petrograd)—nobody taking any notice of the incident, and the driver resignedly trying to amend whatever mistake had brought the chastisement on him—and not feel something of the kind.

What interested me most in the streets—apart from the beautiful aspect of the city, with its streets and roofs white with snow and its many glittering spires—was to hear the talk of the people. Once I was standing on the platform of a tramcar, next to three women, obviously from the provinces, who were excitedly expatiating on the vastness of Petrograd and the difficulty of finding one's way through the maze of its streets. The conductor came up to them with a request for fares. "Here are our fares," one of the women blurted out, "but-do-not-fail-to-warn-us-when-we-reach-such-and-such-a-street, for-here-we-have been-three-days-roving-about-and-always-losing-our-way-in-this-enormous-bewildering-city!" "Well, *golubushki*," the conductor retorted (*golubushki*, 'little doves', is a form of address which may be used with inferiors or equals but never with superiors), "you've only got to ask your way and you'll be told." "*Golubushki*, indeed!" the woman retorted haughtily, "are *we*, then, to be little doves for the likes of you?"

Another time a car, nearly full, arrived at a stopping-place where a crowd was waiting. After a few had got in, the conductor stopped the rush, and when some of the

Street dialogues

people protested, he tried to soothe them with the assurance that another car was close behind "with plenty of empty seats, ladies and gentlemen—seats for everybody". A woman in the crowd complained: "But I'm already an hour late for dinner!" "God help us!" the conductor exclaimed in turn. "How can one be an hour late for dinner?" And he moved aside to allow the woman in.

The Russian people, as a rule, are anything but laconic. Yet, once at least, I heard a tram-driver speak with admirable conciseness. On the front platform, a woman laden with parcels was fumbling with the folding door, trying to open the catch and at the same time to find the step. Over his shoulder the driver let fall the words: "*First* open, *then* get off!"

There was, also, the traditional haggling with sleigh-drivers. When you hailed one, you told him where you wanted to go and he named a price—always preposterous. You offered a third of that, he came down five kopeks (about twopence), you raised your bid by five, and eventually a bargain was struck, to the disappointment of other drivers waiting behind in the hope of getting a look in. Once a driver stuck at fifty-five kopeks, and I at fifty, which I knew was ample. At last, he accepted the fifty with a groan of despair. Soon I noticed all the other sleighs were outdistancing us, and I asked him: "It is impossible to go faster?" "You would not give fifty-five kopeks," he retorted, "and yet you show yourself exacting." He whipped his horse; and when he arrived, he said: "You would not give fifty-five kopeks, and yet I drove you fast." Some evil genius prompting me, I gave him the fifty-five kopeks. He swept me with a glance of withering contempt and drove away. Alas! at the eighteenth hole, I had lost the game.

CHAPTER XXVII

A parenthesis on my musical likes and dislikes—My impressions of Richard Strauss's music—The value of first impressions—Spontaneous, taught *and* caught *opinions—The critic and his readers.*

I

The telling of my story led me to refer to my loathing of Scriabin's music and of most—but not all—of Tchaikowsky's. And I shall have to mention, in conjunction with one particular experience of mine, my similar feeling with regard to Richard Strauss's orchestral works. It may be felt that all this, however lightly it is touched upon (or perhaps, precisely because I content myself with touching upon it as lightly as possible) is out of place in a book such as this. And, in a way, it is. To mention my musical loves was unavoidable; they are part and parcel of my story. They were the dominating influences which determined, not only my career, but a good many of my actions and subsequent adventures. But for them, I should have had no reason to write these memoirs, and no materials. My loathings, too, are part and parcel of my story, but only so far as they led to more or less noteworthy experiences. And this was not often the case.

As regards, for instance, living composers: if their music interested me, I strove to know more about it and them, to make it known, to get into contact with them if necessary. Often I came into contact with them in the natural course of things. But if on the contrary I felt sure that I had no good to say of their music, I naturally kept clear of them so far as possible.

Musical likes and dislikes

Again, there is no unfairness in just mentioning my admirations and leaving it at that. The worst that can ensue is that somebody or other may ask: "What does the fool find to admire in *that* stuff?" But to declare that I dislike and despise the music of So-and-so without even attempting to show good cause is unfair both to So-and-so—whom I seem to be brushing aside as unworthy of discussion; and to myself, by making me appear, maybe, a bigger fool than I might after having explained myself.

However, I shall not attempt to set forth the reasons I find for my feelings with regard to these three composers among many others. There is no room in this book for critical essays, disguised or not. And all I ask readers to take for granted is that I happen to feel thus and not otherwise—whether rightly or ill-advisedly is another question.

But perhaps, by way of a parenthesis, a chapter on what I have been able to observe as regards the evolution of my views, in proportion as I advanced along my path, will not be out of place. Indeed, I hope that a chapter of this kind, together with other confessions I make as to my own ideas and feelings, may serve as a complement to (or, at any rate, prove useful as a subject of comparison with) Mr. D. M. Rorke's *A Musical Pilgrim's Progress*—a little book which I consider most instructive.

Needless to point out that if a professional critic attempted to write a book of the same kind, his first difficulty would be to recapture, in view of accurately describing his "progress", his first impressions in all their particulars, and above all, their freshness. After years working upon them and testing them in all possible ways, he is, ninety-nine times out of a hundred, as unable to do this as a sculptor would be to recapture the various stages through which a block of stone has passed under his chisel before becoming a statue. I can recapture my first impressions of a few works—of the Toccata in Bach's

My impressions of Richard Strauss's music
sixth Partita, of certain movements in Beethoven's quartets, and certain portions of Wagner's lyric dramas, of Balakiref's *Tamara* and Mussorgsky's *Nursery* or *Dances of Death*, to name only a few of the things I heard in my earliest days as a music-lover; and not only recapture them, but live them afresh, in all their first strength and more. I can reconstruct, but not recapture, my first impressions of other works—for instance, of the final scene in Wagner's *Dusk of the Gods*. But others (be it, let us say, my irritation at Debussy's quartet or my bewildered delight at his *Prélude à l'après-midi d'un faune*), are past both recapturing and reconstruction, as are the stages through which I passed with regard to Haydn, Mozart, and Chopin. Moreover, a book of this sort from a professional critic's pen would necessarily be very long (since his duty is to leave no stone unturned when really wishful to make a point) and also very controversial. So that the remarks I offer here are likely to constitute my one and only attempt in that particular direction.

II

I began by speaking of my evolution. In most cases there has been no evolution. I was repelled from the outset by Tchaikowsky and Scriabin, exactly as I was attracted by Wagner and Bach; and I never changed. I was also repelled by Richard Strauss. Before having heard his *Domestica* I wrote, in disparagement of his art, a good many things which other people started saying after the *Domestica*. Was I right in my censures? Had I seen more clearly than those other people, or did I simply, while seeking to account for a thoroughly instinctive dislike, score, by a mere fluke, a forecast of the future? I cannot tell: most of the people who object to the *Domestica* and *Alpine Symphony* seem to continue to like *Ein Heldenleben* and *Zarathustra* and other works of Strauss upon which

My impressions of Richard Strauss's music

I based my impeachment. *Til Eulenspiegel* was, and still is, the only one to find grace with me.

Then one day, in 1907, I was sent to Brussels by the *Grande Revue* to attend the first performance there of *Salomé*. To my surprise this work impressed me deeply. I began my article by confessing that I had been strongly prejudiced against Strauss, and continued it in a vein of unqualified praise. A little later I heard *Salomé* in Paris. I found it just endurable. I was annoyed with myself, of course, but could no more help this second impression than the first. Then I heard *Salomé* a third time, and found I had no further use for it.

This, for me, was a new experience; and it has remained unique of its kind. As a rule, when I have changed my views, it has been definitely in the opposite direction—by adding to my loves and admirations. To go through the inverse process ought to have been most instructive, but I have never been able to determine what had happened. All I could be sure of was that I had been caught napping, but a lot of good that was: a critic always knows in advance that he should beware of being caught napping. Anyhow, I had the consolation of telling myself that my final opinion of *Salomé* was more in keeping with my general opinion of Strauss's art than my first impression had been. And, as luck would have it, I was not called upon to write up those Paris performances of *Salomé*: so that this is the first time the cat is out of the bag.

III

I have never had the experience of coming to detest or despise music which I had really and consistently loved. To have this happen (as Debussy with regard to Wagner) must be very painful, and far more so for a music-lover (that is what I consider myself, rightly or wrongly, despite the fact that I am a critic by profession—and I hope that what I have been telling of myself will have made it

Spontaneous, "taught", and "caught" opinions

clear that if I became a critic, it was solely on account of my loving music) than for a composer. A composer works towards his own ideals and may always hope to come close to them. The music-lover's ideals cannot materialize except by proxy—in the music of others. And, no matter how much he may find elsewhere, a lost ideal must leave him permanently the poorer, unless he loses it only because he has found in some music the very substance of which he had known, so far, only the shadow—as might happen to anybody acquainted only with Beethoven's imitators and suddenly discovering Beethoven. This, of course, does not mean that a capacity to realize the significance of Beethoven's music should lead to underrating any other music, or to despising any but that which is written in slavish and self-conscious imitation of Beethoven's. On the contrary, it should, in the very nature of things, increase our capacity to feel the spuriousness of the imitations (and, as a corollary, to open our eyes to Beethoven's own occasional weaknesses) and also to respond to genuine music of other kinds. I remember a lady friend of mine ending a conversation on Franck and Debussy and other contemporary composers with the remark: "Well, Beethoven is good enough for *me*!"—which made me wonder whether anybody who feels thus could be good enough for Beethoven.

To resume the thread: I have been spared, so far, the pangs of disenchantment. The nearest I came to that particular kind of experience (but it was not really near) was with Wagner's music. Eventually (after the war) I found that, while preserving all my admiration for it, I had ceased to long to hear or read most of it, and that it no longer haunted my mind. I ascertained, with rueful interest, that this had not happened simply because at one time I had thrown myself too thoroughly into Wagner's music and, in consequence, reached the saturation point. Many works which I learnt to love as early as Wagner's,

Spontaneous, "taught", and "caught" opinions which I have heard as often, and know backwards, are as needful to me to-day as they were in the 'nineties. I discovered more positive reasons, and reasons good enough to satisfy me that it meant no reversal of feeling, as in the case of *Salomé*. I was not even tending to regard as mere shadow that which had so long been, for me, genuine, wonderful substance. The substance was still there, and I had not appreciably changed: all in all, I was still looking for the same things as before in music. But my imagination was no longer taking in its stride all that it had taken in the past. Some of the reasons I allude to I found in the music, and some in myself. If ever I write a critical essay on Wagner, I shall refer to the former without ever mentioning the latter—they are nothing to build on for critical purposes. And their biographical interest is too slight for me to dwell on them here.

IV

Apart from this one partial instance, all the music I loved from the first I continue to love in exactly the same way, although maybe a little more discerningly. And all the music I disliked—by which I mean, actively disliked, for positive reasons, not merely because it irritated or bewildered me, or meant nothing to me, but because I felt that, understanding it perfectly, I saw through it[1]—I still

---

[1] It was only in 1930 or so, when already far advanced in the preparation of the second edition of my *Principles and Methods of Musical Criticism*, that I grasped the significance of this distinction. I am convinced that, when all is said and done, the critic—exactly as the music-lover pure and simple—has nothing but his feelings to go by, for better or for worse. Experience and suggestions from other people may modify these, of course. But, as a rule, experienced and sensitive music-lovers and critics may safely accept their first impressions as forecasts of their final judgment, provided these impressions are either enthusiasm or positive dislike coupled with a reasonable certainty of having seen through the music. Anger and bewilderment alone mean nothing. Nor does indifference, for it may be a mild form either of dislike or of bewilderment.

Spontaneous, "taught", and "caught" opinions

dislike. Maybe this means that I am pigheaded, or too much a creature of habit, or that I was endowed at the start with a certain amount of intuition and no more, with definite tastes which experience could not alter to any great extent.

I believe that in this respect I do not differ in kind, and differ but little in degree, from most other music-lovers. Perhaps my calling has rendered me just a trifle more conscious of being as I am. I think that practically all of us have intuitive dislikes as well as intuitive enthusiasms. Not all dislikes which run counter to general opinion are worth building upon, but some may be: it is the critic's business to find out, and then take his chance boldly.

I also feel sure that all of us have spontaneous admirations—which may have come suddenly or gradually—taught admirations, and admirations simply caught from the surrounding atmosphere. The same applies to our dislikes, of course. But if any one of us is capable of entertaining taught or caught dislikes, then there is something fundamentally wrong with him: for surely he must feel, while so doing, that he is not quite true to himself. It is not so easy to feel the same with regard to taught or caught admirations: one may have the impression that they correspond to something latent in one's own true self. And they often do. I have lost a few of mine (for instance, for some of the music written by not very inspired followers of César Franck, which at the time of my début was very much in fashion among some of my friends); but others—such as my tardy love for Haydn, Mozart, and Chopin—have become permanent and treasured assets.

On the other hand, neither objurgations nor sarcasms, nor the strongest arguments of musicians and writers whom I most respect and trust, have lessened my admiration for the much-criticized Liszt, or led me to change my mind as to Tchaikowsky, Scriabin, and Strauss. And yet,

Spontaneous, "taught", and "caught" opinions
I have always been eager to know and think over what others had to say on music of any kind.

V

The question of taught or caught enthusiasms became of paramount importance to me from the moment I started writing—and quite naturally, since after all a critic, however detached and indifferent to popularity he may be, hopes to exercise influence by his writings, and therefore should study *in anima vili* (that is, upon himself) the workings of influence by suggestion. So I have often tried to remember what befell me, in this respect, before and after I had become case-hardened. As it happens, I have plenty of materials to go by in this attempt at self-analysis. Mr. Rorke, in his progress, was guided and otherwise influenced exclusively by the music he heard or studied. Judging by his book, he never encountered or sought advice; nor did he make a practice of reading books on music. I did the very reverse, and not only from the moment when, having become a critic, I felt responsible to others and no longer to myself only. I read all the critical and historical writings I could get hold of: on Wagner, Ernst and Chamberlain and Wollzogen and so forth; on Bach, Spitta and Riemann and even Förkel (Schweitzer and Pirro's books were not yet written); on modern composers, what little I could find in musical journals. And when I began to move in musical circles—whose atmosphere, as I said in the first chapter of this book, was one not of interest only, but of excited partisanship—I had to hear all kinds of views about all manners of music.

Well, I tried since then to find out how all this had affected me; and the result of my efforts proved, on the whole, reassuring. Wagner, Bach, Balakiref, Borodin had found me unprepared and aroused my admiration. After having developed a dislike for Liszt on the strength of

Spontaneous, "taught", and "caught" opinions
some poor works of his, I admired the *Faust* and *Dante* symphonies without priming except for Fred Partington's enthusiastic forecasts. I loved d'Indy's *Fervaal* at first contact, although expecting, on the strength of all I had heard and read, to find it dry and empty. The enthusiasm of others had made me ready to admire César Franck's music long before I heard any of it; but my enthusiasm must have been genuine for all that, because it has not varied. I disliked Strauss forthwith, although I had heard and read much in his favour. He had many admirers in France, among them Romain Rolland; and his works did not come unheralded by preliminary boosting then any more than they do nowadays. Pierre d'Alheim certainly prepared me to admire and love Mussorgsky.

Most of Berlioz's music I heard round about 1904, when, on the occasion of the centenary of his birth, there was in France a revival of interest in it very similar to that which is taking place in England just now. I also had read almost as much about it as I had about Wagner's. By rights, I ought to have caught the fever of enthusiasm—which is half the battle in the case of a composer such as Berlioz, on the subject of whom everybody seems bound to feel passionately one way or the other. Indeed, I wished then, and have often wished since, that I could like his music better. There is nothing in it to which I object fundamentally. I just find most of it wanting, falling short of its goal. I think I know exactly why; and I have now and then stated my reasons in print, but always as moderately and objectively as I could. I have no desire to make a case against him; rather the reverse. And yet I know by now that I am unlikely to derive fresh experiences from his music.

VI

Dutifully following the advice of wiser judges, I studied the works of many composers of temporary or permanent

The critic and his readers

reputation without getting anything for my pains except the conviction that they would never mean anything to me; or sometimes, that I could make as good a case against them as had ever been made in their favour.

As regards modern music of the more difficult order, I often turned to other people's writings, and seldom found them helpful. I was greatly interested by what I read on Schönberg; but, after getting to know his music, I felt that none of those comments affected my impressions, or could go to the forming of my own opinion. In fact the only really favourable impression I have received, so far, from a work of Schönberg—the orchestral pieces Op. 16—remains, so far as I can make out, as unrelated to anything I have read as any other impression of mine has ever been. And I am quite sure that my indifference or aversion to the greater part of his output is as much my own, and is not final.

The important thing is that the writings calling attention to Schönberg's music led me to study it carefully, to give it every chance of working upon me—or, to put things less egotistically, to give myself every chance of accepting it. And this is all that criticism should be expected to do. Maybe my own articles in praise of certain "difficult" contemporary works will now and then do that much, even if in the end their conclusions are not endorsed. The reasons that a critic gives are good, in the last resort, only for people who, by virtue of their nature, are prepared to feel as he feels. If anyone reads violent diatribes of mine against Strauss's *Ein Heldenleben* or Tchaikowsky's first piano concerto or Scriabin's *Poème de l'Extase* and, hearing these works, is thrilled, he will think as poorly of me as I think of people who cannot see the beauties of Liszt's *Faust* and *Dante*, Balakiref's *Tamara* or Bartók's string quartets. If my diatribes deter readers from going to hear the works I run down, it will be a pity, but the risk has to be taken by me—and by them if they

The critic and his readers

choose. I should be the first to remind them, however, that no music-lover in his senses should pin his faith in the dicta of any one critic. But if they have only a taught or caught admiration for these works, and my writings induce them to think things out for themselves, they will be the gainers, and so shall I.

I may as well add that I find no pleasure in running down even the music which I despise most. I had far rather write on music I love. When I go for a work viciously, it is always because I think it may be exercising an influence great enough to stand in the way of the appreciation of better music, exactly as indulgence in bootleg brandy or grocer's port will spoil the palate for fine vintages. And with this confession, I bring this long parenthetical chapter to its close.

CHAPTER XXVIII

Arnold Bennett in Paris—His interest in music—His home at Fontainebleau—A poem by Meredith discussed—What I discovered in Bennett's diary—My preface to a privately printed booklet of his—Plans for opera libretti—Bennett at work and play—Questions of attire—Bennett on Boris Godunof.

I

I first met Arnold Bennett in 1903, at the house of Henry D. Davray, the literary critic, in Moret—a beautiful little town whose boundaries are, on one side, the river Loing and, on the other, the Forest of Fontainebleau. He lived at that time in a small flat in the Rue de Vintimille, Paris. When he heard that music was my job, he invited me to come and see him. When I called, one of the first things he did, besides asking me a hundred and one questions about music and musicians, was to suggest our playing piano duets. He had no technique to speak of, but played adroitly enough and intelligently—he was, all told, far better at duets than I.

His musical library consisted almost exclusively of transcriptions of classical orchestral works, at which he would peg away with great zest. Of contemporary music he knew little, apart from Richard Strauss. Modern French and Russian music were unknown quantities to him, but he eagerly drank in all I told him about them; and he soon procured a quantity of music by the composers whom I had particularly recommended. Whenever I entered his flat, I was sure to be dragged to the piano—for, strange to say, his first experience of duet-playing with me had not discouraged him. The first book of his which he gave me to read was *Sacred and Profane Love*. He asked me my impressions of it, and I confessed that I did not care for it. He did not seem surprised. "Yes," he said, "I know. People, as a rule, don't like it. They're wrong: it's a very good book; and I am going to publish a new edition with a preface which will make this clear."

A little later he moved to a bigger flat in the Rue d'Aumale, and used to spend a good part of the year at Moret, where I often went to spend a few days with him. We talked of music not a little, and of books a great deal; indeed, from then on until 1914, I drew as freely on his extensive knowledge of literature as he on whatever knowledge I had of things musical.

II

We often discussed the works of Russian authors. But of our talks on this subject, as I remember them, the one point worth recording here is that he did not respond much to Russian poetry—the short poems especially struck him as unfinished, fragmentary. No argument of mine could make him reconsider this verdict.

I availed myself of an early opportunity to bring him into contact with Ravel and most of the members of our little circle. When we developed the habit of spending our Sunday evenings at the Godebski's house, he was often to be met there.

After his marriage, he took a house at Fontainebleau. Thither he transferred his library; and, under his guidance, I was able greatly to increase my knowledge of contemporary English literature—a knowledge which, before that, did not go far beyond Hardy, Kipling, Wells, Meredith, and a few things of Conrad's; apart, of course, from Bennett's own books, which I always read as soon as they appeared. I gratefully remember his many useful sugges-

What I discovered in Bennett's diary

tions to me; and I feel specially indebted to him for having called my attention to George Bourne's admirable *Bettesworth* books.

Once, we had a great argument about Meredith's poems, which I declared contained many obscurities, whereas he contended that they were perfectly clear and that I was merely revealing the shortcomings of my knowledge of the English language. I got hold of the poems, and, hitting upon *The Lesson of Grief*, asked him to explain the first stanza:

> Not ere the bitter herb we taste,
> Which ages thought of happy times,
> To plant us in a weeping waste,
> Rings with our fellows this one heart
>   Accordant chimes.

"Why, certainly," he retorted. He grabbed the book, glanced at the passage, opened his mouth, then closed it again, knit his brows, and muttered: "Mm, yes . . . what does it mean?" And then, O glee, I, who was looking over his shoulders while he stood pondering, suddenly saw light, and was able to parse the lines first. He had to agree that perhaps they were, after all, a little involved. Of course, if I did score off him on this occasion, it was because I had happened to catch his mind napping. But we were always trying to score off one another; and, needless to say, he usually gained the advantage over me—even when French, and not English, literature was the subject of our discussions.

III

One fine day I noticed, on a shelf of his library, a set of ten or twelve beautifully bound little manuscript volumes—his diary. I asked leave to dip into it, and his reply was: "You may, but I warn you that it is at your own peril"—a reply which, he told me, he uniformly gave

My preface to a privately printed booklet
to such requests. I soon found out that there were good reasons for his so doing.

I had sometimes told him stories quite unfit for publication—not smoking-room stories, but accounts of actual happenings which had chanced to come to my knowledge and which I thought singular enough to be of interest to him. To my horror, I encountered in the diary a long paragraph, beginning with the words, "This afternoon Calvo said . . ." and setting forth one story (a particularly strange, almost nightmarish one) in all its details. I remonstrated, and he retorted with a grin: "Calvo, people who tell me stories always do so at their own peril"—thereby closing for ever, had he but known it, one source of exclusive documentation. Anyhow, I had the consolation of feeling quite sure that, come what might, this particular portion of his diary would never be published.

IV

It is to the existence of that diary that I owe, at least in a measure, the privilege of being one of the very few people to whose lot it has fallen to write a preface for a book by Bennett. He conceived the delightful idea of having little books printed, under the title, *Things that have interested me*, specially for distribution to his friends at Christmas. The contents consisted of excerpts from the diary and the edition was limited to one hundred numbered and signed copies.

He paid me the unexpected compliment of inviting me to contribute a preface to one of the series—of which three in all appeared—in 1907, 1908, and 1909, I think. Rather to my mortification, but very wisely—for I had practically no experience of writing in English—he stipulated that the preface should be in French. "Write it just as you like," he added. "Don't be afraid of going for me if you wish to." One of the ways in which I availed myself of the permission consisted in referring to his practice

Plans for opera libretti

of including unprintable stories in his diary. I did this in a few colourless words, hoping that he would either appreciate the tactfulness in tactlessness of my little revenge, or be lured into protest—when of course I should have had him on toast. But, alas! In alluding to those stories, I had used the designation "Kryptadia"(quite a current one on the Continent, although used mainly by students of folklore and booksellers), and this conveyed nothing to Bennett—was, in fact (if I may be forgiven the mild pun) doubly Greek to him. So when reading my manuscript, instead of spontaneously reacting to the passage, he raised his eyebrows, and asked me plaintively: "Calvo, what does it all mean?"

V

It was I who first turned his thoughts (but, unfortunately, without practical results) towards writing an opera libretto. Florent Schmitt had expressed a longing to compose an opera after Shakespeare's *Anthony and Cleopatra*. I suggested to him that I could prepare a libretto in French for him with Bennett's aid, and the notion pleased him greatly. Bennett willingly contributed a whole plan for the adaptation; and my share of the work was already far advanced when Schmitt declared that, all things considered, he did not feel like writing an opera, though he wrote incidental music for the play some years later.

When Ravel told me of his idea for a *Don Quixote*, I again approached Bennett and explained to him what Ravel's requirements were; and again he expressed his readiness. But Ravel, as I have said in another chapter, told me that he was decided, if he ever did tackle the subject of *Don Quixote*, to write his libretto himself.

VI

When at Fontainebleau, Bennett used to rise at 5 a.m.,

Questions of attire

go for a long solitary walk "to think things out", and start writing at about seven. At nine or so, over breakfast, he would proclaim that he had written two thousand, or two thousand five hundred words, or whatever the figure was—seldom a smaller one, so far as I can remember. At that point, his work for the day was finished—that is to say, his work at the book he happened to be writing. Later in the morning, and in the afternoon, when he was not engaged in reading, or in writing letters or articles, he was always ready for another walk, no longer solitary, or for some mild form of diversion such as hunting in the forest for fungi, of which his wife knew many edible varieties. He devoted a good deal of time to turning out water-colour drawings—mostly aspects of the rooms in his house, which were prettily furnished in Empire style.

He devoted to questions of attire the meticulous care to which, in post-war years, the "Society Gossip" columns of several London newspapers often paid tribute. One winter day (he had just come back from England, and was staying at a fashionable hotel, Place Vendôme) he called my attention to the brown boots he was wearing, and asked: "Don't you think they're rather nice?" I, who was always on the watch for opportunities to get even with him in the matter of leg-pulling, replied: "They are nice, certainly: but brown boots are not worn in Paris during the winter months." This disconcerted him a little, and he turned to his wife, who confirmed my assertion. For quite twenty minutes after that, he evinced a tendency to keep his feet well under his chair.

Then there was the time when he appeared with a beautiful waistcoat made of a thick, soft cloth, deep crimson in colour. He invited me to admire it, and that time I uttered no discordant note: on the contrary I was so favourably impressed that a few days later, seeing a similar cloth in a tailor's shop-window, I rushed into the shop, and in turn became the proud owner of a beautiful crimson waistcoat.

There also came a moment when he was longing to have a tie similar to one which he had seen worn by Albert Roussel, a big floating bow of the kind called "Lavallière", made of some kind of dull black silk net—"grenadine" I think the material was called. I had the luck to find one in a Paris shop, and I bought it for him, to his great delight.

VII

In 1908, when Mussorgsky's *Boris Godunof* was given at the Opéra, I was eager for him and his wife to attend a performance. He began by declining, and I made a special journey to Fontainebleau in order to persuade him. He remained a long time reluctant, because it meant, he declared "wasting" (how I writhed under the word!) quite twenty-four hours, besides the bother of spending a night at a Paris hotel. But I pressed him so hard that at last he grumbled: "Well, I suppose we shall have to humour you." And they came. After the performance, I joined them for supper at the Café Napolitain, and he sang a very different song. He was bubbling with enthusiasm. He said: "Sorry I had to be dragged, Calvo. But really, however highly I think of your views on music, I thought that you were just fussing over one of your Russians as usual. I simply couldn't believe that one of the world's masterpieces had existed for nearly thirty-five years without anybody but a handful of specialists being aware of it." But even so he got a bit of his own back for having been dragged away from his beloved Fontainebleau, by chaffing me mercilessly on the highly official aspect I had worn when coming down "in solitary grandeur" the steps of the *Grand Escalier* of the Opéra, just before the opening of the gates behind which he and his wife were waiting—and watching me. After that,

Bennett on Boris Godunof

however, he never declined my invitations to attend performances of the Russian opera or ballet.

During the war, I did not see him at all, although I had, in connection with Russia, to do some work for the Ministry of Information, of which he was in charge. After the war I saw very little of him despite the attempts which I made, on various occasions, to revert to our former intimacy. We met at concerts now and then, exchanged nods, or maybe a word or two, and that was all. There were, I suppose, many calls upon his time; and I certainly had my hands full with the task of adjusting my work not only to post-war conditions, but to conditions in England, where I had never lived before.

CHAPTER XXIX

*Criticism—My meditations on the vocabulary of my craft—
The effect of a misused word—My lectures on "programme"
music and criticism—A course on contemporary music—
First Paris performance of a Bartók quartet—A perplexed
board—A would-be critic checked in his career—A handicapped music-lover—My books on Musical Taste and on
Criticism.*

I

I had never planned to set up as a teacher of criticism, either in writing or by word of mouth. At the time I began the investigations which eventually led to my being lured into so doing, the idea was practically unheard of. Alone, so far as I know, the Director of the Berlin *Seminar für Musik* had organized a musical-criticism class at that institution: this initiative of his had not been noticed abroad, and it had nothing to do with starting me on my track.

Looking backwards, I can see that it all originated in the merest of flukes. There was in Paris a dealer in music and books on music, Costa-Borgnia by name, who was also a violinist and a well-informed music-lover. While inspecting the contents of his shelves, one could chat with him on musical topics of all kinds. One day I asked him whether he knew Ravel's String Quartet (this was in 1904, shortly after the first performance). He replied that he did, and remarked: "C'est de la musique descriptive." I offered no comment; but, walking home along the Seine embankment, I started asking myself what reasons or pretexts could have led him to apply so in-

My meditations on the vocabulary of my craft appropriate an epithet to the Quartet in question. I remembered how often I had caught critics in the act of using, for purposes of praise or detraction, terms which, while seeming quite definite, were given either a meaning different from that in which other critics used them, or no clear meaning at all. And of course, as soon as this notion had begun to run in my head, I discovered that I too had often been guilty of the same practice; so, it became obvious to me that the first thing critics should learn was to ascertain, and make clear to their readers, the exact meaning they gave to the terms they used.

II

These meditations of mine gave birth to the leading idea of the lectures on programme-music which I delivered in 1907 at the Ecole des Hautes Etudes Sociales. I, who so wholeheartedly loved the *programme* or *descriptive* music of Liszt, the Russians, d'Indy, Debussy, and Ravel—to name only those few—felt sure that I had found the joint in the armour of the people who brushed aside *programme* music with the allegation that it was of an inferior type. I had seen that no two writers, whether they approved or disapproved, in principle, of *programme*, music, gave the same definition of it, or saw any difference between the various types lumped together under the definition they gave. For instance, nobody had ever thought of drawing a distinction between music inspired by one single poetic or picturesque or dramatic idea— which idea may influence the character of the music, but not its form—and music inspired by an actual *programme* or succession of such data, which would affect both character and form. Then, all these writers took it for granted that *programme* or *descriptive* music must needs be something different, in some way or other, from *pure* music, and that necessarily the composer's object in writing it was to suggest the *programme* to listeners—to make them

The effect of a misused word

aware of the exact moment when, in the story, the spinning-wheel begins to revolve, or the princess is chucked into the water. No doubt this is true enough of certain works by composers such as Kuhnau in olden times, or Richard Strauss in our own; but had the writers to whom I am referring defined their subject-matter, and the epithets they used with regard to it, less loosely, they would have realized at once that *programme* music never need be, and very seldom is, different in any essential respect from *pure* music, either in form or in substance, and that both should be listened to in exactly the same spirit, and must stand or fall by the same standards.

But the root of the trouble lay in the fact that there was also something wrong with the standards which those people, and many others with them, applied to *pure* music, and so a further confusion ensued. When my friend the music dealer said that Ravel's Quartet was *descriptive* music, he meant, simply, that it contained things which did not correspond to his private conception of music pure and simple, and had to be accounted for in some other way. Learned professors have committed the same kind of mistake in their books on programme music, and in other books too. It was a set of definitions capable of dispelling all ambiguity in debates on programme music that I set out to supply, long before starting to tackle the more general problem of the vocabulary of musical criticism.

III

No doubt all this is of very slight importance nowadays, except as regards the education of tyro music-lovers, because we are in a period of *pure*, abstract music; hardly any composer worth noticing turns his mind to the other kind (I am talking of instrumental music only, of course), and the older works of the *programme* or *descriptive* order have, more or less, fallen into place. But a quarter of a

My lectures on "programme" music and criticism
century ago there were still excellent reasons for wishing to deprive the antagonists of the new music of at least one weapon in their armoury. Readers who may be interested in the way I adopted of dealing with the matter will find my exposition of it in the columns of the *Musical Times* for 1913, and also in a forthcoming book of essays—or, if they do not mind hunting for it abroad, in the tenth volume of the *Encyclopédie Musicale du Conservatoire*. If I refer to the matter here, it is solely because this was the starting-point of my quest for some way of introducing method in the practice of musical criticism generally. I noticed with interest, by the way, that as late as 1929, no less an expert than Mr. T. S. Eliot, referring not to musical, but to literary criticism (which rests on a far firmer basis, has a far longer tradition to look back to, and whose very technique, apart from other questions, has long been an object of study and debate) remarked that "there is room for an experiment in criticism of a new kind, which will consist largely in a logical and dialectical study of the terms used." This is exactly the line which I tried to follow when, in 1909, the Director of the journalism section of the Paris Ecole des Hautes Etudes Sociales having asked Romain Rolland—then the Director of the music section—for a lecturer who could undertake to deal with musical criticism for the benefit of his students, Rolland suggested me.

These lectures of mine, although public and not for the students only, did not attract much notice. Indeed, the attendance was quite small, and only a few brief notices (but these most encouraging, I must say) appeared in the French Press.

IV

A year or so later, it occurred to me that it would be possible to give a practical sequel to this exposition of principles and methods, in the shape of lectures devoted

First Paris performance of a Bartók quartet
partly to the study of new works, partly to the study of the comments to which these were giving rise. Romain Rolland agreed, and the course became a regular feature of the year's curriculum.

It was great fun. Besides offering my own comments and comparing and discussing the comments of others, I was able, thanks to the ready cooperation of many players and singers, to give plenty of illustrations; and every year my lectures were marked by first Paris performances of quite a number of works—by Schönberg, Bartók, Kodály, Wellesz, Ornstein, Binenbaum, and Vaughan Williams among others.

One day, for instance, I received from Budapest a letter in which Waldbauer, the leader of the Hungarian Quartet, informed me that this Quartet was coming to Paris, and would very much like to play a Bartók Quartet at one of my lectures if possible. I immediately arranged for an extra lecture devoted to Bartók, and so it came to pass that the first Paris performance of his first String Quartet took place at the Ecole des Hautes Etudes Sociales.

This led to my getting acquainted, shortly afterwards, with Bartók. On his return from North Africa, where he had been collecting Arab music, he passed through Paris, and tried to find a publisher there for this collection. He came to see me, but unfortunately I was unable to offer a helpful suggestion.

V

My lectures on criticism led to my obtaining, under very amusing circumstances, a private pupil, who was sent to me by Pierre Aubry. Here is the beginning of the story as Aubry told it to me.

One afternoon, the board of the Schola Cantorum—Vincent d'Indy, Guilmant, Aubry and others—were engaged in a conference when the porter came into the

A would-be critic checked in his career

boardroom holding a card and wearing a puzzled look. "If you please, gentlemen," he said, "there is somebody out there who wishes to see the Director. I can't quite make out what he is after." He was told to show the visitor in, and a young man appeared, who asked diffidently: "Please do you give lessons in musical criticism?"

"What do you mean?" they exclaimed.

"Well, I want to become a musical critic, so I thought I'd like to learn . . . attend a class or something." Whereupon the Directors bit their lips and vainly struggled to maintain their composure. There was an explosion of laughter. When it had subsided, they looked at one another rather perplexedly. This idea of tuition for budding critics—which apparently had never occurred to any of them—was not so absurd after all. But what were they to do? They were rescued from their quandary by Pierre Aubry, who, remembering my exploits at the Ecole des Hautes Etudes Sociales, suggested that the candidate be sent to me. The motion was carried *nem. com.* and he called on me armed with an introduction from Aubry. He told me that he had attended my lectures, but wanted more direct tuition; so I undertook to give him private lessons.

These lessons took the following form: I analysed musical works for him, commenting on them as I went on; I made him read certain books and talk them over with me; and I sent him to certain concerts—chiefly to those at which new or little-known works, and works which I had not yet gone through with him, were performed—and asked him to write notices of these without having read notices by other people. Then, at the next lesson, I would take to pieces his notice, and others as well, analyse, compare, and show him how to trace judgments back to their sources. In short, I tried to teach him to think out things, and not merely to write them up.

I dearly wish I could record here that these lessons

A handicapped music lover

bore wonderful fruit, and that the recipient of them speedily rose to heights unexampled in the annals of musical criticism. But as a matter of fact, they ended abruptly at the end of three months or so, with a letter from him saying: "I am very sorry to have to inform you that I am compelled to discontinue my enjoyable lessons with you because I am getting married."

Thus once again it was forcibly brought home to me how impossible it is for a teacher of musical criticism to foresee all the obstacles that may lie in his pupils' path.

In a way, I was not sorry. It had been interesting to build up and test, experimentally, a practical method of teaching the craft on which my own interest and ambition centred, and it would have been equally interesting to see results; but I had begun to realize that my lessons were hardly likely to lead this particular pupil anywhere, and they took it out of me quite a lot. All told, however, I learnt a good deal from the work they had compelled me to do.

VI

It proved far easier to teach another pupil who came to me simply to learn the craft of building up and delivering lectures—primarily on music, but also, in the long run, on a variety of other subjects: one of them, I remember was a comparison between Loti's *Pêcheurs d'Islande* and Kipling's *Captains Courageous*. That kind of teaching, of course, did not teach *me* much; it had the merit, however, of affording a welcome relief from more arduous work.

But another really instructive experience was in store for me. One day a man called upon me and said: "I enjoy music more than anything else in the world. I know nothing whatever about it, and I feel that I could enjoy it ever so much more if I did know something. Do you think you could help me?"

After asking him a few questions, I told him that I

A handicapped music lover

could promise nothing, but thought it might be worth while having a try.

To decide how to set about it was no easy task. He was about thirty years of age. His ear and, so far as regarded music, his mind, were utterly untrained. He had no conscious musical memory whatever, and eventually proved unable to acquire even a rudimentary one. He was, moreover, so shy that in certain respects I never could quite make him out. But various points I was able to ascertain forthwith: he did love music, and enjoyed it in musicianly wise—it aroused in him no non-musical (or, as I prefer to call them, anti-musical) associations, no thoughts of premature burials or little cottages by the riverside or enigmas of the universe or Fate knocking at the door. Nor did it (I carefully made quite sure of the point) merely tickle his senses: it really stimulated his imagination, gave rise to eager, active enjoyment, to momentous though unformulated and almost subconscious inner experiences.

A particularly interesting point was that, contrary to what is to be observed with the immense majority of inexperienced and wholly impulsive music-lovers, he had neither all-embracing and indiscriminating, nor narrowly restricted sympathies. His likes were wide and catholic in range, and as definite as his dislikes. His instinct stood him in remarkably good stead; for the music that appealed to him was always of a kind which no experienced and sensitive judge would dream of calling shallow or meretricious. Nor could his preferences ever be accounted for by signs of a leaning towards certain particular qualities such as austerity or sensuousness, restraint or effusiveness, abstractness or poetic and dramatic suggestiveness, and, in modern music, boldness in innovation or adherence to established practice. In short he was, in more ways than one, very much what the ideal music-lover and—in theory—the ideal musical critic ought to be at the start.

A handicapped music lover

On the other hand, he was so utterly lacking in theoretical knowledge that I could not use, without having to explain it, a single technical term—not even words so simple as "chord", "arpeggio", "third", "octave", or "modulation"; and he never learnt to associate more than a few of these with the musical facts for which they stood. He certainly ought to have begun by studying at least the vocabulary of elementary theory; but he could not afford the time, and was, moreover, loth to do so. Technicalities not only bewildered him, but were repugnant to him.

According, I resolved to exclude from our plan of work not only these, but all generalizations and labels, however convenient they might have been under other circumstances; and relying upon the workings of his subconscious mind and memory, not to explain, but to make him feel, the significant relations upon which the value of music depends.

It would have been perfectly futile to talk to him of Sonata form or Rondo form: but, taking a Sonata or Symphony (and for choice, one which he would have an early opportunity of hearing) I could, at the piano, give him a chart of that work, call his attention to important points in it, invite his comments, and show him how his impressions could be extended, or corrected, or connected with one another. I took great pains never to run the risk of inducing him to believe that the significance of a musical work could be accounted for by mere technical considerations, by analysis, or by reference to rules or laws. And I always urged him not to bother about trying to remember themes or points of form, or watching for landmarks while listening, but on the contrary to let himself go and listen wholeheartedly. And when I offered such imaginative comments as corresponded to my own feeling, I never failed to remind him that these were intended only as possible stimuli to his own imagination, which might eventually work in an altogether different direction.

My books on Musical Taste and on Criticism
I had satisfied myself that far from unsettling him by its appearance of indefiniteness, this cautious policy served his purpose well, because he happened to be endowed with much of his own to go by.

He also was quick to perceive many of the musical facts which he could not learn to pigeonhole and label. He did not know, for instance, what a modulation was; but when one occurred, I found that he always felt a difference, and expressed it by speaking of a contrast of light and shade, rise and fall, or tension and relaxation. Or if while playing a piece I inserted something that did not belong to it (either extemporized bars, or portions of some other pieces), almost invariably he would detect it at once and say: "Là, ce n'est plus la même chose!"

I was longing to study his case thoroughly, with the help, if possible, of some expert psycho-physiologist. But the war came. In 1915 I received from him a post card in which he said: "In the trenches, I often remember my pleasant hours with you, and the musical joys I owe to them." So I had the satisfaction of knowing that my work had borne fruit.

VII

To myself this work proved very useful when, years later (in 1925) I wrote my little book, *Musical Taste and How to Form It*. This being a primer, and as short and simple as I could make it, I did not attempt to include in it views of my own or any form of imaginative comment on any particular musical work; but I tried hard to convince readers that musical enjoyment depends upon nothing but musical imagination, and to make it clear that no cut-and-dried recipes can act as substitutes for this—that indeed they may mislead instead of helping. I also pointed out that many of the suggestions offered in certain "Appreciation" books (such as descriptions of musical

My books on Musical Taste and on Criticism

works in terms of "stories" or anecdotes about composers) drew the pupils' attention away from the music instead of inviting them to concentrate upon it.

My book, I soon found out, displeased a number of "Appreciation" teachers. One, I remember, accused me of trying "to kill the Appreciation movement." I assured him that, on the contrary, I was trying to help it along to the best of my ability, and to make its course safer; and that I did not believe things to be so far gone that this should be a case of kill or cure. When, in 1931, the Music Educational Conference at Lausanne passed a resolution to the effect that the aim of the study of Musical Appreciation should be, first and foremost, to foster "the ability to hear music in its own terms, and not in terms of association with other experiences", I was glad to see that they, who certainly could not be suspected of trying to "kill the Appreciation Movement", thought exactly as I did.

But even so, there are ways and ways of dealing with music "in its own terms". One reviewer complained that in my *Musical Taste* I did not even "tell readers what to listen for in the music". He was quite right: it was the last thing I should have dreamt of doing. I might be able to tell a tyro what to listen for in a given piece of music. I do not mind doing the same kind of thing in critical writings, but I do not wish to do so for directly educational purposes except verbally, when I can ascertain the effect that my suggestions will have, and qualify or justify them if necessary. As for telling people what to listen for in music generally, it is quite another matter. I once heard a music teacher explain that he could make nothing of Schönberg's music, "because he could find neither a tonic nor a dominant in it." Obviously, he knew, with a vengeance, what to listen for. Systems of musical appreciation which not only fail actively to promote, but may, if narrowly interpreted, directly impede the development of

My books on Musical Taste and on Criticism
an unprejudiced attitude towards the music of to-day and that of to-morrow (and who could tell people "what to listen for" in the music of to-morrow?) stand in great need of improvement.

VIII

The point is even more important as regards the training of embryo critics; and indeed it was for that purpose that I first strove to make it clear. As I have said at the beginning of this book, the first thing I was asked to do when I embarked upon my career as a critic was to deal with new music; but this accidental circumstance really corresponded with my own desires. In fact, I have always made a point of devoting, if not the greater part of my work, at least the greater part of my writings, to music (not necessarily new) which I considered had not yet come into its own.

I have heard it said that this was by far the easier path. I have never asked myself, and I do not care, whether it is or not: but I doubt it. To rhapsodize about music which covers new ground is not more difficult than to rhapsodize over music that has already been the subject of investigation and also of rhapsodies. But if one attempts to tackle new music in earnest one has all the spadework to do; and as regards older music that has not won the favour of which one thinks it worthy, the very fact of its remaining overlooked or disparaged proves that obstacles do stand in the way—such is the case with the music of Mussorgsky, and, according to many excellent judges, with that of Berlioz.

It was, at first, for my own benefit only that I started on my quest of principles and methods which would render the task less difficult. The first impulse to coordinate results for the benefit of others was given me, as I have said, by Romain Rolland. The second I owe to

My books on Musical Taste and on Criticism
the late Charles Volkert, then the head of the firm of Augener's. In 1921 I mentioned to him that I had vague plans for a book on musical criticism. Much to my surprise, he urged me to write it at once, and offered me attractive terms for the publishing rights. A little later, he informed me that the Oxford University Press wished to acquire those rights, and generously offered to cancel my agreement with him if I concurred with his view that this would serve my interests better.

I accepted, and my book appeared in 1923. It runs practically on the same lines as my lectures of 1909 and after, but with one big difference. My early investigations had shown me that critical judgments fall into two categories: some are, or appear to be, statements of facts apart from any question of opinion, whereas others obviously are mere expressions of opinion. I thought I had found the key to the whole matter. But, carrying my analysis further, I came to the conclusion that the critic, whenever he points to a "fact" in the music, necessarily implies that the fact is significant, so that a judgment of "opinion" always lurks behind his judgments of "fact". So, in my *Principles and Methods of Musical Criticism*, I tried to show that the distinction was useful as a first step only, as a warning not to mistake points of opinion for points of fact. I am the last person in the world to believe in the "sensitized-plate" type of criticism; but I am convinced that it is only by an act of imagination (that is, by forming an "opinion") that a critic can usefully decide which facts in the music are significant. On the other hand, I noticed that while I was ascribing less and less importance to the distinction, other critics had come to believe in it even more than I had done in 1909.

However, I kept forging ahead in the same direction. I was greatly encouraged by the attention given to my book, and I wish to record my gratefulness for the trouble which my colleagues took to discuss my suggestions. In

My books on Musical Taste and on Criticism
fact, their comments proved so useful that I was able to prepare, for a second edition, fresh chapters in which I dealt more thoroughly with various difficult and debatable points.

CHAPTER XXX

How I came to be attracted by England—Early attempts at writing for the English public—First visits to England—Thomas Hamond—At the Royal Academy of Music—Professor Corder on French Taste—Vaughan Williams and Ravel—A music Congress in London—Bathing in the Serpentine in 1911.

I

Talking of these two books of mine has carried me far beyond the time when I settled in England. Remains to tell how this happened.

For many years I had been drawn closer to England. During my childhood I had been brought up almost exclusively on English books, and had been in contact with many English people (children and adults) met at Hyères, where we used to spend the winter, or at watering places during the summer. I had English governesses, and used to speak far more English than French—so much so that, apparently, at the age of five or six I spoke French with an English accent marked enough to cause much amusement around me (this was recounted to me by my mother, much later; but I remember, without help, that when I asked in French for a candlestick, I would insist on calling it "*Le bougie-bois*" and declared that this was bound to be the right name for it). England, from what I heard and read (especially in *Little Folks* and afterwards in the *Boy's Own Paper*, whose delivery in wrappers addressed to my own self was every month an event of paramount importance) seemed a wonderful land where children were allowed to go about on their own and keep pets and build

Early attempts at writing for the English public
huts and have picnics and adventures instead of being for ever held in leading strings as I and my Marseilles playmates were.

During my later school years, I came to have a number of English friends, among whom an altogether delightful one, Thomas Hamond, whom I first met in Auvergne, and who shared my taste for long rambles and hill climbs. Summer after summer we used to join forces, exploring craters and lava fields and fishing the Sioule; and although he was over thirty years my senior, never did I have a more congenial chum. He invited my mother and myself to his Norfolk home. She was unable to accept at the time; and it was only in 1902 (the year when, having become a musical critic, I felt a free man after a long period of bondage and uncertainty) that I came to England, as his guest, spending part of a wonderful month of May at his house in Swaffham and the remainder at that of his brother, Admiral Hamond, at Westacre.

I hardly saw London on this first visit to England. But afterwards I made many journeys to London in order to collect information on modern British music—in those days quite unknown on the Continent—and also to study the ground with the hope of finding outlets which I badly needed for my own work. My first articles in English had appeared, it will be remembered, in the Paris *Weekly Critical Review*. In 1905, John Shedlock, at that time the musical critic of the *Athenæum* and the editor of the *Monthly Musical Record*, came to Paris to read, at a meeting of the French section of the International Music Society, a paper on a Scarlatti manuscript. I told him my hopes and asked his advice; and he very kindly invited me to contribute to the *Monthly Musical Record*. I wrote a first article on modern French piano music—Debussy, Ravel, de Sévérac and so on. When it appeared, I was not pleased with it. I had not at all succeeded in doing what I wanted—partly, it seemed to me, because I was unable

Early attempts at writing for the English public
to think in English when writing in English (apart from any question as to the quality of the English), and partly because I had not tackled the subject from the English point of view. A critic, whether he knows it or not, always asks his readers to take a number of things for granted—things which are part of the culture, mode of thinking, and ordinary experiences of one country but not necessarily (and indeed very seldom) of another. Then, there is a question of tone. Nothing could be more different in tone and manner than articles on the same subject (even viewed from the same angle) by English, French, German, and Russian critics respectively. And, unless the right tone is struck, an article will lose much of its cogency as soon as it crosses a frontier. For these and other reasons, my article struck me as strangely different from those I was accustomed to read in the English musical press, and I decided to submit no further specimens until I could see my way about more clearly. I did write a second in 1907, on the occasion of Balakiref's seventieth birthday, but this was far less ambitious, and, I think, a little less inadequate.

II

I continued to work hard in view of future attempts; not only because of my need for more outlets, but because, from what I read and heard, I felt that England would be a favourable field for the very things I was most eager to do—in fact, the only possible field outside France. I was not yet in touch with Russia (from which, as I have told, I was to receive much encouragement); and Germany did not seem to know, or to wish to know anything about the modern French and Russian music which was my favourite subject of study. Indeed in 1906, Busoni having given in Berlin a series of concerts of modern French music, the torrent of indiscriminate abuse poured on d'Indy, Franck, and Debussy in the German Press was

At the Royal Academy of Music

enough to show that it would be superfluous to hope for outlets for articles on these composers in that country. And so far as I could find out, it would have been equally useless to come forth with articles on Mussorgsky, Balakiref, Borodin, or Rimsky-Korsakof. Germany seems to have discovered Mussorgsky round about 1922.

In England things seemed very different. Connoisseurs were developing an interest in the very music about which I wished to write. And as a subject upon which to write for France, British music, an unknown quantity, seemed far more attractive than the more or less known quantity, modern German.

In the task of improving my English, Bennett helped me a good deal, although he was chary of encouragement. "Of all non-English people I know, barring Joseph Conrad," he told me, "you are, after Marcel Schwob, the one who knows English best. In time you might learn to write quite good English, and even better English than that of many English writers: but you will never write as an English-born writer would. Not even Conrad has succeeded in doing it. There is hardly a page of his in which one does not encounter something which gives him away." This was in 1906, I think. I do not know whether, later, he changed his views on Conrad. Nor did I ever have an opportunity to find out what (if anything) he thought of my post-war work.

My first French article on English music was one on Elgar which appeared in 1905. When collecting materials for further articles, I was greatly helped by Theodore Holland, whom I had met in Paris, and who, as soon as he heard of my intentions, got busy on my behalf. He introduced me to musicians and publishers, and took me round to the Royal Academy of Music, where I met J. B. (now Sir John) McEwen, who showed me, among many other things, the new British works published in the Avison edition. This was my first introduction to the

Professor Corder on French taste

music of Arnold Bax, Benjamin Dale, York Bowen, and McEwen himself. He gave me much information, and kindly invited me to stay to lunch and meet his colleagues. Many musical subjects were touched upon during this lunch hour. And I was thoroughly enjoying myself when, across the table, Professor Frederick Corder shot at me the question: "And are the French still exclusively fond of light music?" Alas, I rose to the fly—not with a rush and splash, but enough to be lured away from the safe waters. I started talking—maybe a shade too eagerly —of Franck and d'Indy and Fauré and Debussy, of the Bach cult in France, of the interest in Monteverdi and Marc Antoine Charpentier, and of critics such as Romain Rolland, Henry Expert, and Pirro and Lionel de la Laurencie. When I had quite done, he half raised his head, uttered a semi-resigned, semi-dubious grunt, and relapsed into silence. But, naturally, someone came to the rescue with a remark or question, and the conversation drifted into other channels.

After lunch McEwen handed me over to Benjamin Dale and York Bowen. We were given a room with a piano and I had a delightful time talking music with them and hearing them play. They knew a lot about modern music, and were as eager to ask me questions as to answer mine. I often met them after that; but, to my great regret, found no opportunity to come across either of them after the war.

III

I also met Edwin Evans, who was already then a splendidly informed specialist on modern music. He gave me invaluable information on British music, and I contributed what small additions I could to his extensive knowledge of French and Russian music. In the course of one of the long conversations we had together, he mentioned that Vaughan Williams, who had recently come back from

Vaughan Williams and Ravel

Germany, was planning to go to Paris in order to work a while with some teacher who would help him to acquire additional practical experience and technical ease. He had thought of going to Vincent d'Indy, and Evans asked for my opinion. Despite my great admiration for d'Indy, it occurred to me that considering Vaughan Williams's special object—which was, I understood, to cast off the cramping influence of strict technical training under a German master—d'Indy's class at the Schola Cantorum might not quite fulfil requirements. I had no reason to feel sure that I was right on the point; but I had been witnessing the amazing results achieved by Ravel with Maurice Delage, and I knew quite well what his ideas on the teaching of composition were. So I did feel sure that he would be the very man for Vaughan Williams and said so. The idea struck Evans as novel, but not bad (I doubt whether six people could have been found in England to approve of it), and he asked me whether I would care to talk it over with Vaughan Williams.

This was done a day or two later over dinner at the Savage Club. I cannot recall the details of the conversation, but the upshot was that I promised to find out whether Ravel would be willing. I must have shown myself very eager to gain my point. Otherwise Edwin Evans would never have dared coolly to set down in print (as he did many years later) that when the whole thing had been fixed and Vaughan Williams came to Paris, I was at the Gare du Nord awaiting his arrival, so as to make quite sure that he would not, at the last minute, tell his taximan to drive him straight to the Schola Cantorum after all. This story is not true. If someone was at the Gare du Nord, it must have been some particularly subtle enemy of Ravel (or maybe, of myself) impersonating me in order to throw discredit upon the whole affair.

The letters that I received from Vaughan Williams during his stay in Paris (he had put up at an hotel bearing

A music Congress in London

the amazing designation Hôtel de l'Univers et du Portugal, which up till then I had thought could exist only as a skit on the improbable names which certain Continental hotels bear) show that my surmise proved correct. "Ravel," he wrote, "is exactly the man I was looking for. As far as I know my own faults, he hit on them exactly, and is telling me to do exactly what I half felt in my mind I ought to do—but it just wanted saying." And again: "I am getting a lot out of Ravel. Only I feel that ten years with him would teach me all I want."

IV

Another person to whom Holland introduced me was Alfred Percival Graves, the authority on Irish folk music. He asked me to lunch at his house near Windsor, told me lots of interesting things, took me to see Windsor Park, and brought me back for tea. Alas! After tea we started talking music. I gloated over the treasures in his library, time flew, and suddenly, to my dismay, I heard a voice saying: "Now, Mr. Calvocoressi, won't you have supper with us?" I poured forth apologies; I asked to be allowed to take my leave, but in vain. I was pressed to remain, and did so—firmly resolved not to start again on music after supper.

The worst thing is that a few years later, and again in England, I committed exactly the same sin. It was during the International Music Society Congress in 1911. I had been invited to lunch at the home of a very charming friend. After lunch, we started going through music, and tea was served before I had dreamt of looking at the clock. Even for so notoriously absent-minded a person as I am in certain matters, this is a terrible record.

Last, but not least, among the people whom I met, Dr. W. G. McNaught should be mentioned. He was most kind and helpful to me from the first, and for years afterwards. As soon as he became the editor of the *Musical*

British works in Paris

Times, he invited me to become a regular contributor to this paper, for which I have worked ever since except during the war.

V

As it happened, despite my ambitious plans and all the fuss I had made about collecting materials, I was not able to do much for British music in France or elsewhere. I wrote a few articles, I delivered a couple of lectures at the Ecole des Hautes Etudes Sociales and elsewhere. I helped, from France, Nouvel and Nourok to select a few works for performance at the Petrograd Contemporary Music Evenings, and that was about all. I had arranged (then or later, I cannot recall the exact date) for a series of big articles under the general heading *Musique et Musicologie Anglaises* in the monthly *S.I.M.* with its editor, Ecorcheville. But he changed his mind about this—he was rather liable to do such things—and only one or two of the projected set appeared. Then, in February 1906, the London Symphony Orchestra and Leeds Chorus had come to Paris, and the modern British works on the programmes of the concerts it gave (excerpts of Elgar's *King Olaf*, Stanford's *Irish Symphony* and *Requiem*, Parry's *Blest Pair of Sirens*, and minor things by Cowen, Mackenzie, and Sullivan) had created so unfavourable an impression that thenceforth none of the French conductors who sometimes consulted me on the subject of new works suitable for their programmes would consider doing an English work. They simply refused to believe that, on so important an occasion, the organizers could have failed to select the very best and most live of the contemporary British output.

A few years later when Guéritte, a French music-lover living in England, where he had done a tremendous lot to make modern French music known, started in Paris a

A music Congress in London

"British Concert Society", I was able to help him a little by advising, making certain moves, and lecturing at the Society's first concert. But the concerts, despite the genuine interest of the programmes and the performers' splendid quality (they were Mrs. Swinton, Myra Hess, and Lionel Tertis among others) attracted little attention; neither the Press nor the public supported Guéritte, and the Society vanished, never to reappear.

Other things—mainly the advent of Diaghilef and the increasing demands made upon my time by other work in connection with Russian music—prevented my pursuing my plans with regard to writing on British music.

For the same reasons my plans concerning contributions to English papers remained in abeyance until 1911. In 1908 or 1909, however, I made an effort, chiefly in order to prepare the way for Diaghilef's forthcoming Russian seasons in London. I offered the editor of a certain journal articles on the Russian Opera and Ballet. His reply (which I kept as a curio, but have mislaid) was that "these subjects could not be of the slightest interest to the British public."

However, I was not to be disappointed in my hope that my writings might find favour in England. My first lectures on the principles and methods of criticism marked I think, the turning point. As I have said, they had not created much of a sensation in Paris. Nor did they when —chiefly in order to secure copyright—I published a synopsis of them in a French periodical. But then, I was surprised and delighted to see the interest aroused by them in England. Although the journal in which the synopsis had appeared was not a very big one, everybody whom it might interest seemed to have read it. A whole column in *The Daily Telegraph*, and long articles by Arthur Hervey, Ernest Newman, and others, in the *Musical Times* and other papers, were devoted to stating and discussing my views. And when I came to London

A music Congress in London

to attend the International Music Society Congress, I found myself, to my surprise, in great request.

VI

The Congress turned out to be not only an interesting but a lively affair, from both the professional and the social points of view. Our hosts had done things on a huge scale, and they certainly succeeded in giving us a busy and a happy time.

The sectional meetings (devoted to debates and to the reading of papers) took place in the great hall of the University of London, partitioned into sections by screens which excluded sight but not sound, so that a general din formed a background to the proceedings in each particular compartment. The effect was more picturesque than satisfactory; and one day I heard one of my French colleagues say to the Secretary of the Congress, Dr. Charles Maclean: "Nous n'avions jusqu'ici que la polyphonie musicale; mais vous, Messieurs, vous nous avez donné la polyphonie musicologique." I was told, later, that Dr. Maclean thoroughly enjoyed it all, and went about remarking gleefully: "Isn't this a *lovely* muddle! I like it." Whether this was true I cannot tell. What I do know is that he was most active, obliging, and hospitable. Although kept very busy by his duties, he found time to take me round a good deal, and invited me to lunch or dine at several of the clubs to which he belonged. He told me many amusing stories about the London musical world.

The paper I read was entitled, *Psycho-physiology the true road to progress in musical æsthetics*. When I read, in a Press notice, that surely I must have done it on purpose, I could not help thinking: "Serves me jolly well right!" But I had not done it on purpose. For years I had been reading treatises and monographs on musical æsthetics, and had found ninety-nine per cent of what I

A music Congress in London

read bitterly disappointing. On the other hand the research work of psycho-physiologists such as Féré, Dogiel, Vaschide, and Lahy among others, had filled me with eager anticipations. Unfortunately, what most of these people had to say about music struck me as no less preposterous than a musical critic's utterances on psycho-physiology would, no doubt, have appeared to them. Dr. Ingegnieros, for instance, in the course of a disquisition on musical genius and talent, selected as an example of "genius", Ambroise Thomas; and as one of "talent", Liszt. But I felt sure that a cooperation between specialists in musical matters and specialists in psycho-physiological investigation would prove fruitful—nothing more complicated lurked beneath the formidable title of my paper.

Since then, two and twenty years have elapsed, and, so far as I can see, psycho-physiology has done nothing of what I hoped for. And meanwhile, I reached the conclusion that it is not to that science, but to the branch of psychology pure and simple which deals with the imagination that we should turn when investigating the mysteries of musical æsthetics. But I could not foresee all this in 1911.

Among the people I met at the Congress were Percy Scholes and Barrett, then the musical editor of *The Morning Post*. Barrett asked me to become the Paris musical correspondent of this paper—a post I held until the outbreak of the war. Scholes invited me to contribute to his very useful little periodical *The Music Student*, and to lecture on modern music at the "Musicians' Holidays" which he organized. This led to my spending two very enjoyable holidays—one at Bideford, the other at Port Ballantrae. My mother came with me both times, and she too enjoyed herself heartily despite her handicap—Scholes and his wife proving most charming and thoughtful hosts.

Scholes also got me engaged, to my delight, to lecture

Bathing in the Serpentine in 1911

on French music at Oxford in the summer of 1913. He attended the lectures, and, knowing how wishful I was to amend my shortcomings as a lecturer in English, took the trouble to jot down all my mispronunciations and other errors. His notes, with which he presented me at the end of my fourth and last lecture, filled several sheets of foolscap.

VII

There is one memory of my visit to London in June, 1911, which I shall jot down "just in order to note" I shall say, in imitation of Bennett on the *Bal des Quat'z-Arts* "what bathing-time in Hyde Park was in 1911". I was staying in rooms near Marble Arch, and during Congress week had to cross Hyde Park three or four times a day, going to or coming from South Kensington. As often as not, there was a biggish crowd on the Hyde Park side of the bridge over the Serpentine. This bridge overlooked the unroofed enclosure in which women bathers undressed and dressed, and so loafers would stand there staring, and obey as slowly and reluctantly as possible a police constable's ever-repeated invitation to "Pass along, please!"

I told Arnold Bennett how very much that sight had amazed me. I also referred to the couples sprawling and cuddling on the grass in broad daylight. He said, "Oh, it's always like that in Hyde Park, and can be far worse," and proceeded graphically to describe various scenes he had witnessed there one August bank-holiday afternoon. I could hardly believe my ears. I do not know whether he recorded his observations in his diary—but I can remember his narrative word for word.

CHAPTER XXXI

My situation in 1914—Léon Vallas and the Revue Française de Musique—*The war—I join the British Intelligence —Results of studying Edgar Allan Poe—Code-picking— Examining candidates—My marriage.*

I

In 1913, I was commissioned to write two books in English: one on Russian music for Novello's, the other on modern French music for Methuen's. The war came before these were written, and after the war, for various reasons, I did not feel like tackling them afresh. Anyhow, these commissions, jointly with my regular work for the *Morning Post*, the *Musical Times*, and *Musical Record*, were more than I had ever hoped for when trying to find outlets in England. And I was looking forward to more engagements for lectures.

Meanwhile things had been happening in France too. A small job which I had been given in 1909 as musical critic to the fortnightly *Comœdia Illustré* had developed, thanks to the enterprising spirit of its proprietor and editor, Maurice de Brunoff, and his generous treatment of his collaborators, into a really good one from all points of view. Then, in 1913, an old friend of mine, Léon Vallas, who for years had been running a musical periodical (and a remarkably well-informed and live one) decided to transfer this to Paris and asked me to become its joint editor and manager.

Vallas is one of the most interesting members of my profession I have ever met. He was a doctor by profession; and, having small means of his own, gave up

Vallas and the "Revue Française de Musique"

practising medicine to become a professor, historian, critic, and editor. A shrewd observer, endowed with strong convictions and the saving grace of a keen sense of humour, he kept a close watch on the turmoil around d'Indy, Debussy, Ravel and others, now and then taking part in the fray dispassionately but to excellent purpose. The files of his *Revue Musicale de Lyon* reflect the musical France of the last decade or so of his century far more fully and faithfully than those of any other periodical. After the war, he published, for several years, a small, bright one-man journal, *La Nouvelle Revue Musicale*, whose contents consisted entirely of pithy summing-ups and crisp, generally merciless, judgments. And nobody else could have written the exhaustive, splendidly balanced, powerfully interesting book on Debussy's life and works which appeared, in French and English editions, a short time ago (January, 1933).

I had been, by request, one of the earliest contributors to the *Revue Musicale de Lyon*; and never did I respond so readily to an invitation to contribute unpaid articles (except, of course, in the case of the *Art Moderne* which gave me my start[1]). And I gladly agreed to join forces

---

[1] Bennett, in his journal, records a story I told him, which illustrates the evils of amateur journalism (by which I mean, journalism by people to whom seeing their name in print is sufficient reward) in France. But he did not remember it quite rightly. The truth is even funnier. A friend of mine (or rather, of my family) thought that he could make a little pocket-money by running a small periodical, partly financial, partly theatrical. He asked me to contribute paragraphs on music, and said that a number of his friends paid to have their articles printed in it, but that of course I should not be asked to pay. My reply was that, being a professional, I should have to be paid. After much haggling (for I did not wish to refuse his pressing request) we agreed upon a small fee payable half in cash, half in chocolate and bottled lager beer which he received as payment in kind for advertisements. The chocolate was quite good; the lager beer poor.

Since I have mentioned one lapse of memory on Bennett's part,

ETHEL, 1933
[*Elliott & Fry photograph*]

The war

with him in the matter of the *Revue Française de Musique*, as the periodical in its new form was to be named.

We made a splendid start—although I must confess our issues did not always appear at the fixed dates. Not only subscriptions, but also advertisement contracts (mainly from foreign music publishers) poured in readily. By way of advertising our review, Vallas organized a series of four *Conférences-Concerts de la Revue Musicale*, which took place in a big hall, and at which modern music ranging from Fauré to Ornstein and from Mussorgsky to Schönberg and Bartók was performed. My two lectures on this occasion were entitled: *Géographie Musicale de l'Europe*, a subject with which I had previously dealt, upon Vallas's invitation, at the Lyons Conservatoire.

II

So, all was well under way when the war broke out. Vallas took service as an army doctor. I offered my services to the French Government, but on account of my Greek nationality these were not accepted (according to French law, children born in France of non-French parents could, on coming of age, decide whether to accept French nationality or not; I had selected the latter course). I graduated as first-aid and stretcher bearer with the French Red Cross, but even so they refused to send me to the front.

I had various funny adventures in the course of my attempts to break through the barrier, though they did not strike me as funny at the time. I tried to see Cruppi, the War Minister, whom I had known for years. But he, of course, had other things to do, and I only gained access to his secretary's secretary. Discovering that there existed a department of the Ministère de la Guerre, entitled Field

---

I shall mention another. I was astonished to see that he, who knew Viñes so long and so well (Viñes was his guest in England as well as in France) should have spelt his name "Vignés" in his journal.

Result of studying Edgar Allan Poe

Hospital Organization, I went there with my certificate in my pocket, and, to my surprise, was forthwith admitted into the head's private office. He listened patiently to my explanations, gravely examined my certificate, and then said that it was gratifying for France, in her need and woe, to have friends such as myself, and that my feelings deserved the highest commendation. "But, Monsieur," he continued, "unfortunately I can do nothing in the matter. You see, this department's only duty is the sending out of supplies and stores."

And days flew by, and all my friends had enlisted or were being called up, and the rumble of the Marne guns reached us, and within three or four hundred yards of our house trenches were being hastily dug and trees felled. Then came a letter from Hamond, asking whether my mother and I would not care to come to Norfolk. This gave me an idea. I accepted the invitation (my mother preferred to stay in Paris) and with his readily granted help soon entered the British service, he and Lord Fitzmaurice (whom I had known in Auvergne too—I still have a snapshot, taken by Hamond of him, Major [afterwards Lieutenant-General Sir William] Pulteney, and myself on the top of the Puy Chopine, near Royat) being my sponsors. This was the first step towards my making England my home and becoming naturalized.

III

My languages, of course, were my chief asset. But it is incredible how everything that one happened to have learnt could turn out to be useful in wartime. For instance, I had always been greatly interested in Edgar Allan Poe and especially in his critical writings, which I had studied with care, and found as helpful to my own formation as those of any other critic I have ever read. The only articles I have written, and the only lectures I have delivered, on non-musical subjects, were on Edgar Allan

Code-picking

Poe (chiefly on the occasion of his centenary). And the last piece of work I finished before the war was a volume of translations into French of those tales of his which Baudelaire had not dealt with. This was to be the first of a series which Vallete, the editor of the *Mercure de France*, had agreed to publish. The following volumes were to include the critical essays, the letters, and so on. But a second one never came out.

Now, what chiefly interested me was the question of the workings of Poe's mind (I had not come across J. M. Robertson's admirable chapter on this point in his *Essays towards a Critical Method*). He had an uncanny gift for deciphering cryptograms, which enabled him to carry on sensational journalistic "stunts" in American magazines, solving all puzzles sent in by readers and afterwards publishing articles explaining how the thing was done. In order to study this aspect of his mind, I had gone into the subject of secret writing, and had learnt enough to be able to test Poe's theories and methods, and also to do some deciphering on my own. I sometimes practised on examples given in detective novels—most of them absurdly easy even when readers were told that the best Scotland Yard experts had pondered over them for weeks—and also on those which appeared in the "personal" columns of French dailies (later, perusing a new book by Rémy de Gourmont, I found that he too had indulged in this pastime, obtaining equally startling and revolting results as I had—his disclosures, I believe, led to cryptograms being banned from these columns.)

This working knowledge of cryptography (which I steadily strove to increase) served me in good stead. I did, in various departments, a fair amount of code work. But, so far as my experience goes, this was not carried out as described in the Press at the time. I remember a journalist's account of a visit to a "code department" in the course of which he was allowed to watch "a pale,

Examining candidates

scholarly-looking man with fiery eyes" intent on a piece of deciphering. After a time, he saw the man lay down his work and, with a sigh of relief, cut a fresh notch into an already much-dented penholder—the fate of another spy was sealed.

Once I had the good fortune to decipher a really exciting message; and as it happened, the code being a new one, I had to indite explanations for the benefit of the people who were to give the communication its sequel. But when I asked (in the hope, I must confess, of learning more about the matter) whether my explanations had been adequate, all the reply I received was: "Oh, yes, it's quite all right. We're following it up"—and small wonder!

That such knowledge should prove useful is only natural. But I was amused to find that even casually acquired information on odd subjects could come in handy —in my case, for instance, a very slight and rusty knowledge of mineralogy. Once I was asked to translate a batch of papers referring to certain ores. Shortly after delivering my work I was called up to a certain room where the spokesman of an imposing little assembly informed me that I had given none of the required information. "What we want to know", he explained, "is how much of such-and-such stuff can be obtained from that place within so many months. Don't the documents tell you that?"

They did not, but I was able to work it out by referring to technical handbooks in the War Office Library.

IV

The first department I entered was the Postal Censorship. Then I was transferred to another and again another. Once I was sent abroad, but after that they kept me in London, in a department in which it was thought my various languages—by then I had rubbed up my

My marriage

Italian and learnt a certain amount of Spanish, Serbian, and Ruthenian—would be useful.

During part of 1915–1916, one of my duties was to examine candidates for interpretships and posts as translators or examiners. One day a man came to be examined for Greek, in view of taking up some office job or other. I placed a manuscript in front of him, and asked him to read it out. He hesitated a while, then started laboriously spelling out syllable after syllable at a very slow rate. When he had reached a full stop, I invited him to translate. He stared at me and asked: "Is it absolutely necessary?"

"What do you mean?" I exclaimed in amazement.

"Well, you see," he replied, "I was told that people who could read Greek were wanted. I can read Greek all right, but I don't understand it. I am a type-setter."

One or two candidates were young officers with little or no knowledge of modern Greek, but so efficient in ancient Greek that with a little coaching (which I was allowed to give them as part of my work) they were able to qualify within an incredibly short time. And, more generally speaking, my own experiences of that period have left me with the impression that there is little truth in the current notion that England produces few good linguists.

One candidate, a Russian, did not take things as meekly. Within a minute, or perhaps less, I had satisfied myself that he would do. So I said: "Thank you, that will be all." He flared up. I found him more fluent than ever. "All? Do you call *that* examining me? Do you imagine you have found out what I can do?" and on he went until I managed to cut in with the remark that if he wished to be rejected, maybe I could find a test which would ensure the desired result.

In May, 1916, I married. My fiancée and I, far from sharing the general superstition, considered May a delightful month in which to get married—and our view

My marriage

was confirmed by the loveliness of the Norfolk countryside all abloom with hawthorn and buttercups around Westacre Abbey, Hamond's home, lent to us for the occasion.

In the autumn, the department I worked in was broken up and I was sent back to the Postal Censorship, where I spent a dreary eighteen months or so doing work of the dullest kind in a very depressing atmosphere. Then I was transferred to a better department, and after the Armistice again to another, in which I worked until the autumn of 1919. Then I was released for good, and an entirely new chapter of my life opened.

CHAPTER XXXII

Reverting to music after the war—Musical France and England: retrospects and comparisons—The Press and public, there and here—On hissing at concerts—The genuine Boris Godunof *published—What broadcasting may do.*

I

From August, 1914, to the time of my marriage, I had not touched music. But as soon as Ethel and I had settled in a little flat in Chelsea, I procured a piano, had a few of my favourite scores, and other music, sent from Paris, and we went through them all in my spare time. It was a great joy for me to acquaint her, who loved music but had heard very little so far, with the things I loved best. Our first explorations ranged from Wagner's operas to *Boris Godunof* and *Fervaal*, and from Bach's Partitas to Erik Satie's *Morceaux en forme de poire* for piano duet, which we played together, and Bartók's lovely pieces for children. But still I did not go to concerts, nor did I write a line. I did not want to think of music much, lest I should be attracted by it again at a time when it was important for me to concentrate on other things. As regards concerts, however, there was one exception: we went to the Queen's Hall to hear Liszt's *Faust* Symphony conducted by Busoni, and Ethel enjoyed it as much as I did.

Then once, I was given tickets for Rimsky-Korsakof's *Golden Cockerel* at Covent Garden. There I met, among other people, Dr. McNaught, who pounced upon me and said: "So there you are, Calvocoressi! I heard only the other day that you had been killed, but thought I'd wait for more information before publishing your

Reverting to music after the war

obituary." He dragged me along to "show me" to Ernest Newman and to other friends, asked me to lunch the next day, and wanted me to resume my contributions to the *Musical Times*. This I declined: although my work at that particular moment was very dull (or perhaps for that very reason), it took up all my available energies.

Later, I found out that an obituary of me had actually appeared, at the same period, in the American *Etude*, whose editor, in reply to a letter offering him contributions, informed me of the fact. He was, unfortunately, unable to send me a copy of this document. How the rumour spread I cannot guess: so far as I know, no Calvocoressi was killed in the war, although several (not relatives of mine) were serving in the British Army.

II

After the war I remained reluctant to revert to musical criticism. I took up other work, but this bored me terribly. And in 1921, urged not only by a few of my friends but, very pressingly, by Ethel, I went back to what was really my job.

The situation, at first, seemed rather frightening, not only from the practical point of view, but also because I had so thoroughly lost touch with things and had so much to catch up. Even with regard to subjects that I had studied most carefully, I felt very much at a loss. I no longer wished to write the books on modern French and Russian music that I had planned eight years earlier. Most of the information and critical views that I could have put into them had become common property, and I doubted whether I could supply what was still wanting. With regard to Russian music especially, I felt that I knew far too little to be able to write an adequate book.

Moreover, interesting things had been happening, during the war and the first after-war years, in Central Europe as well as in the allied countries. And to find out what

THE AUTHOR FISHING THE LAC DE TIGNES

THE AUTHOR AND HIS WIFE
AT THE COL DU PALET,
ABOVE THE LAC DE TIGNES

they were, to procure information and music, seemed an almost insuperable task.

With regard to Russia, it proved easy, thanks to the ready help of my good friends Andrei Rimsky-Korsakof, Findeisen, and, a little later, of Professor Victor Belaiev, with whom I got into touch. And little by little, other information and new music began to trickle in.

Among the people who helped me then in my quest for work was Dr. Eaglefield Hull. I had not met him before. During the war I had accepted an offer (I did not know from whom—it came through my French publisher) for the English rights of my book on Mussorgsky; and the translation, for which he was responsible, had turned out to be most unsatisfactory. In 1921, when I went to the *Monthly Musical Record* to offer contributions, he spontaneously opened the matter. "I know that I have done you a very bad turn," he told me. "I can't explain how I came to make such a mess of your book. I can only say that I am very sorry, and shall do my best to make it up to you." And he did, finding me many outlets at a time when I stood in great need of them.

III

From the time when I resumed my work, I was able really to study Ethel's impressions of music, and especially of the new works which so many of us find baffling in the light of previous experiences. I had often wondered whether it would be possible for Schönberg's music, for instance (I mean the "difficult" Schönberg, not the Schönberg of early, overripe romantic works such as the *Gurre Lieder* or *Verklärte Nacht*) to make upon listeners with little or no previous experience impressions as positive and deep as, for instance, Debussy's *Pelléas et Mélisande* (then deemed by many practised judges no less "abnormal" and cruel to the ear than anything of Schönberg was deemed later), had done in 1902, when, to my own knowledge, others besides Delage had suddenly developed a love for music under its influence. I knew quite well that, as I have mentioned in a previous chapter, a number of young men such as Berg, Wellesz, and Webern had mustered around him from the first, feeling that his music corresponded more closely than any other to aspirations latent in themselves: but so far as I know, these young men were, at the time, no tyros. I have yet to meet anybody whose musical imagination was fired for the first time by a work of the mature Schönberg; but Ethel, who heard *Pierrot Lunaire* after having become acquainted with a fair variety of music old and new, all heard for the first time within a short period—so that she could have acquired no set habits—was the next best thing for observation purposes. I was greatly interested to note that she could see no reason why *Pierrot Lunaire* should be more "baffling" than, say, Debussy's Quartet or a Bach fugue. If music appealed to her imagination, she felt at home in it. And this, I must repeat it, is the only valid test for critics as well as for music-lovers pure and simple. That the imagination can be trained is unquestionable. How it can be profitably trained is another matter. My own feeling is that never was a greater truth uttered than is embodied in Debussy's saying: "J'essaie d'oublier la musique (que je connais) parce qu'elle me gêne pour entendre celle que je connaîtrai demain." And I feel that all books on Musical Appreciation, after having duly told readers "what to listen for" in the classics and other already charted music, should quote this sentence in big block letters.

IV

To revert to music after an intermission of several years must be a curious experience in any circumstances. To do so in surroundings different from those in which I had grown and had worked made it doubly strange and in-

The Press and public, in France and England

structive. I found myself missing much that had become a matter of course with me, and I encountered much that I had not been accustomed to take into account. There was much to be learnt. I doubt whether I learnt as much as I might have done, but a few things certainly struck me and showed me in which direction it would be advisable to steer—which does not mean that I acted accordingly. I shall content myself with mentioning here a few differences which may be of more or less general interest.

One, which naturally I had realized long before the war, was on the attitude of the daily Press towards music. It had always been a source of amazement to me that even at a period when interest in music was progressing by leaps and bounds throughout the country, so little space should be devoted to it in French dailies. Taking the files of any of these from, say, 1890 to 1914, it would be impossible to obtain from them even the faintest idea of what the musical life of France was during the period—which concerts were given, which artists appeared, which new works were written by French composers, which new foreign works introduced, which books on music published. Most critics seemed to live in blissful ignorance of a good many things that took place. They were expected to notice only first performances of operas and other musical plays, and Sunday symphony concerts. Had they written up recitals and concerts of new music they would only have provided fodder for the sub-editorial waste-paper basket.

It is true that the French dailies are far smaller than the English, and give scanty information even on subjects of more general and more immediate interest than music. I remember Arnold Bennett asking me, "Do French papers ever spend a cent on getting news?" But there was a more special reason for their attitude towards musical events other than those which it was customary, and compulsory, for them to notice—they viewed them ex-

The Press and public, in France and England

clusively as potential sources of advertisements—not merely legitimate advertisements announcing the particulars, but "*communiqués*" or "blurbs" proclaiming how wonderful the events promised to be, and, after they had taken place, how wonderful they had been, these after-the-event "*communiqués*" appearing as substitutes for *bona-fide* critical notices.

Accordingly, many editors and managers lived in fear of giving for nothing a notice which otherwise might be paid for. And, unavoidably, there must have been a few so-called critics who took views similar to those of their employers. The results were, at times, curious. In the early days of my career, practically all recitals and chamber concerts took place at one of two halls, each belonging to a firm of piano manufacturers. In one of the Paris dailies which did not restrict the activities of its musical critic to the usual minimum, only the concerts taking place at the Salle X were noticed; in another, only those taking place at the Salle Z. Once, the critic of the pro-X paper wished to notice, for some special reason, a performance at the Salle Z: he did so, but without stating where the performance had taken place. Others never alluded to concerts given by certain societies.

That the evil existed is undeniable. From time to time, the situation was frankly described in the independent Press, but protests remained ineffectual. Quite recently, I had proof positive that the tradition had not altogether died out. I was in charge of an important and unusually interesting case of international copyright which came before the French courts—a case affecting a well-known musical masterpiece. Not a word on the proceedings appeared in any Paris daily; and our counsel told me that this was because, in the editors' eyes, reports would have constituted free advertisements for one of the parties if not for both.

There were exceptions, of course. The critics of a few

The Press and public, in France and England

big dailies such as *Le Temps*, *Le Journal des Débats*, and *La Liberté*, were allowed free scope, and, so far as the space allotted to them permitted, could deal independently with all musical events, and even review published music or books on music. But their articles, as a rule, appeared once a week only.

It surprised me very much to find that English editors made a point of treating musical events as "news" with a vengeance—news that will not keep any more than news of a sensational murder, and must be served piping hot under the pains of losing whatever nourishing value it may possess; and even more so to mark that whereas concerts and performances were "news", music itself and ideas on music—including the possibly valuable conclusions which critics might reach if allowed reasonable time to think things out—were not.

Of course, there is a practical reason for this policy. Artists who appear in London are engaged to appear elsewhere too, or hope for engagements; and societies and agents are on the lookout for artists to engage. In Paris, nothing of the kind happens. Artists who appear there know perfectly well that the best they can hope for is that the notices and the reputation which they earn thus will help them to get engagements abroad. So that, even from the point of view of their own legitimate interests, a day or two makes no difference.

The English practice is certainly beneficial to performers; but I doubt whether it is equally so to music. To hear for the first time a new symphony or chamber work by a composer who may be striking a line of his own—and a disconcerting one at that—and about whom one may know nothing whatever at 9 p.m., and have to hand in a report on it by 11 p.m., is far from constituting an ideal condition of things: especially when one considers that a majority of people do not take in periodicals in which more leisurely reports appear, and so have

On hissing at concerts

nothing to go by but what they read in their daily paper.

V

On the other hand, I had always been amazed at the uncritical attitude of French critics in matters of interpretation—especially of instrumental music. Ninety-nine times out of a hundred, they content themselves with declaring that it was uniformly excellent. "L'exécution fut de tous points parfaite", is as current a formula in their concert-notices as the detective's "This is a bad business" in English murder yarns. I regret to say that I too used it during my critical nonage. It is still to be encountered in the French Press. Indeed, either thirty years ago or to-day, notices of Paris concerts (and not in the daily Press only) convey the impression that practically everything heard there is flawlessly played or sung. Only the other day, I was told that the managing committee of a certain English concert association had held several meetings in order to decide whether to continue issuing Press tickets to a critic who had annoyed them by finding fault with the quality of many of their performances. If there is any truth in the rumour, that managing committee would certainly be happier in Paris.

VI

While living in France, I had attended far too few concerts in England to be able to form an opinion as to the attitude of English audiences as compared with that of the French. In this matter, another big surprise lay in store for me—that of discovering how much greater a part what I shall call, for short, the personal factor, or hero-worship, played in England than in France. It would be natural to think that the more excitable Frenchmen would be far more boisterous in cheering their

On hissing at concerts

favourite singers, players, or conductors, than London audiences. Not at all: it is the very reverse that happens. Before I came to London I had hardly ever seen audiences stand so long clapping and cheering at the end of concerts —often, I regret to say, very indifferent ones. And then, I always felt that the demonstrations originated in the desire to offer a warm personal tribute to the performers.

English audiences, besides being generous in their gratitude, are always courteous. French audiences can be very rude. In theory, of course, courtesy is all to the good; but in practice it may be carried too far. That a soloist, a conductor, or a composer introducing works of his own should be assured of a pleasing welcome is only as should be: but it strikes me as unnatural that audiences should never express their dissatisfaction even at music which irritates or disgusts them. Hissing at concerts, so far as I am aware, is unknown in England. I am suggesting, not that it is a commendable practice, but simply that excitable audiences should, in the normal order of things, be excitable both ways. Otherwise their applause loses much of its significance. And, as regards demonstrations reflecting the listeners' impression of the music, not of the performance, I wish to add this: the people who heartily hiss a piece of new, strange music are not the worst kind of public a composer could wish for. They may be presumed, at least, to have a live outlook and to feel strongly. For aught one knows, they may come to take an altogether different view of the works they began by hissing. It is rather the listeners who stand politely indifferent who are hopeless.

There are, however, protests and protests. The people who hissed at *Pelléas et Mélisande* in 1902 were certainly hopeless. Their demonstrations expressed a petty, sneering, smug antagonism, very different from the honest, lusty anger which made itself felt in the protests at the first performances of *Le Sacre du Printemps*.

On hissing at concerts

VII

I remember, too, an instance (which created a mild sensation in its time) of hissing dictated by a peculiar fad. A small number of concert-goers had decided that concertos were tedious and ought to disappear from programmes. They made a practice of going to concerts at which concertos were played in order to hiss and shout, "Down with concertos!"—no matter which the concerto was or who played it. They created so much disturbance that more than once some of them were expelled from the hall. Their leader, a certain T——, managed to get in a protest in the Press, coupled with an appeal for support on the part of a long-suffering public. This provided a certain amount of "copy" for the papers, after which the affair died a natural death.

I have known Paris audiences hiss after a composer had conducted a work of his own. One of these composers was a visitor from abroad introducing one of his symphonies—a very insignificant one, but one which did not deserve abuse any more than it deserved applause.

There were disturbances at the Concerts Colonne in 1908, when Debussy conducted his *La Mer*, but this was a case of partisanship pure and simple: admirers and detractors were demonstrating mainly in defiance of one another. They got so excited about it that, after a first outbreak had died down, a second one started while Jacques Thibaud was playing a solo.

But the most incredible instance of bad manners is one of which I read, in a French musical periodical, a description from the pen of its very perpetrator—a critic. A new work had been played, and part of the audience was hissing and booing. He, to quote his own words, "*naturally* (italics mine) was among the first to protest"— and so vehemently did he carry on that the policeman on duty attempted to expel him. Other critics intervened,

On hissing at concerts

and he was allowed to remain in the hall. From the further issues of the paper I found out that he was also allowed to retain his job.

VIII

When Paris audiences get really excited, it is over music rather than over those who compose or perform it. And this, I think, is but one illustration of a fundamental difference between these and London audiences. Another is the fact that, in Paris, no artist would dream of giving a concert without announcing, well in advance, the programme in full. Here, many of them rest content with making it known that they will be heard on such-and-such a day at such-and-such a hall. Often it is impossible to find out what they will play or sing. They, and their agents, seem to take it for granted that this will make no difference—even, at times, in the case of unknown people giving their first recital in London. The first time I came across a concert announcement giving the artist's portrait and excerpts from Press notices, but not the slightest hint of what the programme would be, I was amazed. I continue to think that the practice is very symptomatic.

Maybe the British public have a wider range of interests, and the French more definite preferences. I have often asked myself the question: of the omnivorous —or almost omnivorous—appetite or the fastidious palate, which is it that betokens the more genuine keenness and holds out the greater hope of improvement in taste and receptiveness? There is much to be said either way. In practice there are limits to the elasticity and power of assimilation of the human mind and sensitiveness. I also think that strong and enlightened admiration of certain qualities implies strong dislike of corresponding defects. But I am quite prepared to grant that it may also induce blindness to other very different qualities.

Music to which I devoted much thinking

IX

I have often wondered how I should have developed, as a music-lover and critic, had I grown and started work in England. Even knowing that surroundings and education are bound to exercise an influence, it is difficult to determine what the influence has been. Besides the question of musical outlook, there is one of general outlook, habits of mind, modes of thought, and so on. One thing I know: nowhere but in France could I have developed exactly as I did. I also hold that all my feelings on subjects on which I feel strongly (and in matters of music I hardly ever feel otherwise—lack of interest, with me, is almost as positive a feeling as love or dislike) are so very much part and parcel of my nature that I cannot conceive myself feeling otherwise, even under the strongest influences. And yet reason tells me that this must be an illusion, or at least partly so. And I must acknowledge that had circumstances and opportunities to exercise my mind been other, the development of those feelings might have been hastened or delayed if not otherwise affected. I might have had my attention called to composers with whom, as it happens, I have concerned myself very little: Dvořák, for instance, to whom English experts ascribe far greater significance than anyone I came across elsewhere does. On the other hand, music to which I devoted much thinking and which I found very stimulating at the time when I began to mature—that of Liszt, Balakiref, and Mussorgsky among others—might have escaped my early notice; and this would certainly have meant a difference—for better or for worse—in my evolution.

Another point is that opportunities for critics being far more numerous in England, I should probably not have remained so long a free-lance—a position which has its advantages and drawbacks from the practical point of

The genuine "Boris Godunof" published

view as well as from that of mind development and professional technique.

But, to sum up, what I can say is that I owe a great deal both to France—which, as I said in the first chapters of this book, was, at the time I lived there, a wonderfully stimulating centre—and, for the many reasons which I hope I have made clear, to my country of adoption. And I shall always remember with special gratitude John Shedlock and Dr. McNaught, who gave me my first chances in England; and Charles Volkert, who by volunteering to publish my *Principles of Musical Criticism* (a book for which I should have been hard put to it to find a publisher in any other country) made me sit down to write it instead of continuing to think, more or less vaguely, that it ought to be written.

X

Among the things I did after the war, this was, to me, one of the most interesting. But the most exciting of all was resuming work on Mussorgsky under entirely new and unhoped-for conditions.

In 1925 I read in a paper that Professor Lamm was preparing to publish the full genuine text of *Boris Godunof* and, subsequently, of all Mussorgsky's other works. This meant that the materials most needed for my new book were coming forth. It also meant much more. I had failed in my previous attempts to secure recognition for the genuine *Boris*. I had seen the revised version spread, and the original sink deeper and deeper into oblivion. Here at last was the chance of things righting themselves; and even, maybe, of my dream of translating *Boris* coming true. I had longed to attempt a translation which would be as flowing and natural in style as the Russian, and so faithful that not only Mussorgsky's metres and rhythms would be respected, but there would exist, as nearly as possible everywhere, the same reasons as in the original

The genuine "Boris Godunof" published
for his subtly devised rises and falls of pitch, variations in emphasis and colour, and so on—an impossible ideal, no doubt: but I could at least hope to come within measurable distance of it. And, when I had succeeded in persuading the Oxford University Press to acquire the rights for the English and French editions, I was given the chance to try my hand at the translation into both languages.

I did the greater part of this work during the summer of 1927 at Tignes, in the heart of the mountains of Savoie, in a small refuge by the banks of a lake, 7000 feet up, where my wife and I used to spend happy holidays every year. Never have we seen finer scenery—lake and torrents, rocks and glaciers, meadows gorgeous with alpine flowers and all peopled with lovely birds and butterflies.

One day, I was hard at work in the common-room, mentally cursing the words which would insist on having a syllable too few or too many, or an accent in the wrong place, when in stepped a visitor, an Englishman. He watched me a while, and then said: "How wonderful it is, in these romantic surroundings, to behold a composer at work! What beautiful music this incomparable setting should inspire! It reminds me of Svengali in Du Maurier's *Trilby*." It was sad to have to disillusion him by confessing that there was no romance, but hard grind, and that my dictionaries, not the lake and glaciers, were the source of my inspiration.

We had to leave Tignes before the work was finished, other duties calling me back to London. Alas! The refuge is now sold and closed to the public, and we can no longer hope for holidays by the wonderful lake.

XI

After the genuine *Boris* had appeared, complications of all kinds arose, and delayed its performance. All I have heard of it so far—apart from excerpts which were

What broadcasting may do

performed to illustrate lectures of mine—is a broadcast from Berlin, which came very faint and much spoilt by interference. But no doubt, the chance to hear it will come sooner or later, and then I shall be able to know, finally, how far I was right or wrong in preferring it to the remodelled version.

Having mentioned wireless, I may as well explain, by way of conclusion, that if I have not discussed more fully the differences between London and Paris as musical centres, it is mainly because, even as I write, conditions, under the influence of broadcasting, are continuously and speedily changing—especially in England, where it is conducted on a different basis and plays a far greater part. A comparison of past conditions would therefore be pointless. And, obviously, the time is not far off when further and more radical changes will be taking place. Only the other day (November, 1932) the critic of a London paper was able to discuss in detail a concert relayed from Warsaw. Musical events taking place all over the world will be accessible to us all, and there will be no excuse for ignoring them, for restricting our interests, maybe, under the influence of our surroundings, or for losing our sense of proportion. But, nevertheless, we shall remain, one and all, true to our own nature; and this will be, as it was before, the only valid excuse for our shortcomings, and the only hope for us of discovering something of the truth about music.

THE END

INDEX

Académie des Beaux-Arts, 18, 49, 50, 204
Adam, Adolphe, 220
Adès, Jehan, 86, 88
"Affaire Dreyfus", the, 80, 90–91
Akimenko, Theodore, 158
Albeniz, Isaac, 95–97, 136
Alheim, Pierre and Marie Olénine d', 39, 149–152, 254
Alice in Wonderland, 25
Amyot, Jacques, 78
Annunzio, Gabriele d', 57
Antoine, André, 86, 87
Arensky, Anton, 207
L'Art Moderne, 41, 44, 292
Aubry, Pierre, 75, 76, 82–85, 269–270
Auric, Georges, 133

Babaian, Marguerite, 87, 158
Bach, J. S., 19, 21, 24, 34, 43, 109, 247, 248, 253, 299, 302
Bakst, Léon, 79, 167, 170, 171, 182, 186, 195, 205, 207, 219
Balakiref, Mily, 39, 54, 57, 77, 138, 148, 149, 153, 155, 164, 170, 235, 236, 238, 248, 253, 255, 281, 282, 310
Barrett, J. M., 289
Bartók, Béla, 171, 228, 255, 269, 299
Bathori, Mme. Jane, 69
Bax, Arnold, 18, 190, 283
Beethoven, L. Van, 34, 42, 48, 53, 101, 109, 162, 248, 250
Belaiev, Prof. Victor, 301

Bennett, Arnold, 200, 209, 257–264, 282, 290, 292, 303
Benois, Alexandre, 79, 167, 182, 186, 190, 205, 220
Bérenger, Senator, 196, 204
Berg, Alban, 302
Berlioz, H., 54, 157, 162, 254, 276
Bertrand, L., 125
Bessel, Ivan, 153, 154
Bielsky, N., 238, 241, 242
Binenbaum, Ianco, 102–106, 269
Binet-Valmer, Gustave, 41, 82
Bizet, G., 111
Bles, Arthur, 74, 82, 83
Bliss, Arthur, 18
Blumenfeld, Felix, 175, 181, 192, 193
Bolm, Adolf, 212
Bordes, Charles, 20, 107, 112–114, 137
Boris Godunof, Mussorgsky's, 76, 88, 117, 143, 149, 153–156, 167, 169, 173–175, 177–179, 181–193, 207, 243, 263, 311, 312
Borodin, Alexander, 39, 54, 77, 149, 206, 236, 253, 282
Bourgault-Ducoudray, L., 136–139, 157, 159, 161
Bourne, George, 259
Bowen, York, 283
Boy's Own Paper, the, 279
Brahms, J., 228
Brayer, Jules de, 149, 151, 154
"British Concert Society" (Paris), 287

Index

Broussan, L., 182
Brown, Sarah, 196, 198
Bruneau, Alfred, 56
Brunoff, M. de, 291
Busoni, Ferruccio, 230, 281, 299

Cabezon, A. de, 94
Calvocoressi, Ethel, 297, 299, 300, 301, 302
Caplet, André, 98–102
Caran d'Ache, 213–215
Carmen, Bizet's, 24
Caruso, Enrico, 144–145
Casa-Miranda, Marquis de, 38 (see also Partington, Fred)
Casella, Alfredo, 98
Castillon, A. de, 107
Chabrier, Emmanuel, 54, 57
Chaliapin, Feodor, 88, 141–144, 169, 184, 192, 193, 207, 215
Chamberlain, H. S., 253
Chanteurs de Saint-Gervais, 20
Charpentier, Gustave, 56
Charpentier, Marc Antoine, 283
Chopin, F., 34, 42, 159, 163, 206, 248, 252
Cicero (quoted), 223
Claveau, Eugène, 34, 37
Cobbett, W. W., 102, 240
Collet, Henri, 95
Collins, Arthur, 217
Colonne, Edouard, 29, 90
Combarieu, Jules, 198
Comœdia Illustré, 291
Concerts-Colonne, 37, 90–91, 308
Concerts du Conservatoire, 48, 159
Concerts-Lamoureux, 33, 34, 37, 161, 163
Conrad, Joseph, 258, 282

Conservatoire, the Paris, 18, 19, 40, 48, 50, 98–100, 133, 135, 138
Cooper, Emil, 205, 207
Corder, Prof. F., 283
Cortot, Alfred, 38, 39
Costa-Borgnia, E., 265
Coutts, Francis, 97
Cowen, Sir Frederic, 286
Cruppi, Jean, 293
Cruppi, Mme. Jean, 63
Cui, César, 233, 237, 238

Daily Telegraph, the, 287
Dale, Benjamin J., 283
Dargomyjsky, Alexander, 239
Davray, Henry D., 257
Debussy, Claude, 18, 20, 35, 36, 37, 42, 44, 46, 51, 56, 57, 58, 61, 63, 67, 68, 90–92, 100, 101, 115, 117, 118–123, 124, 127, 129, 130, 133, 135, 137, 173, 175, 224, 228, 234, 237, 248, 249, 250, 266, 280, 281, 283, 292, 301, 302, 308
Delage, Maurice, 61–62, 64, 66, 81, 284, 302
Delibes, Léo, 111
Diaghilef, Serge, 58, 62, 76, 79, 88, 100, 104, 136, 146, 150, 154, 165–194, 195, 205–226, 242, 287
Dogiel, H., 289
Domengie, L., 187
Don Quichotte, Massenet's, 143
Don Quixote, Ravel's plan for a, 78–79, 261
Dukas, Paul, 96
Dulac, Charles Marie, 108
Duparc, Henri, 107–110
Durand, A. et fils, 76, 122

Index

Dvořák, Anton, 310

Ecole Monge, the, 26–27
Ecole des Hautes Etudes Sociales, the, 31, 85, 103, 268, 269, 270, 286
Ecorcheville, Jules, 176, 286
Elgar, Sir Edward, 282, 286
Eliot, T. S., 268
Encyclopédie Musicale du Conservatoire, the, 268
Engel, Emile, 69
Erlanger, Camille, 140, 141
Ernst, Alfred, 253
Espagnat, G. d', 64
Etude, the, 122, 300
Evans, Edwin, 283, 284
Evocations, Roussel's, 59
Expert, Henri, 283

Falla, Manuel de, 55, 64, 95
Fargue, Léon-Paul, 55, 62–63, 66, 88, 126,
Farlow, 84
Fauré, Gabriel, 50, 54, 76, 96, 97, 132–136, 175, 234, 283
Feodorova, Sophia, 212
Féré, G., 289
Ferrer, Francesco, 56
Fervaal, d'Indy's, 39, 53, 111, 112, 254, 299
Findeisen, Prof. N., 150, 238, 239–240, 301
Fitzmaurice, Lord, 294
Fokin, Michael, 62, 79, 104, 167, 170, 205, 206, 211, 213, 220
Förkel, N., 253
Fra Angelico da Fiesole, 195
Franck, César, 18, 19, 47, 52, 54, 56, 107, 108, 250, 252, 254, 281, 283

Fromont, Eugène, 36, 38

Galland, 78
Garde Républicaine, the, 145
Gauthier-Villars, Henry, 125
Gérardin, Léon, 27
Genée, Adeline, 212
Gheltzer, Catherine, 221
Glazunof, Alexandre, 54, 57, 87, 160, 176, 207, 232, 233
Glinka, Michael, 77, 86, 153, 157, 159, 177, 206, 232, 236, 239
Godart, Aimé, 26, 27
Godebski, Cyprien and Ida, 64, 258
Godet, Robert, 149, 155, 156
Gogol, N., 194
Godowsky, L., 148
Gounod, Charles, 53, 111
Gourmont, Rémy de, 74, 295
Grande Revue, the, 67, 177, 249
Grassi, Eugène, 59
Graves, Alfred P., 285
Gray, Cecil, 102
Gretchaninof, Alexander, 234
Grieg, Edvard, 90–92
Guéritte, 286
Guerrero, Francisco, 94
Guilmant, Alexandre, 269
Guimet, E., 197
Gunsbourg, Raoul, 144–147
Gunzburg, Baron Dimitri de, 218, 221

Hamond, Admiral Richard, 280
Hamond, Thomas A. H., 280, 294, 298
Hardy, Thomas, 258
Hardy Brothers, 84
Hauptmann, Gehrardt, 77
Haydn, F. J., 34, 248, 252

Index

Hérédia, J. M. de, 35–36
Hérold, A. Ferdinand, 78
Hervey, Arthur, 287
Heseltine, Philip, 102
Hess, Myra, 287
L'Heure Espagnole, Ravel's, 67
Holland, Theodore, 282, 285
Honegger, Arthur, 65
Houville, Gérard d', 36
Hull, Dr. A. E., 301
Hungarian Quartet, the, 269
Huysmans, J. K., 216

In Bohemia, Balakiref's, 161
Indy, Vincent d', 19, 21, 37, 39, 43, 47, 53, 58, 59, 99, 107, 111–117, 118, 121, 133, 135, 137, 173, 175, 234, 254, 266, 269, 281, 284, 292
Ingegnieros, Dr., 289
Inghelbrecht, D. E., 55

Jean Christophe, Romain Rolland's, 17, 21
Journal des Débats, Le, 305

Karatyghin, V., 238–239
Karsavina, Tamara, 211, 212
Kipling, Rudyard, 61, 258, 271
Kodaly, Zoltan, 72, 122, 269
Kuhnau, Johann, 267
Kussewitsky, Serge, 155

Ladmirault, Paul, 175
La Fontaine, Jean de, 100
Lahy, 289
Lalande, André, 30–31
La Laurencie, L. de, 283
Lamm, Prof. P., 236, 311
Lamoureux, Charles, 38
Landowska, Wanda, 21

Langen, Albert, 90
Leeds Choir, the, 286
Leroux, Xavier, 46, 98–99
Liabeuf, 80
Liapunof, Serge, 158, 163, 164, 235, 236
La Liberté, 305
"Ligne contre la licence des rues", the, 196–197, 204
Lipkowska, Lydia, 207
Liszt, Franz, 38, 43, 77, 109, 115, 116, 234, 236, 237, 252, 253, 254, 255, 266, 289, 299, 310
—, his centenary celebrated at Marseilles, 87
Little Folks, 279
Loiseau, Paul, 188, 190, 192
London Symphony Orchestra, the, 286
Lopokhova, Lydia, 221
Loti, Pierre, 271
Louÿs, Pierre, 35
Lycée Janson de Sailly, the, 27–28

Mackenzie, Sir Alexander, 18, 286
Maclean, Dr. Charles, 288
Maeterlinck, Maurice, 134
Mahler, Gustav, 228
Mahomet II, the Sultan, 161
Maindron, Maurice, 35
Makowsky, Serge, 155
Malherbe, Charles, 155, 157
Manuel, Roland, 64, 81
Mardrus, J. C., 78
Marty, Georges, 48, 159
Masque of the Red Death, Binenbaum's, 103
Massenet, Jules, 143
Mata-Hari, 197–198
Maurel, Victor, 141
Mans, Octave, 41

317

Index

McEwen, Sir John, 282–283
McNaught, Dr. W. G., 285, 299, 311
Melba, Dame Nellie, 33
Meredith, George, 258, 259
Messager, André, 182
Methuen's, 291
Meyerbeer, G., 177
Milhaud, Darius, 65, 133
Monteverdi, Claudio, 21, 283
Monthly Musical Record, the, 280, 291, 301
Morales, Cristoforo, 94
Mordkin, Michael, 212
Morning Post, the, 289, 291
Moscow Choir, the, 167, 184–185, 190, 191, 193, 195, 212
Mozart, W. A., 34, 38, 42, 101, 248, 252
Music Student, the, 289
Music Educational Conference at Lausanne, 1931, 275
Musical Taste and How to Form It, the author's, 274–275
Musical Times, the, 285–287, 291, 300
Musiciens d'Aujourd'hui, Rolland's, 17
Mussorgsky, Modest, 39, 54, 76, 88, 89, 117, 142, 143, 147, 149–156, 157, 162, 168, 169, 173, 174, 178, 180, 207, 224–225, 235, 236, 238, 239, 243, 248, 254, 263, 276, 282, 301, 310, 311

Newman, Ernest, 74, 287, 301
Newmarch, Mrs. Rosa, 157, 181
Night on the Bare Mountain, Mussorgsky's, 235, 236

Nijinsky, Vatslav, 79, 209–211, 216, 219, 223, 224
Nikisch, Arthur, 177
Nourok, Alfred, 76, 166, 169, 242, 286
Nouvel, Walter, 76, 166, 169, 172, 188, 208, 218, 221, 242, 286
Nouvelle Revue Musicale, the, 292
Novello's, 291

Oberdoerffer, Paul, 103
Oberon, Weber's, 24
Obukhof, N., 81
Orfeo, Monteverdi's, 21
Ornstein, Leo, 269
Ossowsky, Alexander, 172, 238, 242
Oxford, lecturing at, 290
Oxford University Press, 277, 312

Pagliacci, Leoncavallo's, 119
Parry, Sir Hubert, 18, 134, 286
Partington, Fred, 38, 42, 254
Pavlova, Anna, 211, 212
Pedrell, Felipe, 93–96
Péladan, Josephin, 124, 125
Pelléas et Mélisande, Debussy's, 20, 35, 44, 56, 61, 115, 116, 118–121, 173, 301, 307
Pernot, Hubert, 75, 160
Peter, René, 121
Pétremand, Eugène, 188, 190, 192
Pinchon, Eugène, 199
Pirro, André, 253, 283
Poe, Edgar Allan, 100, 102, 294, 295
Poulenc, Francis, 65
Principles and Methods of Musical Criticism, the author's, 31, 251, 277, 311
Prokofief, Serge, 240–242

Index

Prudent, E., 24
Prunières, Henry, 105
Pulteney, Lieutenant-General Sir William, 294

Ralli, Mrs. Julie, 29
Rameau, J. Ph., 184
Ravel, Maurice, 18, 20, 21, 37, 42, 43, 46–81, 87, 88, 101, 115, 121, 124, 127, 133, 135, 152, 153, 162, 163, 169, 173, 175, 224, 227, 234, 258, 261, 265, 266, 267, 284, 292
Régnier, Henri de, 35–36
Régnier, Mme. Henri de (Gérard d'Houville), 36
Renaissance Latine, the, 41, 82, 118, 119
Revue Française de Musique, the, 293
Revue Musicale, Combarieu's, 198
Revue Musicale de Lyon, the, 292
Riemann, Hugo, 113, 253
Riesmann, O. von, 155
Rimsky-Korsakof, Andrei, 173, 219, 225, 301
Rimsky-Korsakof family, the, 173, 238, 242
Rimsky-Korsakof, Nicholas, 39, 47, 54, 77, 117, 122, 143, 148, 149, 153, 155, 156, 157, 168, 169, 172–175, 178, 179, 181, 207, 218, 224, 225, 236, 238, 240, 241, 282, 299
Risler, Edouard, 38
Robertson, J. N., 295
Rodin, Auguste, 146, 202
Roerich, N., 207, 223
Roger-Ducasse, 234
Rolland, Romain, 17, 21, 83, 152, 254, 268, 269, 276, 283

Rorke, J. D. M., 247, 253
Rosé Quartet, the, 227
Roussel, Albert, 55, 58, 59, 64
Rubinstein, Anton, 109
Rubinstein, Ida, 57, 213
Runciman, John, 74

Saint-Foix, G. de, 38
Saint-Saëns, Camille, 53, 56, 186
Sakhnovskaya, Mrs., 239
Salome, Strauss's, 249
Samuel, Harold, 21
Sanin, Alexandre, 167, 186, 187, 188, 205
Satie, Erik, 47, 54, 72, 124–131, 299
Scarlatti, D., 72, 280
Schaeffner, André, 224
Schmitt, Florent, 55, 56–58, 59, 64, 76, 175, 261
Schola Cantorum, the, 21, 59, 83, 114, 116, 284
Scholes, P. A., 289, 290
Scholes, Mrs. P. A., 289
Schönberg, Arnold, 122, 127, 223, 227–230, 255, 275, 301, 302
Schweitzer, Dr. Albert, 253
Schubert, Franz, 142, 162
Schumann, Robert, 142, 162
Schwob, Marcel, 282
Scriabin, Alexandre, 176, 234, 246, 248, 252, 255
Séguy, Emile, 55
Selva, Blanche, 21
Senilof, V., 240, 241
Sévérac, Déodat de, 55, 59, 60, 64, 280
Shakespeare, William, 261
Shedlock, J. S., 280, 311
Sibelius, Jan, 92–93
Sjögren, Emil, 92

Index

Sobinof, 168
Sorbonne, the, 29
Sordes, Paul, 55, 66
Stanford, Sir Charles Villiers, 18, 286
Stassof, Dimitri, 236
Stassof, Vladimir, 153, 155, 236
Steinberg, Maximilian, 240, 241, 242
Strauss, Richard, 54, 173, 246, 248, 249, 252, 254, 255, 257, 267
Stravinsky, Igor, 56, 122, 171, 218, 221, 223–225, 227
Sullivan, Sir Arthur, 286
Swift, Dean, 151
Swinton, Mrs. George, 97, 287
Symons, Arthur, 74

Tamara, Balakiref's, 39, 46, 148, 153, 157, 159, 170, 171, 255
Tchaikowsky, P., 54, 148, 168, 169, 171, 206, 236, 237, 240, 242, 243, 246, 248, 252, 255,
Tcherepnin, N., 147, 205, 206
Tebaldini, G., 95
Le Temps, 305
Tertis, Lionel, 287
Thibaud, Jacques, 308
Thomas, Ambroise, 19, 289
Thomasset, Louise, 75
Tignes, Lac de, 312
Titian, 195
Trilby, du Maurier's, 312

University of London, 288
Vallas, Léon, 92, 119, 291, 293
Vallete, Alfred, 295
Van Dieren, Bernard, 102
Vaschide, N., 289

Vaughan Williams, Ralph, 81, 269, 283–285
Vauthier, Gabriel, 28–30
Veronese, 195
Victoria, T. L. de, 94
Vidal, Paul, 161
Viñes, Ricardo, 55, 63, 66, 87, 107, 124, 127, 152, 153, 159, 293
Vladimir, the Grand Duke, 165, 190, 191, 217
Vladimir, the Grand Duchess, 165, 190, 191
Volkert, Charles, 277, 311
Vuillermoz, Emile, 20, 64, 133, 135

Wagner, Richard, 19, 32, 33, 34, 35, 37, 38, 39, 42, 43, 46, 53, 103, 110, 111, 112, 125, 148, 177, 237, 248, 249, 250, 251, 253, 254, 299
Waldbauer, Emerich, 269
Walton, William, 18
Waltz, Charles, 168, 188, 192, 205
Weber, C. M. von, 24
Webern, Anton, 302
Weekly Critical Review, the, 280
Weingaertner, Felix, 157
Wellesz, Egon, 228, 269, 302
Wells, H. G., 258
Widor, Ch. M., 19
Wolfurt, Kurt von, 155
Wollzogen, Hans von, 253
Wyzewa, Téodor de, 38

Ysaye, the Quatuor, 42

Zambelli, Carlotta, 212
Ziloti, Alexandre, 232, 233
Zimmermann, J. H., 153, 159

www.ingramcontent.com/pod-product-compliance
Lightning Source LLC
Chambersburg PA
CBHW021052080526
44587CB00010B/224